To a wonderful Mom.

Happy Mother's Day.

Marilyn +
Lowell

GEORGE ROMNEY *60, 1967 July 8*

Books by CLARK R. MOLLENHOFF

Washington Cover-Up
Despoilers of Democracy
Tentacles of Power
The Pentagon
George Romney: Mormon in Politics

GEORGE ROMNEY
MORMON IN POLITICS

By CLARK R. MOLLENHOFF

MEREDITH PRESS / New York

First edition

Library of Congress Catalog Card Number: 68–19030

Manufactured in the United States of America
for MEREDITH PRESS

To Raymond Mollenhoff
Who I hope will find some inspiration
in the life of George Romney.

CONTENTS

vii

GEORGE ROMNEY

ONE

A Prime Target

Political sharpshooters of both parties had selected George Wilcken
Romney as the prime target by mid-1967. Obviously he was the
man to beat for the Republican nomination in 1968, and as such
became fair game for those pushing the candidacy of former
Vice President Richard M. Nixon, California Governor Ronald
Reagan, and Illinois Senator Charles Percy.

The consistent strength Romney displayed in political surveys
through the summer of 1967 was irritating to the poll-conscious
President Lyndon B. Johnson, who had become painfully aware
that he had lost his consensus and that his popularity had skidded
to such a low point that his political future was precarious. Organization Democrats—Democratic National Chairman John
Bailey, Senate Majority Leader Mike Mansfield, of Montana;
House Majority Leader Carl Albert, of Oklahoma; House Speaker
John McCormack, of Massachusetts; and Representative Emanuel
Celler, the veteran New York legislator—started early to chip
away at Romney in an effort to destroy or mar the golden public
image acquired in three terms as Governor of Michigan.

3

Although George Romney was far from a shoo-in for Republican presidential nomination, Democrats considered him a serious-enough contender to take advantage of every controversy to try to deflate him. Nixon, the other front runner, had been buffeted by the Democratic organization for the better part of twenty years, and in the last two times out it had managed to defeat him, for the presidency in 1960 and for the governorship of California in 1962.

If Richard Nixon won the Republican nomination, the Democratic organization was well stocked with old cartoons, old political positions, old facts and old myths. If Nixon became the Republican presidential candidate in 1968, the Democratic arsenal hoped to roll out old weapons used when John F. Kennedy won by a narrow margin in 1960, and when Edmund G. "Pat" Brown won by a convincing margin in the California gubernatorial race in 1962. Nixon had been beaten, and Democrats were confident they could do it again.

Michigan Governor George Romney presented a different problem, and certainly one that the Democratic organization in Michigan had been unable to solve even with the money, men, and expertise of Walter Reuther's United Automobile Workers Union. In his first try for elective office in 1962, Romney had defeated the incumbent Democratic Governor John B. Swainson by 51.4 percent of the vote. He boosted his victory margin to 55.9 percent of the vote two years later despite the fact that he ran on a ticket headed by Senator Barry Goldwater. President Johnson overwhelmed Goldwater by an unprecedented 1,076,463-vote margin in Michigan, but Romney won reelection as Governor by sweeping 382,913 votes ahead of his opponent.

Romney's 1964 victory was largely a one-man show, in which he kept at arm's distance from Republican presidential candidate Goldwater and kept his Republicanism out of sight, but in 1966 he demonstrated his power as a team player with the coattail strength to carry other Republicans into office. His victory over Zolton A. Ferency by a margin of 588,000 votes was a whopping 61 percent of the votes cast. His victory returned Robert Griffin to the United States Senate and gave the Republicans five more seats in Congress, eighteen seats in the Michigan House, and five additional seats in the Michigan Senate.

Romney's rugged masculine face, his athletic build, and his reputation for personal integrity enhance his image as a political campaigner. He combines experience and youthful vigor. As he turned sixty on July 8, 1967, Romney carried the broad background of a Washington lobbyist for the Aluminum Company of America and the career of a successful executive in the automobile industry. Grinding poverty in his youth and the tiring monotony of the manual labor of thinning and topping sugar beets in the fields of Idaho had disciplined him to complete his tasks. The satisfaction of learning the trade of a lather and plasterer resulting in the higher-than-average wages that come to a skilled workman in Salt Lake City, Utah, inspired him to press forward.

Although he was a college dropout, Romney in his early twenties had valuable experience serving as a Mormon missionary in England and Scotland, where the converts were few and the shouted ridicule for what was regarded as an offbeat religion was often cruel. He had faced the frustration of slammed doors and cynical slurs at the Church of Jesus Christ of the Latter-Day Saints. He had experienced brief moments of depression when he chucked the religious literature into a handy waste container rather than face further disappointment. The excitement of winning a few converts was matched by the challenge of debating with hecklers in London's Hyde Park. He has said those two years as a Mormon missionary were more valuable for him than college. He believed it, and he made it so.

George Romney has come through it all—success and periodic frustrations—with the bouncy optimism of a teen-age boy, and with the patient strength of a man who believes that sincere honest work will win over all adversity.

The fringe of white hair at his temples gives a hint of Romney's age, but his muscular fitness projects the appearance of a man ten years younger. On the golf course or on the dance floor, he carries his five-foot eleven-inch frame with the springy step of a man in his forties.

Most of his closest advisers are active young men in their thirties or early forties, but it strains their dedication to keep pace with the dynamic, fast-striding Michigan Governor who has set his sights on the White House.

No miracle accounts for the good health and well-being that Romney exudes. Daily golf or a brisk early-morning jog near his home in the Detroit suburb of Bloomfield Hills keeps Romney's waist slim. In line with the teachings of the Mormon religion, he does not drink tea, coffee, or liquor. The ability to catch a quick thirty-minute nap restores his full energy.

George Romney tackles any job with inquisitiveness and dogged persistence. This quality has brought success, whether in pursuit of Mormon converts, wooing the girl who became his wife, or fighting for the survival of American Motors in what seemed hopeless competition with the Big Three of the automobile industry.

While Romney is not unaware of the worst in men, he still holds out a trust to most men with hope and some conviction that the vast majority of people will respond in good faith if they are met in good faith.

As a life-long member of the Church of Jesus Christ of the Latter-Day Saints, he has frankly declared that religion is the single most important force in his life. He served as president of the Detroit Stake of that church, which is equivalent to being a bishop. He uses no profanity, but an occasional "damn" or "hell" escapes his lips in periods of anger or crisis.

When he launched his political career in 1962, some staff members carried respect for the Mormon prohibition against smoking or drinking to an extreme which made Mr. and Mrs. Romney seem a bit too pious to some admirers. No smoking or drinking of liquor or even coffee was permitted in the presence of George and Lenore Romney, which seemed an undue hardship to many otherwise enthusiastic boosters.

Among newspaper reporters and politicians invited to the Romney home there developed the practice of downing a few extra Scotches or bourbons to tide them over the evening. The fortifications of some guests arriving at a Romney reception were often obvious, and after he became Governor, associates convinced him that having liquor available for his guests was a lesser evil than continuing with a practice which resulted in guests making their initial appearance wobbly from overindulgence.

By the summer of 1967, Governor Romney had unbent to the extent that at a press party on Mackinac Island the liquor flowed for the guests with the same freedom that would have prevailed in the presence of a more traditional presidential political aspirant. Governor Romney and Mrs. Romney retained their own personal religious standards with regard to liquor, but they did not insist that others adhere to their views.

It is doubtful that any man in public life in recent years has been more deeply devoted to his religion than Governor Romney, and yet he does not wear his religion in a manner to make others self-conscious. His brief grace at a Sunday breakfast is as natural as a warm greeting to a friend. He easily avoids the sing song repetition which robs some prayers of their meaning, while also avoiding the pretentious sanctimoniousness that makes some prayers ring hollow.

A George Romney prayer comes through in quiet, unaffected conversational tones and in simple words direct to the point. This sincerity also comes through from the platform when he speaks for good government, and it comes through even more forcefully with the warm, firm handshake, the open smile, and the steady gaze of his piercing blue eyes.

Romney is not a wealthy man in the manner of New York Governor Nelson Rockefeller and Senator Robert F. Kennedy, who could finance presidential campaigns out of family funds without making a significant dent in their fortunes. But Romney is well to do and could probably be classed as a millionaire as a result of stock options and bonuses acquired when he took American Motors out of the red in 1957, remaining with that company until being elected Governor of Michigan in 1962.

Upon becoming Governor of Michigan, his salary dropped from more than $200,000 to $27,500. When he said that he entered politics for more effective public service, the drop in income alone speaks for the honesty of his statement. While he was president, chairman of the board, and general manager of American Motors, Romney voluntarily had taken a prorated pay cut of more than $75,000 a year because he was giving considerable time to a nonpartisan citizens group he had organized, the Citizens for Michigan.

From a political standpoint, his financial status was ideal. His money had been acquired honestly, and was not inherited. There was none of the taint on his wealth that so often accompanies large profits from liquor, questionable sharp business dealings, or exploitation of poverty-ridden employees. In short, it was clean money, obtained in the best American tradition.

One of his greatest assets as the 1968 election year approached was the contrast he represented to the wheeling and dealing political professional, President Lyndon B. Johnson. The high ethical standards that seemed to characterize all of Romney's known financial dealings stood out even more sharply against the much publicized $14-million Johnson family fortune which largely flowed from the government-regulated radio and television industry. That fortune, held in the name of Mrs. Johnson, was acquired during the time Johnson was holding federal office as a Congressman, Senator, and Vice President. And key acquisitions were made during the time Johnson was a member of the Senate Interstate and Foreign Commerce Committee, which had policing jurisdiction over the Federal Communications Commission, and when he was serving as Majority Leader.

Equally important was the contrast in the men around Romney and those men around President Johnson. Romney's closest associates appeared to be an energetic, high-minded, and even slightly naïve group of public-spirited men who had been untouched by a taint of scandal in his three terms as Governor of Michigan. President Johnson's most intimate political associates had included Walter Jenkins, a twice-convicted homosexual whom Johnson had placed in charge of security at the White House, and Robert G. (Bobby) Baker, denounced by the Senate Rules Committee for "gross improprieties" and convicted in federal court on charges of fraud, conspiracy, and federal tax evasion. The relationship between Bobby Baker and Mr. Johnson was not imaginary or overdrawn, as everyone familiar with the Capital knew. Bobby

Baker had been referred to as "Little Lyndon" because of his effort to imitate the master manipulator from Texas.

Certainly, Governor Romney was not the only Republican hopeful with an admirable record, but the whole image of the man reporters called Mr. Clean offered clear contrast to the hard-eyed Texan whom President John F. Kennedy had said reminded him of "a riverboat gambler." Public-opinion polls indicated that the riverboat-gambler image had come across to the voters with a steadily mounting distrust. This wariness was counteracting admiration which had credited Johnson as "a man who gets things done."

As serious questions were being raised about President Johnson's much-lauded "ability and effectiveness" on both domestic and international matters, Governor Romney was demonstrating that the talents he had exhibited in rescuing American Motors from decay and ruin were applicable to the chaotic fiscal picture in Michigan, resulting in financial reform and sound management of the state.

Romney's background as a corporation executive brought his favorable comparison with Wendell Willkie, a man without prior political experience who had captured the Republican presidential nomination in 1940. Others compared him with President Dwight D. Eisenhower from a standpoint of personal attractiveness and the heroic image of a winner.

In addition to the assets of a Willkie or an Eisenhower, Romney had demonstrated ability as a vote getter which neither of them had at the time they were nominated as GOP standard-bearers.

But, in viewing George Romney as a potential candidate, it must be remembered that Eisenhower, the only Republican winner since 1928, had an international reputation as a World War II leader and as a postwar Supreme Commander of the occupation forces in Germany and as Supreme Commander of the Allied Powers in Europe. Rightly or wrongly, General Eisenhower was regarded as a man with a depth of understanding in international affairs little short of Churchillian. Nevertheless, with that towering Eisenhower reputation, and with the full power of the still-intact organization of Thomas E. Dewey, it took a series of acrimonious primary battles and a bitter national-convention struggle for the so-called eastern internationalist wing of the party to win the nomination from Senator Robert A. Taft, the Ohio conservative.

Many similarities appear between George Romney's political position in 1968 and General Eisenhower's position in 1952. Both have the backing of the more liberal wing of the Republican Party. New York Governor Thomas E. Dewey was a major backer of Eisenhower, and New York Governor Nelson Rockerfeller has become one of the chief promoters of Romney's candidacy.

General Eisenhower faced the opposition of Senator Taft, an organization Republican who had supported the GOP candidacy for years and had campaigned tirelessly. It was "Mr. Republican" and the conservative tone that brought joy to the most conservative delegates. Romney's chief foe is former Vice President Richard M. Nixon, who has a record of twenty years as a regular Republican and more than a dozen years as a national political figure willing to go into the boondocks to help local Republican candidates or GOP fund-raising affairs.

Certain segments of the Republican Party refused to support Senator Taft because they contended he could not win a national election, but that argument was made against a background of Taft's consistent pattern of victory in the heavy industrial state of Ohio. The Romney candidacy is bolstered by the talk, even among some Nixon admirers, of doubt that the former Vice President can win. But this talk of possible Nixon loss was against the background of his narrow loss to President Kennedy in the 1960 election, coupled with the devastating defeat he suffered in his effort to be elected Governor of California in 1962. The former Vice President was vanquished by a 296,758-vote margin by Governor Edmund G. "Pat" Brown in the same year that Republican Senate whip Thomas Kuchel, also a Californian, was being reelected by a quarter of a million votes.

The fact that Romney was elected three times as Governor of Michigan would seem likely, on first examination, to give him rapport with Republican regulars not enjoyed by Eisenhower, who had never run for office, had never supported a Republican office seeker, and had never indicated a party affiliation prior to 1952.

However, running for office in Michigan and serving the better part of three terms in that trouble-plagued state had created for Romney many serious political liabilities within the national Republican political organization.

While Eisenhower had no political record to defend, Romney had an action-packed political career, with controversy in every race, and every major domestic issue on his doorstep every month of the period of time he was in the Capitol in Lansing. Labor problems, tax policies, civil rights, racial riots, automobile-safety legislation, and teachers' salary disputes were only a few of the issues he faced in administering the business of the state of Michigan.

In the practical political business of being elected and reelected, Romney had been an unorthodox political performer. While victory will wipe out the memory of much unorthodox political posturing, the Romney independence was difficult for party regulars to swallow. He ran in 1962 as a Republican, but it was not apparent in his literature, for he felt, and possibly rightly so, that the name Romney had more appeal than the Republican label at that time.

Deviation from party regularity could have been forgotten quickly on the national scene, even though it might have caused long-time bitterness among Republican conservatives. But the 1964 campaign brought an unorthodoxy not so easily forgotten or forgiven by the conservatives.

Romney refused to endorse Senator Barry Goldwater, the Republican presidential candidate, because of real or imagined differences on the civil-rights issue. Senator Goldwater and his closest associates considered this a low blow and a demonstration that the Michigan Governor cared little for the Republican Party but was only concerned with his own political skin. It has been argued that the Johnson landslide would have smothered Senator Goldwater just as effectively even if Governor Romney and New York Governor Nelson Rockefeller had come forward with warm endorsement. It has also been argued that endorsement of Goldwater would have been a futile gesture for Goldwater and might have lost the Michigan governorship to the Democrats.

Regardless of the merits of various arguments in this Republican squabble, most of Romney's problems within the Republican Party can be traced to his decision not to endorse Goldwater.

Some of the enthusiasm for Richard Nixon, who had not won an election on his own in seventeen years, was actually a strong stop-Romney sentiment persisting among potential convention delegates. The emphasis on the "wide knowledge" of Nixon in the foreign-affairs field was often an effort to downgrade Romney as lacking experience in international matters. But, significantly, Romney's lack of experience in foreign affairs was emphasized as a drawback by some Republican political figures who did not view California Governor Ronald Reagan's lack of experience in foreign affairs as worthy of the same concern.

The sudden surge of support for California Governor Reagan owed a great deal of its impetus to the deep dislike some conservatives continued to harbor against Romney for not endorsing Goldwater. Certainly Reagan was an attractive person and an effective speaker for Republican causes, but a few months at Sacramento was hardly the test necessary to project a political unknown into the role of a serious contender for the Republican presidential nomination. It was possible he would emerge as a man with qualities worth serious consideration, but that was not the reason behind immediate intense interest. He represented only a new conservative face, which might be an alternative to the much-used face of former Vice President Nixon in stopping George Romney. Stopping Romney was the total objective of many ardent Goldwater fans, and reasons for supporting others could be made up to meet the circumstances.

Romney, target of Republicans, became a target of President Johnson and other Democrats as his general popularity moved ahead of Johnson in many areas and it appeared that he was a front runner for the Republican nomination.

Representative Emanuel Celler, the crusty Brooklyn Democrat who headed the House Judiciary Committee, raised the question of Romney's eligibility for the presidency because of his birth in Mexico. The New York Congressman offered his own opinion that it was necessary under the United States Constitution to be born in the United States to be eligible for the nation's highest office.

President Johnson and a dozen other leading Democrats took great pains to slash at Romney, ranging from his comments on the war in Vietnam to the handling of the rioting in Detroit. Such attention would not have been directed at anyone but a potential candidate who they felt would be a dangerous opponent. From their standpoint, the job of trying to carve up and discredit "Good George" could not start too soon.

The problem presented by a puritan in politics has been best demonstrated by Paul B. Fay, Jr., the former Under Secretary of the Navy. Fay, a close friend of former President John F. Kennedy, relates in his book *The Pleasure of His Company* that President Kennedy once told him,

"The one fellow I don't want to run against is Romney. No vice whatsoever, no drinking, no smoking. Imagine someone we know going off for twenty-four or forty-eight hours to fast and meditate, awaiting a message from the Lord on whether to run or not. Does that sound like one of the old gang?"

Romney doesn't sound like one of any political gang in Washington in recent history.

But with all his virtues, George Romney had a lot of tough hurdles to clear before he would be ready to face campaigning against the Democrats. He was about the same age as General Dwight D. Eisenhower when he agreed to seek the Republican nomination. However, many of their problems were different.

By avoiding politics and political positions, Eisenhower at age sixty-one could seem to be all things to all men. By contrast, George Romney has been a frank critic of big government, big labor, and big business. He has faced the problem of dealing with the ticklish open-housing issue while under fire by ultraliberal Democrats who demanded immediate action, and conservative Republicans who wanted no action.

Dwight Eisenhower was able to sit in Europe as Supreme Commander of the Allied Powers while national political figures beat a path to his door trying to persuade him simply to say he would accept the Republican nomination if it were tendered to him.

George Romney, the activist, would have found it difficult to sit and wait for others to deliver the nomination even if he had been in the position of international prestige from which General Eisenhower was dealing in 1951 and 1952. Success had never reached out for George Romney, and it had seldom come easily to him. He had worked hard and pursued his goals with tenacity. It seemed unlikely he would change what had been a winning style at a time he was pursuing the most prized goals of all—the Republican nomination and the presidency.

Some associates have been quoted as saying that Governor Romney has felt he was destined to be President of the United States, and that God was on his side. Those who know George Romney have no doubt that he believes God is on his side, but they will also say that the energetic evangelistic Mormon has always been willing to give God a helping hand. And when difficulties or hardships crop up, George Romney is a fellow who views these as part of God's method of testing him for later service. Unfortunate developments which would dishearten others would not be likely to discourage Romney in any field of competition.

The Detroit riots in July 1967 could have wrecked the political careers of many skillful and experienced politicians. It could have been disaster for Governor George Romney. However, it brought him to the center of the national and international news stage after it had appeared that public interest in his candidacy was lagging.

The Michigan Governor performed no heroics in those tension-filled days, but he was a man genuinely concerned over the tragedy of violence, burning, and looting. He seemed willing to forget his political aspirations in those tense days of trying to bring order out of the chaos and terror which rocked Detroit.

If Romney was making his decisions from political motivations, it was not apparent in those hours of trial. The effort to cooperate with Detroit's Democratic mayor, Jerome Cavanagh, rang true and in great contrast to the treatment he received from President Johnson when as Governor of Michigan he requested federal troops.

Lyndon Johnson could have gained stature by simple and honest cooperation in getting federal troops on the streets of Detroit at the earliest time possible. The occasion cried out for nonpolitical and straightforward acts which would have been admired, if briefly, by critics as well as faithful Democrats.

Instead, President Johnson, always the political operator, saw a possibility for undercutting the righteous Romney who had surpassed Johnson's popularity in the polls. The movement of the federal troops to the Detroit riot scene was delayed more than twelve hours as a result of red tape, and Administration jockeying to try to force Romney to state that an insurrection existed and that he had been unable to control the rioting with the Michigan National Guard. The troops were requested to avoid insurrection.

When President Johnson addressed a national television audience to announce that he finally was using federal troops, his effort to reflect unfavorably upon Governor Romney was so heavy-handed and political in nature that it backfired in a general criticism of the President. Governor Romney was indirectly the beneficiary.

A distrust of President Johnson's handling of the Vietnam War had resulted in sharp disapproval of the Johnson Administration, providing significant political benefits to the Republican Party. However, despite this, Governor Romney had received little direct benefit from the Vietnam War issue, and there were some indications that he had hurt himself with comments that lent themselves to charges of vacillation and inconsistency.

Seeming inconsistencies were exploited by critics of Romney in both parties. To the faultfinders, it was proof that the Michigan Governor, for all his success as an automobile executive and Michigan politician, was not capable of handling the complexities of modern international relations. Efforts were made to label him as a man who "shoots from the hip," who is "superficial," who "goes as the wind blows," and as a plodding business executive with no intellectual depth.

The outspoken Romney added to his own problems in September 1967, with an unfortunate choice of word that played into the hands of his critics. He blamed a "brainwashing" by the Johnson Administration for seeming inconsistencies in his position on Vietnam. Democrats and anti-Romney Republicans jumped on the term with glee and claimed that when he admitted he was deceived on such an important issue, it was proof he was an incompetent or naïve oaf who should not be trusted with important foreign-policy decisions.

His position in public-opinion polls dropped sharply, and Romney was in serious trouble. He asserted that his brainwashing comment was only another way of pointing up the lack of credibility of the Johnson Administration on Vietnam, but it had little early impact on the political damage caused by that one poorly chosen word. It was to be only one of many problems he was to encounter as opponents within the Republican Party tried to trip and discredit him.

Some of the efforts were fair politics, and some were questionable, but the responsibility was on Governor Romney and his associates to try to keep the record straight and present his case in the most favorable light. That challenge in and of itself was one of the crucial tests for Governor Romney and his political supporters, for there is always the possibility of some opposition effort to oversimplify and distort in the heat of a campaign.

To assess George Romney properly we must explore the background of every controversy deeply enough to provide an opportunity to judge the whole picture of this man as he developed and as he is today. He is an admirable figure in many respects, and none of his critics challenge his personal integrity, his record of business success, and his energetic and capable handling of most of the business of the state of Michigan.

But questions have been raised about his eligibility for the office of President of the United States and about the influence his religion might have on his handling of the business of the Government of the United States. The highly controversial position of the Mormon Church in barring Negroes from the priesthood is certain to be as much an issue as was President Kennedy's Catholic religion with its ties to Rome and its opposition to birth control.

There will also be the question of whether George Romney is a man with enough knowledge of foreign affairs to make decisions

on Vietnam and dozens of other areas where the United States is
committed through a complex series of treaties and regional
agreements. The United States Government with its budget of
more than $140 billion a year dwarfs American Motors and the
state of Michigan.

It would be impossible to predict with certainty that any man
would be a good President, for there is no job on earth that com-
pares with it. It is necessary to explore the facts that seem pertinent and provide in-depth examination of the major controversies
which have swirled about the life of the potential candidate. Then
only will we be able to make an educated evaluation as to
whether George Romney has the background, the capacity for
growth, the integrity, and the stable judgment which should be
found in the man who assumes the office so important to the
future of each of us.

TWO

A Persecuted Minority

"I am a member of a religion that is among the most persecuted minority groups in our history."—*George Romney*

The Church of Jesus Christ of the Latter-Day Saints traces its origin from September 22, 1827, when, according to Mormon belief, the angel Moroni delivered to Joseph Smith, Jr., the golden plates containing what was to become known as the *Book of Mormon*. Although that religion had grown to a membership of 2.5 million by 1967, its first sixty years were a history of bitter controversy. Some elements of controversy still persisted as George W. Romney became the first member of that church to make a serious bid for the office of President of the United States.

Persecution had followed the path of the Mormon religion from that fall day in 1827 when 21-year-old Joseph Smith knelt in a wooded area southwest of Palmyra, New York, through the Mormon trek West, under the leadership of Brigham Young, and the first forty years the church was centered in Salt Lake City, Utah.

18

The first large colony of "Saints" settled in Kirtland, Ohio, in 1831, but the temple was hardly constructed in 1836 when the unorthodox religion kindled resentment among neighbors who followed more traditional religions. Smith and the main body of his followers moved to Missouri, where other Mormon baiters insulted and physically attacked them in "the massacre of Hann's Mill." Twenty Mormons were slain, and Joseph Smith was temporarily jailed. The Saints beat a hasty retreat to Illinois, and there Prophet Joseph Smith obtained from the state of Illinois what has been described as "perhaps the most liberal charter ever granted to an American city." This charter provided Smith and his followers with complete independence in education, and in judicial and military activities in the city which they called Nauvoo.

In four short years, the industrious, well-organized Mormons had constructed a beautiful city on the eastern bank of the Mississippi River, complete with a huge temple, university, and well-trained militia. It was in this thriving midwestern city of twenty thousand that the Romney family first joined Prophet Joseph Smith. As a result of Mormon industry, Nauvoo was then the largest city in Illinois, four times larger than Chicago with its population of five thousand.

In the summer of 1841, Miles Romney, a 35-year-old carpenter from England, his wife Elizabeth Gaskell Romney, and two small sons arrived in Nauvoo. The skilled young carpenter and cabinetmaker and his wife had been converted to the Church of Jesus Christ of the Latter-Day Saints at Dalton-in-Furness, Lancashire, in 1839, by one of Prophet Smith's traveling missionaries. They had sailed from Liverpool on February 7, 1841, arrived in New Orleans in April, and had traveled by boat up the Mississippi to Nauvoo. They were among the more than four thousand English converts who arrived in Nauvoo in a span of only four years.

The Romneys had little money when they arrived, but Miles was proficient in a needed skill. He constructed his own home, worked on the construction of the Mormon Temple, and settled down to establish himself as a stable man in this flourishing community in the New World. Miles Park Romney, grandfather of

Governor George Romney, was born at Nauvoo on August 18, 1843—a few months before tragedy struck the Mormon settlement.

A feud which developed between Prophet Joseph Smith and William Law, Canadian-born member of the Church, shattered the tranquillity of Nauvoo in the summer of 1844. Some historians contend that it was a result of an attempt by Smith to persuade Mrs. Law to become one of his wives.

Law printed a newspaper alleging that Smith was practicing polygamy, and Smith and his associates retaliated against what they termed a libelous charge by wrecking the printing press and destroying all copies of the newspaper.

While Prophet Smith had been the authority within the Mormon colony, a wave of anti-Mormonism was fanned by Law and his friends. It swept the entire area, and Joseph Smith, his brother Hyrum, and two associates were arrested and jailed pending a trial on riot charges.

An anti-Mormon mob stormed the jail at Carthage, Illinois, on June 27, 1844, shooting and killing Prophet Smith and Hyrum.

The murder of the brothers signaled the end of the Mormon colony in Nauvoo. Under the leadership of Brigham Young and other disciples of Smith, the colony remained there through 1845, but anti-Mormon sentiment increased. Early in 1846 the decision was made to leave Nauvoo and to travel west in what was to be one of the most remarkable migrations in the history of the United States.

When thousands of Mormons started the trek west with Brigham Young in early 1846, Miles Romney was too poor to accompany them. With other terror-stricken Mormons, he moved across the frozen Mississippi River to Iowa, traveling only to Burlington in his first move to escape bitter harassment in Illinois. A few months later, Miles Romney moved his family down the Mississippi to St. Louis, and after a brief period there, followed the muddy Missouri River to Council Bluffs, Iowa, stopping there to work and prepare for the long trek west to the Salt Lake area in northern Utah.

In March 1850, the Romney family left Council Bluffs on the

grinding thousand-mile oxcart journey along the sandy Platte River, through the dusty sandhill territory of western Nebraska, and the long Rocky Mountain climb to the Sweetwater River, crossing South Pass, and down the rugged trapper trails to the Wasatch Mountain Range into the valley of the Great Salt Lake. They arrived on October 13, 1850, and seven-year-old Miles Park had walked most of the way.

The Saints had survived an arduous ordeal for freedom to practice their religion, including polygamy. Brigham Young had selected the sandy, arid region near the huge Salt Lake because no one else had wanted it, and because it had appeared to be an isolated place with little possibility of intrusion by others. The Mormons had given up good land and comfortable homes to make the journey, and when Brigham Young had arrived in July 1847, Salt Lake was still a possession of Mexico. It became a United States territory in 1848 through the Treaty of Guadalupe Hidalgo.

In 1849, the year before the Romney family arrived, the Mormons organized the state of Deseret, named Brigham Young as Governor, and prepared their first constitution to be submitted to the Congress of the United States.

Congress rejected that constitution because of the practice of polygamy. Although President Millard Fillmore appointed Young as the first territorial Governor in 1850, a stormy forty years were to follow before the issue of polygamy was settled and the state of Utah was created by Congress.

Brigham Young's good relations with the White House fell apart when James Buchanan of Pennsylvania was elected President in 1856. The following year, President Buchanan appointed Alfred Cumming of Georgia as Governor to break the tight Mormon control. He also sent federal troops into the Salt Lake area to enforce the appointment, and they remained there until the Civil War.

Seeking statehood was pointless under the Buchanan Administration, and when Abraham Lincoln became President the Mormons did not fare any better. In 1861, a large area of what the Mormons called the state of Deseret was given to Colorado on the east, and another expanse constituting most of the state of Nevada was taken from the west.

In 1862, the Mormons drew up their third constitution for another try at winning statehood, but the result was again sharp reaction against the practice of polygamy and passage of a federal polygamy law. Although troops were sent to Salt Lake, the polygamy law was not enforced.

Brigham Young, a most active polygamist, was president of the Church of Jesus Christ of the Latter-Day Saints, and until his death in 1877 there was no possibility of change in Church doctrine, which approved polygamy, and consequently little chance that the Mormon colony would be given statehood by Congress. Unsuccessful efforts were made to obtain statehood in 1872, in 1882, and in 1887.

Each time the Mormons brought the subject before Congress, it opened the old debate, whipped up new controversy, and resulted in additional, tougher laws against polygamy or a new flurry of enforcement of the laws already on the books.

Miles Romney, after a brief period in the Salt Lake area in 1850, was sent by Brigham Young to southern Utah to establish the town of St. George and to supervise construction of a temple there. In 1877, Miles Romney, at age 71, was overseeing final work on the St. George Temple when he fell from a high window and was fatally injured. That temple was dedicated on April 6, 1877, a red stone monument, to Miles Romney, the English carpenter who had carved a place for himself and his family in the Virgin River area in the far southwestern corner of the Utah Territory.

By the time Miles Romney died, his son Miles Park Romney had become a confirmed polygamist. He married his first wife, Hannah Hood Hill, in 1862, when both were nineteen years of age. Five years later Miles Park Romney took a second wife. By the time the Federal Government started a tight crackdown on polygamy, he had moved to St. Johns, Arizona, where he had become a building contractor, businessman, and editor and publisher of a local weekly newspaper, the *Orion Era*.

Aggressive federal prosecutions for polygamy started in the Utah Territory in 1884, and more than twelve thousand Mormons lost their citizenship that year. As the prosecution net broadened in 1885, Miles Park Romney, who now had three wives, lost his status as a leading citizen and, according to author Tom Mahoney, became "a hounded and hunted man."

Helaman Pratt, son of an influential Mormon Church leader and a friend of Miles Park Romney, was in Mexico City on a Mormon mission at the time. He called upon Mexican President Porfirio Díaz and obtained permission for the polygamous Mormons and others to buy lands and establish a colony in Mexico.

Gaskell Romney, father of Governor George Romney, was born September 22, 1871, to Hannah Hood Hill Romney in St. George. Gaskell, reared in the polygamous family in St. George, Utah, and in St. Johns, Arizona, was thirteen years of age when his father left for the Casas Grandes area in Chihuahua, Mexico, to seek a location for a new home and to avoid arrest by United States authorities.

The next year, the young boy helped his mother Hannah drive the horses as they traveled across the barren stretches of Indian territory in southern Arizona and Mexico to join his father in Casas Grandes.

Although they lived briefly at a desolate place called Cliff Ranch in the Sierra Madre Mountains west of Colonia Juárez, the Romney family soon moved into that small town, where Miles Park continued his trade as a carpenter and builder.

The move to Mexico by the polygamous Mormons was in part financed by the Church, and the Romney family and others in the colony retained close ties with the Salt Lake Stake. Gaskell learned the traditional family trade of carpenter and builder, and then returned to Salt Lake City for a year at the old Latter-Day Saints College before returning to Colonia Juárez to marry Miss Anna Amelia Pratt, one of the ten daughters of his father's friend Helaman Pratt. They had known each other since they were children.

The marriage of Gaskell Romney and Amelia took place on February 20, 1895. One year later, Congress finally approved statehood for Utah as the forty-fifth state. Several years before, on October 6, 1890, the Mormon Church had issued a manifesto which by divine sanction rejected the commandment to practice polygamy that Joseph Smith had revealed fifty years earlier. Polygamy became grounds for excommunication.

After living briefly on the outskirts of Casas Grandes, Gaskell and Anna Amelia moved to Colonia Dublán, where five of their seven children were born.

Gaskell Maurice was born in 1897, Douglas Pratt in 1899, and Miles Pratt in 1903. George Wilcken, the fourth son, was born on July 8, 1907, in the two-story red brick home his father had constructed in Colonia Dublán. Lawrence Romney was born two years later in the same house.

Gaskell Romney had one wife, and there was no legal reason why they could not return to the United States. But his building business was prosperous, and his family and closest friends were there in the little cluster of Mormon colonies along the Casas Grandes River only about 150 miles below the border of the United States.

While the Mormon life in Mexico was untroubled and prosperous for more than twenty-five years, it lost its stability in 1911, when the aging President Díaz lost control. A revolution led by Francisco I. Madero erupted in 1911, and on March 5, 1911, the fighting came within six miles of the Mormon colony. The crack of gunfire was heard by four-year-old George Romney as he sat on the porch of his father's home in Colonia Dublán.

There was a brief peace after Madero captured Juárez and traveled south in triumph through Casas Grandes, but a counter-revolution in February 1912 put the entire Mormon community in a state of turmoil. They tried to remain neutral in an effort to avoid being victimized by the violence of the rebel forces of Pascual Orozco. However, their efforts at neutrality were only partially successful, for nine Mormons were killed as Orozco's men seized most of Chihuahua.

Mormon horses were confiscated and among them was Monte, George Romney's Indian pony. The loss of Monte was a tragedy to the four-year-old boy, but the tragedy turned to triumph when the clever little horse escaped from the rebels and returned home. During the spring and summer of 1912, rebel soldiers stole Monte on a half dozen occasions, but each time they made the mistake of believing that normal hobbles would keep him from straying. Monte had learned to run with hobbles, and the little horse simply waited for nightfall, slipped away from the rebel camp, and ran home.

While Monte's craftiness pleased George and other Romney family members, it was one of the few things to be happy about in July 1912, for central Chihuahua became a battleground for federal and rebel troops. As the situation became more and more desperate, rebel General José Inez Salazar demanded a list of all weapons owned by the residents of the Mormon colonies.

Mormon leaders held a late-night strategy conference at the Gaskell Romney home on July 12, 1912, while George and his brothers slept soundly upstairs. The men arranged for Junius Romney, George's uncle, to call on General Salazar to plead that they were genuinely neutral and to ask that they be permitted to retain their weapons for their own protection.

Temporary arrangements ceased on Saturday, July 27, 1912, when rebel soldiers put Colonia Dublán under siege and ordered all Mormon arms to be delivered to the rebels immediately. Junius Romney agreed to relinquish their weapons the next day if assurances were received that all women and children could be evacuated by train to El Paso, Texas. Safe passage for the women and children was guaranteed, and the Mormon men gathered up all weapons except four dozen recently acquired long-range rifles. Those new modern rifles were hidden.

On Monday morning, July 29, 1912, Gaskell Romney put his wife and five sons on a train in Casas Grandes. Anna Amelia Romney was pregnant, so she and the two youngest boys, George and Lawrence, were permitted to ride in a chair car. The older boys, Maurice, Douglas, and Miles, rode in another, less comfortable, car on the long, crowded evacuation train that made use of flatcars, boxcars, and any other available conveyance to increase the load capacity.

As his family left Casas Grandes, Gaskell joined the other Mormon men at a nearby mountain rendezvous. Conditions did not improve, and within a few days they decided it was pointless to try to remain in the dangerous rebel territory of Chihuahua. The 235 Mormon men, under the direction of Junius Romney, made preparation to leave Mexico with a few valuables and five hundred horses. A brief skirmish with one group of rebels highlighted an otherwise tiring ordeal. The men made the 150-mile trek in three days under a blazing August sun. They entered New Mexico a few miles southeast of Hachita, and Gaskell immediately headed east to rejoin his family in El Paso.

In Mexico, Gaskell Romney had been a prosperous business-man, perhaps one of the most prosperous in Colonia Dublán. The large red brick house was considered the finest in the community. But the leading citizen of Colonia Dublán was just another un-employed carpenter in the crowded streets of El Paso.

More than 2,300 of the 4,000 Mormon colonists were evacu-ated in a three-day period, and crowded El Paso was a difficult place to find steady work. Congress provided a relief fund of a hundred thousand dollars to help what George Romney has often called "the first displaced persons of the twentieth century."

Charles Wilcken Romney was born on August 26, 1912, into what was a newly poor family. Comforts had been left behind, and Gaskell and his older boys worked at odd jobs. In the late fall of 1912, Gaskell and his brother, George S. Romney, moved their families to Los Angeles, California, to find more lucrative employment.

The Romney family was starting over again. Gaskell Romney at forty-one was beginning as a carpenter in Los Angeles in the same fashion that Miles and Elizabeth Gaskell Romney had started anew in Nauvoo, Illinois, and again in St. George, Utah, and as Miles Park Romney had to begin again in Mexico after tighter enforce-ment of the polygamy law had forced him to flee the United States.

THREE

Poverty and Idaho Potatoes
(1912 – 1921)

Los Angeles offered better opportunities in late October 1912 than El Paso, which was jammed with displaced persons, and Gaskell and his oldest son, Maurice, were soon able to find enough work remodeling houses and business places and doing other small carpentry projects to make an adequate living. Much of the work was on an hourly basis, as Maurice recalls it, with Gaskell receiving roughly one dollar an hour and Maurice receiving "fifty cents an hour, or it might have been a little less."

"We weren't poverty[-stricken] in the sense of us being in want," Maurice recalls. "There was always enough food in the house, and the home at West Twenty-first and Main streets was a well-built white frame house. It wasn't in a slum area, but it was on the fringe of an area that was colored and oriental."

There were few luxuries for five-year-old George Romney, and even as a small boy he was aware that there was no longer any money for many of the things he and his brothers had enjoyed in Colonia Dublán. It was out of the question now to think of a horse to replace the much-loved Monte he had had as a daily

27

companion in Mexico. The changed status was especially reflected
in the fact that the older boys were required to work to supplement
the family income. While Maurice was the only son old enough to
help his father on remodeling jobs, Douglas Pratt had a fruit-and-
vegetable stand a block from the Romney home, and Miles sold
newspapers and worked as a vendor at a nearby park and recreation area.

The few luxuries that came into the life of young George Romney were treasured and remembered. Incidents that stand out
most vividly in his memory more than a half century later are
a visit by his maternal great-grandfather C. H. Wilcken, of Salt
Lake, attending the Ringling Brothers Circus, and his first dinner
at a cafeteria.

Great-grandfather Wilcken, a tall and white-haired former soldier in the German Army, made a lasting impression on all of the
Romney children. The six-foot four-inch Utahan had served as a
bodyguard for the Kaiser in Germany, and after coming to the
United States had served in an American Army unit recruited in
New York and was sent to Utah to quell the independent and
often arrogant antics of Brigham Young in Salt Lake.

The tales that Grandfather Wilcken told were exciting, and at
times chilling for the young Mormon boys. As Maurice recalled it,
the old gentleman had never heard of Mormons until he was recruited into the Army in New York to help Col. Albert Sidney Johnson take control of the Utah Territory from Brigham Young and
the Mormon Church. President James Buchanan named Colonel
Johnson for the assignment shortly after taking office in 1857, and
the troops arrived in Utah the next year.

It was a bloodthirsty group of young soldiers who accompanied
Colonel Johnson, according to the stories their great-grandfather
told them in Los Angeles more than sixty years later. Whether it
was part of the recruiting propaganda, or simply the self-induced
emotion of the young militiamen, the old soldier told the young
Romney boys the mission was to "kill the Mormons—and wipe
them off of the face of the earth." After the detested Mormons had
been properly slaughtered, some of the young adventurers planned

to join the Gold Rush in California or in the Rocky Mountain states.

Maurice related that Great-grandfather Wilcken pictured himself as no less bloodthirsty toward Mormons than his companions as they entered Utah, but there was a happy ending for his story. He concluded the Mormons were such fine, industrious people that he was converted and became a bodyguard for Brigham Young.

Great-grandfather Wilcken was also remembered for more than his fascinating tales of the history of early Utah. He took the Romney boys to their first vaudeville show, where trained ponies and dogs performed. With him the boys also attended a Ringling Brothers Circus which set up its tent in a huge recreation and park area a block from their home.

Equally vivid in the mind of George Romney is his first meal in a cafeteria. As George recalls it, his father and Maurice had remodeled a cafeteria, and the owner had invited the entire Romney family for a huge dinner. The children were permitted to eat anything they wanted, and for little George it was a moment of greatest thrill.

Although Maurice enjoyed the meal, a less pleasant aspect of the cafeteria incident stands out more clearly for him. The dinner was the only pay that he and his father ever received for the job. Initially the free meal for the family was supposed to be a special gesture of thanks for a job well done, but the cafeteria owner later claimed he was broke and could not pay the money he owed for the labor of Gaskell and Maurice. "Father filed a lawsuit, but I don't believe we were ever able to collect a thing," Maurice recalled. "That was a time when every dollar counted."

Although life was not generally unpleasant in Los Angeles, Gaskell Romney was anxious to take his family to a better environment for growing boys. He wanted to return to the type of living they had known in the dominantly rural area of Colonia Dublán, and he wanted close association with friends from the Church of Jesus Christ of Latter-Day Saints.

A potato-and-grain farm in southern Idaho became his goal. He made one trip to Oakley, Idaho, in 1913, in an effort to buy a farm. That brief visit to the area south of the Snake River was unsuccessful. He rejected the only farms available as unpromising because of location or poor soil.

In the fall of 1913, George Samuel Romney, who had been a science teacher in Mexico, was offered a teaching job at the Oakley Academy, a Mormon school. As he left Los Angeles, his brother Gaskell asked him to keep an eye out for a farm near Oakley.

Within a few months, George Samuel wrote to Gaskell enthusiastically, reporting a farm for sale in the Brush Creek area south of Oakley. Following his suggestion that Gaskell send money to bind the purchase, Gaskell scraped together all the savings he could spare, sent it to George Samuel for the down payment, and made preparations to move to Idaho.

In the spring of 1914, the Gaskell Romney family went by train to Salt Lake for a short visit with Grandfather Wilcken and other relatives, and then journeyed north to Oakley, a short distance above the Utah-Idaho border. They were met by an enthusiastic George Romney, but as Maurice recalls it, his father "was sick when he saw the farm that had been bought for him."

"It was a farm that Father had examined a year earlier," Maurice relates. "He had turned it down as the worst farm in the whole valley, but Uncle George had bought it for him and there was no choice but to try to make it go."

Gaskell and Maurice built a house in Oakley, then a little town of about six hundred, and the whole family pitched in to try to make the potato farm pay. It was a futile exercise from the start, with money going out for harness, equipment, seeds, and other necessities, and little coming in. The debts piled up in that unsuccessful farming venture were to hang over Gaskell Romney's head for a dozen years before he was finally able to pay the last of them.

George, who had been old enough to help with the farm work at Oakley, had an accident there which could have cost his life. According to Maurice, the boy fell off a heavy harrow being pulled by a team of draft horses to level the fields. Fortunately, George fell into a deep furrow and so only suffered scrapes and bruises from the heavy farm equipment.

George Romney remembers Oakley as a period of poverty and potatoes. "We ate potatoes for breakfast, dinner, and supper," he recalls. "We fed potatoes to the hogs, and this gave us a little pork for variety in our diet, but it wasn't much variety."

"It was the worst period, and Father finally gave up," Maurice recalls. "We moved to Salt Lake. The only thing we had in abundance was potatoes."

But in spite of everything, the boys had fun riding the two farm horses and swimming in nearby Brush Creek.

The Gaskell Romney and George Samuel Romney families moved back to Salt Lake in 1916, when George was nine. Gaskell and Anna's only daughter Meryl was born in Salt Lake City on May 24, 1917. George Samuel wanted to complete his work on a degree at the University of Utah, in preparation for a better teaching job. Gaskell and his two older sons, Maurice and Douglas, were eager to see if they could reverse their fortunes in construction work in a larger city. The Romneys' financial prospects were better than they had been in Oakley, but they were still far from prosperous when the opportunity came for another move a year later.

In 1917, the Mormon Church engaged George Samuel as president of Ricks Academy, a Church school in Rexburg, Idaho, in the farming country thirty-five miles northeast of Idaho Falls. At the same time, Gaskell was hired to supervise construction for the Rexburg Home Builder, which was flourishing as a result of a World War I building boom. Increased demands for wheat, wool, and sugar beets had brought sudden prosperity to the little town of four thousand.

The booming building business in Rexburg provided the Romney family with the only period of real prosperity that they had known since leaving Mexico. Gaskell Romney became a director of Rexburg Home Builders, and this firm merged with others into the Rexburg Building and Loan Company. Big plans for expanding the firm, with its holdings in farms, houses, and a hotel, to a five-story office building were made in the expectation that the boom would go on indefinitely.

George Wilcken Romney was ten years old when the family

moved to Rexburg, and he started to show promise as a student and as a person of determination. The next year he hired out for a dollar a day to shock wheat, and a dollar an acre to top and thin sugar beets.

With this flush of prosperity, Gaskell Romney bought his first car, a secondhand Maxwell. When he later bought a new Studebaker, Douglas rebuilt the old Maxwell into a racing car for appearances at county fairs in the eastern Idaho region. George Wilcken had a typical boy's curiosity and interest in the family car, and particularly in his brother's tinkering with the old Maxwell.

Those were formative years for George Romney. He recalls them as great years. From his bedroom window at the rear of the family home he could look east to the western slope of the majestic Teton Range. With his father and brothers, he went camping and fishing in the Teton River and swam in the irrigation canals of Henrys Fork of the Snake River. Rexburg had an active Boy Scout troop under the guidance of Scoutmaster Andrew M. Andersen, a former Marine, and both Miles and George were members of this troop at different times.

The economy of Rexburg, based on demands for wheat, sugar, and wool, started to collapse a few months after the end of World War I. Although Gaskell Romney and his business associates held on, hoping for a reversal that would restore the building industry, it was futile. Farmers went broke, businesses went bankrupt, and building stopped. With farmers and businessmen abandoning the area, the price of real estate tumbled, and the Rexburg Building and Loan Company was left with a bundle of worthless second mortgages.

Young George and Miles saw their father's plans for the five-story business building abandoned after the huge excavation had been made for the foundation. They saw streets deserted, and homes and business buildings vacated as the pinch of the depression increased.

Personal sorrow enveloped the family when Lawrence, twelve years old, died on February 12, 1921, following a lengthy illness of rheumatic fever. George was thirteen at the time, and closest in age to Lawrence.

A happy event came for the Romney family that year when George was graduated from Washington Grade School as valedictorian and spoke before an audience of more than eleven hundred people. But pride in the accomplishment of a young son did not shut out the cold economic necessity to leave the ailing Rexburg area and try to make a fresh start in Salt Lake City.

In the late spring of 1921, the Romneys moved back to Salt Lake. At the age of fifty, it had become necessary for Gaskell to try to start over again. By this time, Maurice and Douglas were in their twenties; both were married, and capable carpenters and builders. Miles and George were also being trained as carpenters, and during his high-school years in Salt Lake George became a fast and skillful lather and plasterer.

Miles, closest to George during the high-school years, says he cannot recall any special traits that the younger brother had which indicated he would become an outstanding figure in the business and political world. "He had his little attainments in junior high school and in high school, but they were not so unusual at the time, or even as I look back at them," Miles said. "I can think of other fellows with the same attainments and the same experiences and they are driving milk trucks in Salt Lake City," Miles said.

As they worked together as lathers and plasterers, Miles did note a steadiness that he said has been a consistent trait of his younger brother. "George accepted responsibility, was a good hard worker, and got along with people well, and he enjoyed being in the leadership of the activities."

Maurice said there were no indications of any brilliance in George, but that there was "a determination and a persistence" that was characteristic of everything he did.

Because the older boys played football, and because several cousins were outstanding stars, George wanted to play football. "He went out for the team in Salt Lake when he weighed only about ninety pounds, and he stayed with it until he was finally big enough and good enough to make the team," Maurice said.

Within a family of many outstanding athletes, George Romney was simply one who tried harder. He was never able to achieve
the skill of his older brothers, Maurice and Douglas, in high-school
football, or that of Miles, who became the Inter-Mountain Amateur
Welterweight boxing champion in 1922.

FOUR

In Pursuit of Lenore

In the summer of 1924 seventeen-year-old George Romney fell in love with a pretty fifteen-year-old brunette and never got over it. Occie Evans, a football and basketball teammate, asked George to ride along as he drove his father's car to Holliday, Utah, to meet his girl friend, Genevieve Bird, and several of her friends. Lenore LaFount was one of a half dozen girls who piled into the car for the ride back to the city from an afternoon picnic in a canyon of the Wasatch Mountains.

Pretty Lenore, one of four daughters of Harold Arundel La-Fount, had a ukulele with her, which she strummed as they sang on the way home. The slim, brown-eyed girl was the last to be taken home, and Evans says, "From that time on it was Lenore and George."

As Occie remembers it, George had never had a girl friend. Though he danced and mixed socially, he had been totally absorbed in athletics, high-school politics, and his job as a lather.

Girls had never mattered until that day when Lenore became everything to him. Friends and family members generally agree that Lenore has been a major force in his life as a high-school sweet-heart, an ardently wooed young woman, and his wife of more than thirty-five years.

Teen-age George was shy about asking for a date and sent a friend to ask Lenore if she would accept his invitation to a dance sponsored by the high-school speaking club, to which he belonged. Lenore was surprised when George showed up because his friend had not made it clear he was speaking for bashful George. This Miles Standish won out in the end.

Initially, George was more interested in Lenore than she was in him, but he went about solving that problem the way he tackled any problem—with hard work and persistence.

Lenore and her three beautiful sisters did not lack suitors, and the LaFount home was always crowded with boys. George was present whenever he could squeeze in the time, even if he had to take his seven-year-old sister Meryl along. He arranged to go on double dates with Occie Evans and his girl, Genevieve Bird. When Lenore tried out for a school play, George came tagging along.

"She was taking the lead in the school play," Occie recalled. "He (George) was hanging around so much, they finally had to give him a part." It was the role of her father.

The play called for Lenore to be kissed by the leading man, and George, who had never yet kissed Lenore, lost his temper as a result of what he considered a too enthusiastic rehearsal of the love scene. The play was staged complete with kisses despite the objections of the jealous young suitor. It was only the first of many incidents demonstrating the possessive attitude that George had developed toward Lenore.

Although Lenore was flattered by the attention of this persistent admirer, there were no indications that she was as serious about him.

Lenore and George had much in common as far as pioneer family background was concerned. Her father, Harold LaFount, had come from England as a result of the work of missionaries in much the manner that the Romney family had come. Rosetta Berry,

Lenore's maternal grandmother, had made the trek from Nauvoo to Salt Late City in a group traveling with handcarts.

But there was a difference between the social status of the LaFount and the Romney families.

Harold LaFount had started with a small hardware store in Logan, Utah, but he had moved into land development, had launched a small manufacturing business making earphones for crystal radio receivers, and had become well to do.

The Gaskell Romney family had suffered one financial reverse after another, and was in the process of struggling to make a comeback from the Rexburg disaster as George went through high school. George wanted to go to college, but it was obvious that he would have to work his way through. By contrast, Lenore LaFount, with aspirations to be an actress, had solid family financial support to provide any educational advantage that would be helpful.

Before he met Lenore, George had talked of going to the Atlantic Coast to get a job and work his way through some Eastern university as soon as he was graduated from Latter-Day Saints University High School. His romantic pursuit of Lenore was a factor in his decision to attend the local Latter-Day Saints Junior College in Salt Lake, for Lenore still had another year of high school to complete in Salt Lake City.

Having a pal like Occie Evans, whose father owned a new Nash, was helpful to George and his romance with Lenore. As were Occie and Genevieve, they were constant companions during much of George's year in junior college.

The Romney family suffered its greatest blow in February 1926, when George's mother died of a cerebral hemorrhage at the age of forty-nine. Always devout, George now turned to his religion for comfort in the months ahead and was determined to start a Mormon mission that fall in England.

Although family finances had improved to the point that Gaskell Romney had bought a Chrysler, there was not enough for the family to afford to send two boys on foreign missions at the same time. Miles, four years older, was then on his Church mission in South Africa. George was told he would have to pay his own way if he started that fall.

After discussions with his father indicated that $500 would be sufficient to start his mission to England, he pitched in with the kind of exhausting schedule that would have finished a weaker man. The nineteen-year-old George worked as a lather from dawn until dark throughout the summer and early fall, saved $700, gave 10 percent to the Church for tithing, and with the $630 that remained had more than enough to start his mission.

Although he arose and got his own breakfast at dawn and often worked until after dark, George still managed to drive over to see Lenore nearly every evening in the months before leaving. Lenore entered the University of Utah as a freshman that fall, and she was present at the farewell party and later at the station when George left on October 22, 1926. It was an experience that he was to regard as more valuable than a college education would have been.

On October 29, 1926, George and the other members of the Mormon missionary party sailed from Montreal on a Canadian Pacific liner, the *Montclare*. They landed at Liverpool on November 4.

For two years, the exuberant young missionary trudged up and down the length and breadth of England and Scotland, trying to bring the message of the *Book of Mormon* and the restored true Church to the skeptical, the cynical, and the rude hecklers who only regarded Mormons as polygamists.

George and his companions walked from door to door, gave their little greeting as "a missionary of the Church of Jesus Christ of the Latter-Day Saints" and tried to quickly get across their "very important message about the restoration of the Gospel." Most of the time they were received politely, but coolly enough to make it apparent that the pamphlet on Mormon religion would never be read. Periodically an angry householder would berate the young missionary as a nuisance and angrily slam the door. Occasionally listeners willing and eager allowed the young man from Salt Lake City to explain his religion and the purpose of his mission.

George spent more than three months in Glasgow, an area where his great-grandmother, Mary Wood Pratt, was born. After weeks of weary work in the slums of Glasgow, he was transferred to Edinburgh, where he spoke before hostile crowds on the

"Mound," but in the process had his first experience with golf —a game that was to be his major source of exercise and relaxation in later years.

Romney and a companion, M. B. Langford, had concluded one session on the Mound when a man stepped up, introduced himself, and asked the two young men if they would be interested in borrowing his clubs to play a round of golf on a local course. On that first round, George posted a score of 130 for 18 holes. He concluded it was not bad for a novice, and was back the next day and for several days following, finally paring his score down to 105 for 18 holes.

Golf was one of the few forms of amusement open to the young missionaries. The Mormon religion prohibited them from using coffee, tea, tobacco, or other stimulants. During the missionary period they were not permitted to dance or date, but there was no indication that George had the urge to dance with anyone or to date anyone but Lenore. He wrote her frequently, and carried her picture with him constantly.

A continual flow of letters from Lenore kept him posted on her activities in school, and of her selection as one of six Utah girls chosen to be part of an official welcoming party for Col. Charles Lindbergh when he visited Salt Lake after his historic flight from New York to Paris. In the summer of 1927, she wrote telling him that her father had been appointed by President Calvin Coolidge as a member of the original Federal Radio Commission. The appointment had been recommended by a long-time family friend, Senator Reed Smoot, a Utah Republican. He received the news that the LaFount family was moving to Washington, D. C., with mixed emotions.

During the same time, George received word that one of his older brothers, Douglas Pratt Romney, had died following an attack of appendicitis. He left a wife and small daughter, and a son was born a few weeks after his death.

George also received the news that his father had remarried. The second wife was Amy Wilcken Pratt, younger sister of George's mother and a spinster schoolteacher and librarian.

George learned to keep going whether the news from home

was good or bad, and despite heckling and anti-Mormon slurs. He enjoyed outings at the horse races or the Rugby games. On the best days, he was aware of what it was to be a part of a disliked minority, and he felt the bitterness of those who were influenced by a dramatically anti-Mormon movie, then showing in the British Isles, called *Through Death Valley, or The Mormon Peril.*

His mission ended in late November 1928. He had no money for the tour across Europe that so many of the young Mormons took at the end of their mission. George, who was accustomed to figuring his funds closely, had just enough for a short trip to Paris before taking a ship home. He also managed to squeeze in a two-week visit with Lenore in Washington.

The trip to see Lenore had priority over everything else, for they had been separated two full years. It was a reunion that only convinced George more than ever that Lenore was someday going to be his wife. Although Harold LaFount loaned the family car to George and Lenore, the expense of several days in Washington left George practically broke, and when he boarded the train for Salt Lake City on January 3, 1929, he had just thirty-five cents and his railroad ticket for the 2,100-mile trip home.

With Lenore in Washington, D. C., George made up his mind that he was going to arrange to go to college there. He had no money for a quick decision, so he enrolled for the second semester at the University of Utah. He took a part-time job, and then also enrolled in an evening Speedwriting course at the Latter-Day Saints Business College, with the thought that shorthand would be helpful in landing a job in Washington.

In June, Lenore was graduated from George Washington University in Washington, D. C., and the LaFount family returned to Salt Lake City for the remainder of the summer. It was a happy time for George, but it wrecked his attendance at the evening Speedwriting course. The serious courtship of that summer of 1929 meant that George missed all but six of his night classes.

He had seen her only two weeks in two and a half years, and for once the usually serious-minded George forgot work, school, and his plan to learn Speedwriting.

They dated nearly every night—swimming, dancing, or just driving on the desert and in the Wasatch Mountains. The possessive George did not want to dance with other girls, and he did not want Lenore to dance with other men.

It all ended abruptly when the LaFount family returned to Washington, and George, then twenty-two, made plans to follow at the first opportunity.

The idea of going to Washington, D. C., to attend college also appealed to brother Miles. He had been working with his father in the construction business and had saved enough money to buy a new Chrysler.

Both young men enrolled in night classes at George Washington University, and Miles landed a construction job immediately. It was a little more difficult for George to find a job, but he was eager and confident. Disregarding his lack of consistent attendance at the Speedwriting school, he optimistically answered a newspaper Help-Wanted ad asking for a "stenographer."

Equipped with high-school typing and a Speedwriting course that had been a bust, George went to a designated room at the Senate Office Building to apply for the job. The fact that there were nearly a hundred other applicants for the job did not discourage the young man from Utah, even when a secretary suggested that he might not want to wait.

Long on good looks and personality, but short on office talent, George insisted that he be interviewed by a secretary and by Senator David I. Walsh, the Massachusetts Democrat, who had placed the ad.

Senator Walsh liked George and hired him. The pay was to be $120 a month, but it was only a few days before George was in trouble. The first time he was required to take dictation from Senator Walsh he fumbled through, largely because of the slow manner in which the letters were dictated. When George was called to take a speech, the speed was too much for him, and the results were ruinous.

Some employers would have fired him, but Senator Walsh was a kindly man with a sense of humor and personal experience of working his way through Holy Cross College and Boston University Law School. Instead of dismissing George, he simply arranged to shift him to a job as a legislative clerk on tariff problems pending before the Senate Finance Committee.

Senator Walsh made the shift of assignments at the initial suggestion of James T. Clark, a young private secretary who had previously taken dictation and who had been moved to the job of handling the tariff problems. It was fortunate for George that he found himself among congenial people, and as it turned out, the experience of handling tariff matters was highly beneficial to his career. It was his responsibility to analyze all proposed tariff legislation and prepare a summary, and to interview the Massachusetts constituents and others who came to Senator Walsh's office with information or inquiries about tariff legislation.

He learned how to obtain information from the Library of Congress, the Tariff Commission, foreign embassies, and through various committees of Congress. He accompanied Senator Walsh to the Senate Finance Committee meetings, and had to be prepared to furnish information the Massachusetts Democrat wanted. When tariff matters were being discussed on the Senate floor, he was required to be present with the papers and other documents that Senator Walsh might require.

Those months with Senator Walsh as an insider at the Capitol gave George insight into the working of the Congress that was to be invaluable throughout the rest of his career in business and politics. A cousin, Isaac M. Stewart, was clerk of the Senate Finance Committee, then chaired by Senator Smoot of Utah. George worked with Stewart on many tax matters, and because of the relationship did not feel alone in those first months as a Senate employee.

In that period the great names of the era became simply people with the same strengths and weaknesses of other people he had known well for years. They were only as good as the information that was available to them, George learned. Even in the relatively small bureaucracy of a Senate committee or a Senator's office, it was easy to misplace information or act upon half-information and make a serious blunder. He saw the need for meticulous care for detail in preparing for a hearing on tax legislation, or for debate on the Senate floor. He saw that the strength of most political people was their ability to get along with others and be both courteous and helpful to constituents and visitors to the Senate offices.

Besides Chairman Reed Smoot and Senator Walsh, members of the Senate Finance Committee included Senator Alben W. Barkley, Kentucky Democrat; Senator Robert M. La Follette, Jr., Wisconsin Republican; Senator Walter F. George, Georgia Democrat; Senator Pat Harrison, Mississippi Democrat; and Senator Tom Connally, Texas Democrat.

Other well-known figures in the Senate at that time included J. Thomas Heflin, a rabidly anti-Catholic Democrat from Alabama, and Hugo Black, another Alabama Democrat who had only a few years earlier been a member of the Ku-Klux Klan. Senators Henry F. Ashurst and Carl Hayden represented Arizona, and Senator Hiram W. Johnson represented California. Montana was represented by a team of crusading lawyers—Senator Thomas J. Walsh and Burton K. Wheeler, who had been key figures in exposing scandals in the Harding Administration. Others George Romney watched in action were Senator William E. Borah, of Idaho; Senator Arthur Capper, of Kansas; Senator Henrik Shipstead, of Minnesota; Senator George W. Norris, of Nebraska; Senator Smith Brookhart, of Iowa; Senator Key Pittman, of Nevada; Senator Gerald P. Nye, of North Dakota; Senator Robert F. Wagner, of New York; Senator Charles McNary of Oregon; and Senator Carter Glass, of Virginia.

The courting of Lenore had been a major reason for the move to Washington, but this project suffered a setback when Lenore moved to New York for serious dramatic study at the American Laboratory School of the Theatre. This provided George more time for his job with Senator Walsh, his night school, and his first business venture—a partnership in a small drive-in restaurant on the Virginia side of the Potomac River near the Francis Scott Key Bridge.

Another Utah friend, J. Willard (Bill) Marriott, of Ogden, Utah, had come to Washington a few years before the Romney boys, and had been successful in expanding one A. & W. Root Beer drive-in into three eating places. It was the start of what was to become the multimillion-dollar Hot Shoppes, Inc., a drive-in restaurant chain. Bill Marriott, three years older than Miles Romney, had been on a Mormon mission in the East and had come through Washington on a blistering hot summer day. After his return to Utah he decided Washington was the place to make money by opening a snack bar to sell cold drinks.

The Romney boys failed to duplicate the success of Bill Marriott. Miles made the major contribution in money and time, but George was able to give only a little of either. Among other things, he was too busy trying to squeeze in enough time on weekends to visit Lenore in New York. The job in Senator Walsh's office included Saturday work, and the New York trip was possible only by grabbing an evening train at Union Station in Washington on Saturday night, and returning from New York on Sunday evening.

The travel to see Lenore represented a grueling pace, even though George and Miles lived at the Dodge Hotel, two blocks from Union Station and across the Capitol Plaza from the Senate Office Building, where George worked. But, unsatisfactory as those arrangements were, they got worse before they got better.

Lenore's talent as an actress created the problem. Her work in student productions caught the eye of talent scouts, and she received job offers from the National Broadcasting Company and Metro-Goldwyn-Mayer. Since her father was a member of the Federal Radio Commission regulating the radio industry, Lenore rejected the offer from the National Broadcasting Company.

George was the major impediment to accepting the Metro-Goldwyn-Mayer offer to go to Hollywood, and the two engaged in long and heated arguments before Lenore overrode all of George's arguments and did what she wanted to do. She went to Hollywood.

The 2,700 miles that separated New York and Hollywood might have been too great a barrier for some romances, but George Romney had made up his mind to marry Lenore. His plans for further schooling at George Washington University were forgotten. So was a tentative plan to attend the Harvard School of Business Administration.

George received an unexpected job offer in June 1930 as a result of contacts he had made while working on tariff measures for Senator Walsh. Two officials of the Aluminum Company of America—Vice President Safford K. Colby and J. E. S. Thorpe—had called at Senator Walsh's office for information in connection with pending tariff legislation. George handled their problems, and they were impressed with his courtesy and the extra work he did to take care of their request. They were also struck by the fact that the handsome young man would not accept pay for the additional work he had done.

The Aluminum Company officials offered George $125 a month as a trainee, with a jump to $250 a month when he completed a training program that started at New Kensington, Pennsylvania. The initial agreement had called for George to work in Alcoa's Washington office, but even before the New Kensington program was concluded, George was trying to find a way to be assigned to the West Coast so he could be near Lenore.

In Washington, George called on Mr. and Mrs. LaFount and made a formal request for permission to marry Lenore. Although they liked George, Mrs. LaFount suggested that he wait at least until such time as he had permanent employment.

Abandoning the opportunity to work in Alcoa's Washington office, George asked the company to assign him to sales work in Los Angeles for the last part of his training period. Happily, he moved to Los Angeles, where he spent his days selling and demonstrating the uses of aluminum and his spare time and evenings waiting to drive Lenore home from the movie studios in nearby Culver City.

Jealous and possessive as he was, George could not be happy about Lenore's life as a budding movie actress. He became furious if she went out with anyone else, and on one occasion followed her in his car and parked beside her and her date. Another time, he went into a rage because she went out with another employee of Alcoa when he was out of town. She explained that she had only gone out with the young man because he was George's friend, but it was not a reason that satisfied George at the time.

After that incident, Lenore declared she had had enough of the possessive young man and would never marry him.

It was a short-lived attitude, and Lenore soon gave in to his plea for reconciliation. An attractive three-year contract offer from Metro-Goldwyn-Mayer brought them to a crucial decision point. George asked her to give up a contract worth fifty thousand dollars to her, to give up a career she had been dreaming of and preparing for since her first year in high school, and to marry a $125-a-month apprentice aluminum salesman with a dilapidated 1925 Oldsmobile coupe.

Persuasive and persistent George Romney managed to convince her that marrying him was the best bargain, and she agreed to be married within a few weeks. The wedding took place the morning of July 2, 1931, at the Salt Lake City Temple of the Church of Jesus Christ of the Latter-Day Saints. In the tradition of Mormon marriages, they were "sealed" for "time and all eternity." They started their honeymoon at Pinecrest, the mountain resort east of Salt Lake where they had gone on dates as high-school students seven years earlier.

FIVE

Washington Lobbyist

The marriage of George Romney and Lenore LaFount in July 1931 ended the obsessive chase which had been the most disruptive factor in his life. For seven years his determination to win her had dominated his plans. His efforts to be near her upset college plans, interfered with job plans, and forced him to shirk his duties in relation to the drive-in business he shared with his brother. The whole pattern of pursuit destroyed his long-time plan to attend the Harvard School of Business Administration.

He now found himself in the unenviable position of being a college dropout in an era when more and more stress was placed on the importance of a degree, and being married to a young lady from a better economic background who was better educated than he. His salary was still $125 a month, and he had no backlog of money when they started married life in a small apartment in Santa Monica. However, he buried himself in his work with the same determination with which he had wooed Lenore.

When George finished his apprenticeship in the fall of 1931, he was as pleased to be transferred to Washington, D. C., as with the

doubling of his salary. He was also faced with financial embarrassment, for he had no money for the trip and it was necessary for
Lenore to buy the railroad tickets.

In Washington they moved into the new Kennedy-Warren
Apartments on Connecticut Avenue, where they made their home
for two years. They had only the barest essentials in the way of
furniture, but to the enthusiastic and energetic 24-year-old it was
just another obstacle to overcome.

J. Willard Marriott, then making the first significant moves in
the drive-in restaurant business, remembers George Romney as
mature and responsible even in his twenties. The Marriotts knew
George and Lenore through the many activities characteristic of
the Church of Jesus Christ of the Latter-Day Saints.

"I thought of George as being as old as I was at the time," Mar-
riot said. "I found out that he was about seven years younger, but
he was always mature and had such good judgment."

As second man on the two-man Alcoa staff headquartered
in the Southern Building at 1425 H Street Northwest, only two
blocks from the White House, he was the envy of some of his old
friends who were still working their way through college. In those
depression days of 1931 and 1932, it was a good job.

Gerald Smith, later manager of the huge ZCMI Department
Store in Salt Lake City, watched his high-school friend moving up in
the world of business while he was still in college. They had been
on the same high-school basketball team in Salt Lake, and he had
known George during the one year he attended the junior college
operated in conjunction with the high school. They had also been
together at the University of Utah for one semester when Romney
returned from his Mormon mission before going to Washington.

His friends from Salt Lake knew George not only as a busy and
successful young lobbyist for a large firm but also as a hard-driving
guard on a Mormon basketball team that played in a Washington
City league during 1931, 1932, and 1933. George Romney may
have been short on finesse, but he was long on work and determination.

"The same traits were there—in high school, junior college,
when we were playing on that basketball team in Washington,

ALCOA

and in everything else he did," Smith recalls. "He was a gutty player, not afraid of anybody or anything. He had supreme confidence that he would be a success at anything he tackled, and it didn't make much difference how down things were, he never gave up."

Smith recalls a conversation after a basketball game when Romney confided this bit of advice relative to his own early success: "You know, Jerry, you have to have faith in yourself. You have to have confidence to bet every dollar on yourself."

The $3,000-a-year salary Romney received when he arrived in Washington was one to be envied by college graduates in that depression period, but it was only a starter for the hard-driving young Mormon. His salary increased enough in two years so that George and Lenore were able to move out of the modest small apartment in the Kennedy-Warren Building into larger and more lavish quarters in the Westchester Apartments on Cathedral Avenue.

"That was really plush living as far as the rest of our Salt Lake group was concerned," Gerald Smith explained. "George and Lenore did a lot of entertaining at that time, and some of the fellows from our basketball team were usually included. For us this was really living, but George was always the same guy—with us and with the newspapermen, politicians, and others, who attended."

While George and Lenore enjoyed people, the major purpose of their entertaining was the job of representing the Aluminum Company of America. With his boss, Fred J. Gauntlett, Romney was expected to keep in touch with all legislation and proposals that might jeopardize or help operations of the huge aluminum monopoly. Romney also represented Aluminum Wares Association, a group of cooking-utensil manufacturers with interests roughly the same as those of Alcoa.

The Aluminum Company of America, largest producer and fabricator of aluminum in the world, was a firm of great prestige, but it was also a target of considerable criticism because of its monopoly position within the United States. It made no difference how Romney and his associates argued that Alcoa was "a good monopoly" because the firm showed only a modest 6 percent annual profit, it was to remain the only United States producer of primary aluminum until 1941.

George cultivated a wide acquaintanceship among newspapermen, elected officials, political appointees, career government employees, and various lobbying groups. He joined the Congressional Country Club and methodically devoted himself to becoming a good golfer because he considered the sport essential to his work as a Washington lobbyist. In the first years he often played alone, chasing two or three balls around the course in an effort to perfect his game.

Al Warner, then chief correspondent for the New York *Herald-Tribune,* recalls that he first saw Romney on the golf course at Congressional. Warner was in a foursome which included Raymond Clapper, United Press columnist. Across the course they saw a vigorous young man hitting two balls and then aggressively chasing after them at a fast walk or a lope as if his life depended upon finishing the game by some appointed time. Warner recalls that Ray Clapper quipped: "There is a young man who knows where he is going."

George Romney, constantly competitive, at times carried it to extremes. Harriet Warner recalls that she and Lenore played golf with George and Al on a few occasions, but George Romney's swift-striding determination and impatience to get on with the game didn't change noticeably even with the ladies in the foursome. Deciding it was just too much strain, Lenore and Harriet dropped out.

When it came to dancing, Lenore could keep up and did. Although they were good dancers, they attended Arthur Murray classes at the Congressional Country Club with Al and Harriet Warner and with Supreme Court Justice and Mrs. Robert Jackson and others to learn the rumba and tango, part of a rage of South American dances at that time. For most of the men the lessons were only a limited success, according to Warner. He said this was particularly true of his own dancing and that of Justice Jackson. By contrast, Romney became a good dancer "and the one all the ladies wanted to dance with whenever South American music was played," Harriet Warner reminisces.

Although they did not drink hard liquor, the Romneys were regarded among the gayest and most enthusiastic social companions in Washington. "They retained their own principles under the Mormon religion, but they never tried to force their standards on any of the rest of us," Harriet Warner reflected. "They never made much point of the fact that they didn't drink, and there was never any criticism of those of us who did."

Most helpful to Romney in his first years as a lobbyist in Washington was the little informal group of trade association representatives who met as the Monday Club to exchange information about activities in Congress and various executive agencies. The group met for lunch at the National Press Club or at the Washington Club. The chairman was Nathan Williams, then representing the National Association of Manufacturers.

It was at one of these meetings at the National Press Club that Romney met Pyke Johnson, a former Denver newspaperman who was then the Washington representative and a vice president of the Automobile Manufacturers Association. This contact was to pave the way for George Romney to make an important move to the automobile industry.

Pyke Johnson was a veteran Washington operator by the time he met George Romney in the early 1930's, but he was immediately impressed with the friendly, hard-working young man "who paid attention to business and was so uncompromisingly straightforward and honest."

There were a lot of bright young men around Washington, but most of them lacked the determination, the willingness to work, or the uncompromising integrity that Pyke Johnson saw in George Romney. When Johnson was named to form a Trade Association Advisory Committee to the National Recovery Administration (NRA), he selected Romney as one of the members.

"I considered George Romney a strong man when I named him to that committee," Johnson said. "When the NRA was declared unconstitutional in 1935, we continued the committee because we found it to be beneficial to us in our work."

From their first association in the early 1930's, Pyke Johnson remained close to George Romney and recalls that it was during this period that he commented to Lenore that "as successful as he is in the business world, George is probably suited best for politics."

With all of the qualities of personality and determination that George Romney possessed, Pyke Johnson found "the very charming Lenore to be one of his greatest assets." Pyke Johnson pictured George Romney as a spirited charger "with quite a few rough edges" while Lenore "could hold him down a little, and possessed the social graces that George would have regarded of little importance in his intense desire to get on with whatever he was doing."

"Lenore was, and is, a very charming woman and a very able woman, and her role can't be overemphasized in judging why George moved ahead as he did," Johnson says. "I've always felt she was the one who really elected him Governor of Michigan."

That view of the importance of his wife in the molding of George Romney the Washington lobbyist is also expressed by his brothers, Lawrence and Miles Romney, and by his sister, Meryl, now Mrs. LaVell Ward of Bloomington, Idaho.

Mrs. Ward recalls that George had a strong, stubborn streak in his makeup, and that Lenore was one "who could criticize him and make him listen." Mrs. Ward's devotion to George and Lenore stems in part from the fact that they helped finance her college education in those depression years when other members of the family found it impossible to aid her. She was graduated in music and music education, and taught school in Utah and Idaho before her marriage.

Although Alcoa became the subject of a broad antitrust action in 1937, this did not dim George Romney's enthusiasm for his employer or for the product they manufactured and sold. Even as Attorney General Homer S. Cummings was bringing the antitrust suit charging monopoly and asking that Alcoa be dissolved, Romney was demonstrating his personal faith in aluminum by planning and building his own home with an emphasis on aluminum construction. Because of his experience with his father in the construction business, Romney was able to supervise the building of the large new home near Forty-fourth and Dexter streets in the fashionable area just north of Foxhall Road in northwest Washington.

The Romney family included two daughters by the time they moved into the new home in 1938: Margo Lynn, born on June 6, 1935, and Jane LaFount, born on March 18, 1938.

Although the house was in part to take care of the needs of a growing family, it was also designed for entertaining, and with that in mind George added a huge concrete patio with plenty of room for his energetic dancing.

By 1939, George Romney had moved up the financial ladder to what was then a whopping $10,000-a-year salary. In spite of this, everything was not going his way. When Gauntlett retired, he believed he deserved the job, but Alcoa executives decided to move in an older man. Romney continued in the number-two spot for Alcoa, but kept his eye out for other opportunities.

Pyke Johnson, his long-time friend, provided that opportunity at the time of a reorganization in the offices and activities of the Automobile Manufacturers Association. Alfred Reeves, head of the Automobile Manufacturers Association in New York, retired, and Johnson, the Washington representative, was named executive vice president and general manager. The new general office was to be in Detroit, but Pyke Johnson wanted to remain in Washington. He suggested Romney as the man to head the Detroit office, and took him to Detroit to be interviewed by officers of the Association who would be asked to concur in his choice.

The energetic young Romney was as impressive to the members of the Association as he had been to Pyke Johnson, and Johnson was authorized to offer him $12,000 a year. After talking it over with Lenore and prayerful consideration of the change, George decided to accept the offer, and it became official when he attended a meeting of the directors of the Automobile Manufacturers Association on September 28, 1939.

Gerald Smith, who saw Romney during this period of decision, declared that Romney's "prayerful consideration" of major decisions is often misinterpreted. "As Mormons, our religion is very much a part of our lives, and it is only normal that we should seek

every type of guidance in trying to make sure that the big decisions are right decisions," Smith said. "This isn't a case of waiting
to hear voices from heaven or being struck with some sudden flash
of light. It is simply a matter of asking God's help on any particularly difficult decision."

After the decision was made, there was certainly no indication
that George Romney was content to rest on the results of a prayerful choice. As Pyke Johnson had expected he would do, Romney
submerged himself in a depth study of the history of the automobile industry, the people in the automobile industry, and the
problems of the automobile industry.

Although he had performed admirably as a Washington lobbyist
for eight years, many of his friends still felt he had a certain
naïveté as he and his family left the nation's capital in the winter of
1939 for Detroit. But Pyke Johnson, one of those who knew him
best, insisted that this naïveté was only a surface appearance flowing from a disarming honesty.

"I wouldn't have hired him if I'd thought he was actually
naïve," Johnson said. "I'd come to know George pretty well in
those years in Washington, and I considered him a pretty hardheaded fellow on any project. He wasn't cynical, and he wasn't
an angler. He had good ideas, he was honest, he was loyal, and he
was a fellow who could work with others and get a job done. He
was willing to put out a little more than anyone else, but I don't
think of that as naïve."

In the years between 1929 and 1939, the raw young man from
Utah had become a knowledgeable and effective man about Washington.

Because of the growing importance of Washington and of Washington representation, young Romney had had the opportunity to
work with and advise some of the highest officials in Alcoa. They
had relied upon him to run down the facts they needed, and they
had relied upon his judgment relative to possible governmental
actions. In those years he met men who were among the most
important figures in Government and business, and he dealt with
them in such a close manner that he saw their strengths and their
weaknesses and the qualities that set them apart.

Although apparently handicapped by his lack of a formal education, he did not permit this to hold him back in any way, for he
more than overcame this disadvantage by careful attention to
detail and a willingness to work.

The life of a nondrinking and nonsmoking Mormon from Salt
Lake would hardly seem likely indoctrination for the Washington
party circuit, and yet Romney was able to make the transition
without noticeable discomfort, and he learned to his own satisfaction that even in Washington some of the people who were worth
knowing judged a man on how he produced rather than on how
much liquor he consumed.

In the cynical circles of Washington political lobbyists, George
Romney emerged as a fellow of good common sense who could
make his virtues pleasant to live with.

SIX

Wartime Detroit

Heavy clouds of war threatened the horizon in the fall of 1939, when George Romney made his decision to leave Washington to head the Automobile Manufacturers Association office in Detroit. War and its possible impact on the automobile industry was one factor Romney pondered most seriously, for a shooting war could bring a quick end to auto production and uncertainty to the Automobile Manufacturers Association.

Romney's decision was made during September 1939, when Adolph Hitler was stepping up his land grabbing after seizing the Sudeten area of Czechoslovakia. Hitler had signed a nonaggression pact with Italy and the Soviet Union that fall, and then the German Army had rolled into Poland.

President Franklin D. Roosevelt appealed for an end to the aggression, but they were futile appeals. "When peace is broken anywhere, it is threatened everywhere," President Roosevelt pleaded, but Hitler and Benito Mussolini were not listening, and isolationist attitudes within the United States made it difficult for the President to step up military spending as much as he wanted to.

While any serious problem still seemed months and perhaps years away, Romney opened the new offices of the AMA in Detroit in January 1940. One of the major issues was a reform of the dues system, which bit too deeply into smaller manufacturers while letting larger producers off lightly.

The automobile industry offered the talents of William S. Knudsen, head of General Motors, and B. E. Hutchinson, treasurer of Chrysler, to work with Romney on the problem of a more equitable dues schedule for the AMA. But even in the first months of 1940, President Roosevelt stepped up planning for war mobilization that was to eventually engulf the whole automobile industry. During those months, Knudsen became well acquainted with Romney, and reported to Pyke Johnson that he was pleased with the industry, loyalty, and enthusiasm of this young man whom Johnson had sent to head the Detroit office.

In April 1940, the Nazis seized Denmark and Norway in swift succession. In May, the German war machine swept over the Netherlands, Luxembourg, and Belgium, and started the assault on France. By mid-June, France had fallen and the British were under heavy siege.

In June 1940, in the midst of a campaign for reelection, President Roosevelt took the first active steps to mobilize American industry by establishing the Advisory Commission of the Council of National Defense. Since he was in the heat of a political campaign, the President emphasized "defense" aspects of the mobilization rather than "war," to placate the strong isolationist feeling which still persisted.

President Roosevelt named Knudsen chairman of the National Defense Advisory Commission and made certain that all of the major national interests were represented in the delegation. In addition to Knudsen, the Commission included Edward R. Stettinius, Jr., of United States Steel, Chester Davis, of the Agricultural Adjustment Administration, and Sidney Hillman, of the Congress of Industrial Organizations (CIO).

Rather than ask Congress for new legislation to embark upon the industrial mobilization planning, President Roosevelt reached back to legislation passed in 1916 for authority to set up the Commission.

As Knudsen left General Motors to head the National Defense Advisory Commission, it meant he was to lean heavily on the automobile industry and his experience with the automobile industry to advise on the organization of defense mobilization. And since Knudsen was well acquainted with Romney, it meant that Romney, as manager of the Detroit office of the AMA, was to find himself almost immediately involved in the coordination of auto industry planning.

In the summer and early fall of 1940, the defense work was only a limited part of the production of the automobile industry, although the second half of 1940 was to see the award of $10.5 billion in contracts.

In October 1940, Knudsen spoke at a New York meeting of the Automobile Manufacturers Association, and for the first time placed the full seriousness of the war situation before the automobile industry. He explained a survey he had made of the capacity of the aircraft industry, and the necessity for the automobile industry to take over major responsibility in connection with the production of parts for medium and heavy bombers. A survey of war conditions in England had caused Gen. Henry H. Arnold, then chief of staff of the Air Force, to conclude that the side which would win would be the side with the most medium and heavy bombers.

"I'd like you men—the President would like you men, and I'd like you to agree to subordinate your new model changes and subordinate everything else to the production of subassemblies for medium and heavy bombers," Knudsen told the automobile manufacturers.

The automobile manufacturers unanimously pledged to support the request made by Knudsen and President Roosevelt. The job of drawing the formal pledge of support was left to George Romney and James Cope, then a Washington public-relations man for the automobile industry and later a New York public-relations man.

With the pledge adopted, executives of the automobile industry met with Knudsen, representatives of the Air Force, and representa-

tives of the aircraft industry to discuss the problem of coordinating aircraft production with the production facilities of the automobile industry.

The Automotive Committee for Air Defense was born from that
meeting, and George Romney, as manager of the Detroit office of
the Automobile Manufacturers Association, immediately assumed a
leading role as coordinator of planning between the automobile
industry and the aircraft industry.

Throughout most of 1941, it was only a limited war boom, with
the Office of Production Management reporting at midyear that
three fourths of the contracts were being awarded to fifty-six
major corporations. The public still demanded both guns and butter, and although the automobile industry moved to big defense
production, passenger cars and other general consumer goods
continued to be produced.

George Romney was in intimate contact with all of the problems
dealing with manpower and distribution of raw materials in that
period when Knudsen's Advisory Commission engaged in a futile struggle with the problems of military priorities. President
Roosevelt finally established a new Office of Production Management, with Knudsen and Hillman in control, and an Office of Price
Administration under the direction of Leon Henderson, a New
Deal economist.

Despite considerable chaos in the general administration of
priorities, the United States had made remarkable progress in developing a capacity for war production by the time of the Japanese
attack on Pearl Harbor on December 7, 1941.

Within days after the attack on Pearl Harbor, the Automobile
Manufacturers Association revamped the Automotive Committee
for Air Defense into the Automotive Council for War Production
and pledged "unlimited effort and facilities in aiding all plants in
the industry to get out the mass-production of war materials that
will win the war."

George Romney, then only thirty-three years old, was named
managing director of the Automotive Council for War Production,
which was to operate out of the same offices as the Automobile
Manufacturers Association for the duration of World War II. In

his new position, Romney was in constant contact with all of the leaders of the automobile industry, including Charles E. Wilson, head of General Motors, and Paul G. Hoffman, of Studebaker.

In February 1942, the automobile industry ended the production of passenger cars, and for the next three years essentially all of Romney's time was taken up with the war problems of the automobile industry, ranging from inventories of machinery through personnel and raw-material supplies.

Pyke Johnson, who had continued as general manager of AMA until March 1942, had weekly contact with Knudsen and with leading figures in the automobile industry. He heard nothing but the most favorable reports on the work of his protégé, George Romney.

"They recognized George as bright, enthusiastic, loyal, and totally dedicated to the job that was before the automobile industry at that time," Johnson recalled. "I don't remember a single person in the Automobile Manufacturers Association ever raising any complaint about George. He could get along with people, and it was his job to get along with a lot of different types. He went out of his way to accommodate everyone, and he tried to be fair and pretty much right across the board. Everyone knew that George was saying just about what he thought."

When Pyke Johnson resigned as general manager of AMA to accept a job as president of the Automotive Safety Foundation in Washington, it was only logical that he would recommend Romney for his job as general manager and that the leaders in the automobile industry would follow that recommendation. At that time they had already had nearly three years' experience working with the industrious young Mormon.

In his capacity as general manager for AMA as well as managing director of the Automotive Council for War Production, Romney broadened his scope of activity and knowledge. It was his job to become familiar with the details of operations of the entire automobile industry and allied manufacturing, and to sample constantly the views of the top men in the industry relative to the whole range of policies in dealings between various segments of the industry as well as in dealing with the Government and with labor unions—particularly the United Automobile Workers.

During those war years, George Romney had his first association with Walter Reuther, president of the United Automobile Workers, and his brother Victor Reuther. Although deep ideological differences were apparent from the outset, the relationship was generally pleasant.

Walter Reuther was an important figure to the entire automobile industry, and it took Romney only a short period of time to understand and respect his power. Almost from the outset, Romney was in sharp disagreement with the manner in which the federal labor laws were being administered. He was sympathetic to the need and the right of employees in huge industries to be organized to bargain for wages, hours, and general working conditions. But he shared the views of many others in the automobile industry that the Wagner Act and the New Deal's administration of the labor laws had permitted labor union leaders to accumulate power which was unhealthy and monopolistic.

As early as December 1940, Reuther had proposed a plan for broad general control of the automobile industry in what he contended would represent a more efficient utilization and expansion of the automobile industry for war work. Under the so-called Reuther Plan, manpower and equipment of the auto industry would have been pooled under a single organization controlled by a nine-member board.

This nine-member board would have included three from Government, three from industry, and three from the labor union. The automobile industry was totally opposed to this plan, and Romney was in thorough accord with the opposition to the idea of management entering into an agreement to share management responsibilities with Government and labor.

Enough controversies already existed over what management considered efforts by Reuther and the UAW to usurp the rights of management to manage, and this nine-member board was considered to be an effort to get a foot in the door for greater labor involvement in management in the period after the war.

As far as the major figures in the automobile industry were concerned, the nine-member board proposed by Reuther would amount to turning the management function over to the UAW because of the strong political voice that the Congress of Industrial Organizations (CIO) had in the Democratic Administration.

Although Reuther periodically proposed and pushed his plan, Knudsen was able to head it off through reasonably effective countermeasures from his position as chairman of the National Defense Advisory Commission and with the Office of Production Management. Charles E. Wilson, then head of General Motors and later Secretary of Defense, contended that the Reuther plan would create such a division of management responsibility that it would destroy the whole foundation of industrial efficiency in the automobile industry.

In addition to the job of serving as a spokesman for the automobile industry, Romney also had to take on other public-relations chores in 1943, when a serious race riot erupted in Detroit, greatly marring the image of the automobile capital. Trouble burst forth on Sunday, June 20, 1943, at Belle Isle, an amusement park that had been a minor trouble spot of racial disturbances for three years.

Two Negro youths, chased out of Eastwood Park a day earlier by a group of white youths, went to Belle Isle looking for means of getting even by joining other Negro youths to harass outnumbered white youths. This culminated in some brief squabbling at a Belle Isle entrance as white and Negroes jostled together in leaving, and from there trouble fanned out, with untrue rumors of the rape of a white woman and other incidents adding fuel to the flames.

By the early morning hours of June 21, roaming white groups were searching out Negroes, who were harassed and beaten. Negro groups took similar actions against whites and broke into and looted white-owned stores in the Paradise Valley area, an all-Negro district on the lower east side. Negroes also sniped at police.

The rioting was out of control by 9 A.M. on June 21, as police engaged in a futile battle to isolate the Negroes in the Paradise Valley area while trying to keep white gangs out. A disagreement over the orders needed to bring U. S. Army troops into the area resulted in a twelve-hour delay responsible for a major part of the more than $2 million in damage. The troops arrived at 10 P.M., and within two hours Governor Harry F. Kelly was able to report that the rioting was over.

The final assessment revealed 34 dead, 675 injured, and 1,883 arrested. It took 2,000 Detroit police, 150 state police, and 4,000 U. S. Army troops to bring order to the riot-torn city.

Detroit Mayor Edward J. Jeffries, critical of the unnecessary delay which had permitted the rioting to rage for twelve long hours, declared: "I must know that Detroit will not have to wait twelve hours again for Army troops." The Mayor established an interracial committee of public-spirited citizens to deal with the causes of racial tension.

Walter Reuther proposed a labor-management group to deal with the racial discord, and George Romney and Victor Reuther were given the task of organizing the Detroit Victory Council to explore the special problems of industry contributing to a degree to the unrest in wartime Detroit.

Romney worked closely with Victor Reuther in solving the problems of Detroit, including the training of war workers, establishing child-care centers for working mothers, changing bus routes to accommodate the war plants, and changing the hours of Detroit stores to providing easier shopping for persons on irregular work shifts.

But this congenial relationship in dealing with general civic problems did not bring them any closer ideologically and did not make Romney more content with what he considered to be a power posture unbalanced in favor of labor unions.

Romney, the activist, believed the automobile industry should meet Walter Reuther head on in public debates on a number of matters involving what they considered a union effort to usurp management functions. While conservative business leaders in the automobile industry agreed that national labor policies were unbalanced in favor of organized labor, most of them were cautious and fearful of meeting the firebrand Walter Reuther in any type of public debate on their differences.

As a spokesman for the automobile industry, Romney did not hesitate to engage in direct controversy with Reuther on what he considered to be Reuther's distortions of the responsibility of management for manpower problems in the automobile industry. Frequent exchanges of harsh words typified their relationship, and no exchanges better dramatized the split between the two men than did their testimony before the War Investigating Committee then headed by Senator James M. Mead.

That committee, formerly the Truman Investigating Committee, conducted hearings in Detroit in March 1945 for purposes of probing into allegations of labor hoarding by management and bad union practices that appeared to be cutting war production by as much as 20 to 30 percent.

George Romney first testified on March 9, 1945, in his dual capacity as managing director of the Automotive Council for War Production and as general manager of the Automobile Manufacturers Association. He spoke on behalf of the large automobile manufacturers as well as the dozens of smaller automotive-industry employers operating in cooperation with the major firms. Those employers were spread through thirty-two states and hired a total of more than 1,900,000 employees.

At that time, the automotive industry accounted for about 1,000,000 of the workers, and the industry was delivering 26 percent of all war products made from metal. He pointed out that after Pearl Harbor, when the defense contracts flooded in, the automobile industry was able to convert from car production to the production of totally new products in a period of only four months.

The peak peacetime level of the industry had been $4 billion in production, but by the time of Romney's appearance the automobile industry was producing at the rate of $13 billion a year, Romney told the Mead Committee. The top employment peak had been reached in November of 1943, and from that time on increased efficiency had permitted the automotive industry to cut the number of employees while production had continued to expand.

But Romney explained to the Mead Committee that all the increased production did not represent greater efficiency. The automobile had become one of the least expensive products to build, with most of the work being done within the industry itself, Romney said. War products were often made from more expensive material, and from more expensive parts purchased from others outside the automobile industry.

Romney told the Mead Committee that about 75 percent of the products being delivered by the automobile industry were on fixed-price contracts, with only about 25 percent being delivered on the cost-plus-fixed-fee-type contract. There were none of the straight cost-plus contracts used in World War I, which were so much criticized because they promoted inefficiency, since the higher the cost, the higher the profits.

Senator Homer Ferguson, a Michigan Republican, pointed out that the straight cost-plus contract was illegal. Romney declared that he believed that the public still had the impression that big industry was being paid on the basis of cost plus a certain percentage of the contract rather than on a cost-plus-fixed-fee basis.

"Under a fixed-fee contract, contractors cannot increase their profit by increasing their costs," Romney said.

"Except on the next contract they get, the estimated cost would go up, and their fixed fee naturally goes up on the estimated cost," Senator Ferguson argued.

"Senator, that was true for a short period with respect to a very limited number of contracts, but on the whole the picture now is that the contractor who has high costs is the contractor who is being canceled out," Romney replied.

"I can give you one item where a contractor in Detroit is getting seventy dollars for an article; the same article is produced down in New York for thirty-five dollars," Senator Ferguson countered.

"I agree that there are examples . . . the costs of each contractor differ," Romney replied, "but my point is that the incentive today is for the contractor to keep his costs down."

"What is the biggest item in costs?" Ferguson asked.

"Labor and materials," Romney said, and later modified it to say that even the major part of materials eventually boils down to labor costs.

"Well, do you really think that you get [as] efficient labor production on cost-plus-fixed-fee as you do on fixed price?" Senator Ferguson asked.

Romney replied that many workmen have the idea that the employers are on a cost-plus contract, and that because of this misunderstanding the workers might not feel compelled to be efficient.

"Do you think that the output of management is as efficient under a cost-plus-fixed-fee contract as under a price contract?" Senator Ferguson questioned.

Romney replied that if management is not efficient it "stands to lose . . . war contracts" and that, in addition, "if they permit inefficiencies to develop in the production during wartime, they are likely to lose out in peacetime production, because you can't overcome inefficiencies overnight when you go back to competitive business, and people in this industry know it."

"In other words, as I take it now, your industry is not looking at the present but looking at the future as to production," Senator Ferguson said.

"Just as I look at my health from a standpoint of the present and the future," Romney replied.

Chairman Mead noted that Romney had said costly contracts were canceled and contracts withheld from firms with a high cost per unit. "Do you think that has had a wholesome effect in this area?" Chairman Mead asked.

Romney replied that this system of discipline and rewards had had some good impact on the industry, but that "we don't believe that the administration of these procurement policies is quite as good as it could be."

When Senator Ferguson asked Romney about the "hoarding of manpower" by some industries, Romney replied: ". . . What labor hoarding means is that the manufacturer is guilty of holding more workers than he needs, in anticipation of business that he doesn't have. If that is the definition of the term, I don't know of labor hoarding of any consequence in this area that has occurred for those purposes."

"Has any occurred for any purpose?" Senator Ferguson pressed.

"Not labor hoarding," Romney replied. "There is no way by which a manufacturer in this area can, by himself, hold labor, without the worker himself being willing to be held."

"Well, let's say it is a combination between the workmen and the industry," Ferguson pressed. "Is there any labor hoarding?"

"I don't think there is any labor hoarding," Romney replied. "I don't know of the holding of labor."

"You wouldn't know, Mr. Romney," Ferguson replied, "because you are not out in the plant. You haven't a firsthand knowledge of this employment in the plant, have you?"

"I think I have about as broad a knowledge of that subject as any man in the area here," Romney replied, fully confident.

"Let me give you an example," Senator Ferguson said. "Would this be hoarding, where men are sent home, after they check in in the morning, so they don't have to loaf in the plant, and come back and ring in at night and ring out again?"

"Yes, sir," Romney replied. "I think that would be labor hoarding."

"Has that ever occurred in this district?" Senator Ferguson asked.

"Senator, of course we have failed to keep people fully employed at all times, because there are conditions that arise under which you can't keep people fully employed at all times."

"That would be labor hoarding, wouldn't it?" Senator Ferguson asked.

"I want to add one fact that everyone should understand," Romney replied, "and that is this: that we voluntarily created in this area, before it ever existed elsewhere, a plan that applied to all employees in this area as well as employers, that would permit employees who were not fully employed or who were not employed at their highest skill to transfer from the employer that they are now employed by to another who could use them at full-time employment and at the highest skill."

"Then I take for granted that you boil it down to this: that labor and management are at their highest efficiency in the Detroit area?" Ferguson needled Romney.

"No, sir," Romney replied. "All I am saying is this, and can state it in a nutshell: that if there is any labor hoarding in the Detroit area, it is the result of a conspiracy between the employer and the employee. It cannot take place except where both the workers and the management are parties to the crime."

"All right," Senator Ferguson continued. ". . . Do you know of any labor hoarding under that definition?"

"I think, sir, there may have been some instances of that character in the area," Romney replied. "I think I do know of some instances of that character. I know of instances where workers have been more anxious to stay at the plant that they were employed at, because it was closer to home or because they liked to work there, or other reasons. . . . I don't take the position that all employers are guiltless. I think that the blame is about as much one place as the other. . . ."

Romney testified that despite some poor utilization of manpower he did not consider the problem serious, and he added that he believed that Detroit could have handled more defense contracts than it handled from the very outset of World War II.

Although Romney said he believed there could have been some improvement in the scheduling of materials by management, the most serious problems had been created only where there was a sudden shift in the type of production needed.

"As a result of the change in the military situation in Europe, they suddenly found that their need for certain . . . war products had vastly increased overnight," Romney explained. "So they began to issue a lot of directives that took precedence over the controlled-materials plan setup, to obtain those products as quickly as possible. . . . But what they failed to do adequately, in our judgment . . . is that they failed to cut back on the other programs sufficiently to release the materials needed for these programs. . . ."

Romney testified that such unplanned shifts had upset the scheduling, had caused many firms to be without steel or other raw material, and would be reflected in production for several months ahead. He declared that it had been difficult to get across in Washington one simple message: "That you can't produce any more guns, tanks, planes, and other things than you have got materials available at specific periods to produce them with."

Efforts of the Federal Government to exert tighter control over manpower in the Detroit area met with equally sharp criticism from Romney. He declared that Washington could not do the job of handling manpower problems and that there needed to be emphasis on voluntarism in each locality.

In the face of arguments from Senator Ferguson, Romney came out in opposition to pending legislation that would have created tighter controls over manpower in Detroit and other local areas. This was an area in which management and labor agreed, Romney said. He related that representatives of management and labor had gone to Washington in 1944 "to insist that the War Manpower Commission leave us free enough within this area to work out our own problems."

"We said that management and labor out here knew a darn sight more about these problems than they knew down in Washington, and Mr. [Edward] Cushman helped us get that," Romney said.

Romney said the automobile industry objected to legislation that would provide "for an increased activity on the part of the Government in going out into plants to determine whether the plants are as productive and efficient as they ought to be."

"To boil it down," Senator Ferguson injected, "it is to go out into the plant to see whether there is labor hoarding. You see, this committee has been around and has seen some labor hoarding, and we thought it might be a good idea to have some branch of the Government go out and find it, and expose it."

Romney argued that there was a mistaken impression that "the War Manpower Commission can send some people into these plants and do things that the management of these plants are supposed to do and, if the managements of these plants don't do them, then the Government ought to get rid of those managements, or those managements ought to be deprived of war work."

Romney declared that it would be virtually impossible to find capable men for the War Manpower Commission to send into the plants because "the biggest shortage we have . . . in . . . this war production program . . . is the lack of adequately trained management."

"If he [Cushman] can find any men that can go into these plants and tell the men who are trying to get out production how to do it better, then they ought to be in management themselves," Romney said.

The young spokesman for the auto industry declared that management was "perfectly willing to have . . . any Government people go through our plants. But we say the responsibility for efficiency in that plant should be clearly lodged with the management."

"I agree with you," Senator Ferguson replied.

In answer to questions about unused machinery and unused manpower, Romney replied that it is "utterly impossible to so organize production" that all machines are always in use and that "every worker is working just as hard as he can all of the time."

Romney bristled a bit as he talked about government interference with plant management, and declared that the industry was "very dissatisfied with the fact that its productivity is not what it was when we were producing automobiles."

"I am afraid you might be developing an antagonism that is not justified," Chairman Mead cautioned.

"I don't mean to," Romney replied, but Chairman Mead continued,

"That is not justifiable in your resentment, or apparent resentment, as to what you might call 'governmental interference in the operation and management of the plants.' Don't you think that there is a unity of effort in this emergency in which the Government of the United States has an equal stake, if not a greater stake, than industry in the productivity of war materials?"

"I think we all have an equal consideration," Romney replied. "But I don't think the fact that the Government, . . . workers, . . . agriculture has an equal stake in winning this war . . .

should result in our failing to remember that unless responsibility is clear cut and definite, you create confusion."

"So you would keep Government at the gate, leaving the internal operation of the plant to management?" Chairman Mead asked.

"No, sir," Romney replied. "We believe that the Government should have access to the plants, and they do. I mean we have procurement officers in all of these plants."

"But didn't you point out that this bill gives Government a little too much authority to interfere with management?" the Chairman asked.

"What I mean is this," Romney replied. "I don't see how the War Manpower Commission can find men with the capacity and ability to go into strange plants and determine whether or not . . . the managements are doing all they can do to get production in those plants."

"Suppose a man walked into a plant and he had all his senses and an hour before quitting time one man in fifteen or twenty was working," Senator Ferguson started his question. "Would you think there might be something wrong in the management of that plant or in the labor or something?"

"There would definitely be something wrong," Romney replied.

"Have you ever heard of that?" Senator Ferguson asked.

"Yes, sir, and that is what we want to tell you about, plus the primary cause of it," Romney replied. "We know that exists, Senator."

Romney declared that the loafing in the last hour of a day was a result of union restrictions on the output of employees.

Senator Ferguson demanded to know what management would do under circumstances where there was general idleness in a war industry. "I saw with my own eyes yesterday a man sleeping on a conveyor line three quarters of an hour before quitting time, and about one hundred ninety-nine other idle men around him. Now I want to know what industry and labor are doing here to utilize that labor in this district."

"Senator, the United States Government manacled industry by an outdated, weak, national labor policy, and they deprived management—largely deprived management—of the authority and the responsibility that it needs really to manage these plants."

"Do I understand that industry says today—and you representing them—that they have lost management and cannot manage?" Senator Ferguson asked.

"I am telling you that as a result of the national labor policy and the way it has been applied in this country and has permitted an unrestrained, militant group of unionist representatives to usurp functions and authority of management, management has not been permitted, until relatively recently, to apply . . . necessary discipline.

"Union representatives are demanding and succeeding inch by inch in obtaining the demand that they exercise judgment before management can act."

"Have you ever told that to the procurement department of the Army and the Navy of the United States?" Senator Ferguson asked.

"Yes, sir," Romney responded, "the people of this industry have told them repeatedly. . . . I have told them personally, Senator."

"What do they say about it?" Senator Ferguson asked.

"Well, some of them actually interfere with it," Romney replied.

"In what way does the Army and Navy interfere with your management?" Senator Ferguson demanded.

"The principal deficiency is that they do not feel a direct responsibility themselves for the condition that we are talking about and for that lack of management authority and responsibility," Romney replied.

"What law would you pass?" Senator Ferguson asked.

"We urge you to put an end to the privileged status of unions and their representatives and their exemption from basic laws and principles with which other Americans comply," Romney replied. "Adopt promptly a national labor policy strengthened, completed, balanced, and modernized."

Romney urged that new legislation should "retain or restore to management the ability to manage," and he was critical of labor-union efforts to organize such management personnel as foremen. He charged that the United Automobile Workers Union was at that time trying to promote the unionization of foremen and supervisory personnel.

"Our claim is this, Senator: that the unionization of foremen and their absorption subsequently by the UAW-CIO will make the foremen subject to the direction of the union and not to the direction of the management," Romney stated the industry complaint.

"Don't you think, though, that if both sides to this dispute . . . would look at the present, to produce the war materials to help win the war, and not the future so much, as to what is going to happen in the distant future, that America and the boys at the front would be better off?" Senator Ferguson queried.

"I agree wholeheartedly with you," Romney replied, "and our evidence is that the management of this industry has put war production first and foremost and will keep it there as long as a boy needs a bullet, but since before the war the UAW-CIO has continued to seek its major prewar and postwar objectives and that is to run these plants and to obtain control over them and part of the function of management."

"Then I take it that you admit that management has lost the right to manage?" Senator Ferguson asked.

"To a degree, yes, sir," Romney replied.

Romney quoted George Addes, of the UAW-CIO, as having stated in an official union publication in 1943: "Wartime restriction of the right to discharge employees for disciplinary purposes would eliminate one of the most frequent causes of controversy in the plants and reduce interruptions of production."

He also quoted Richard Frankensteen, vice-president of the UAW-CIO, as having stated to the War Labor Board: "Management should be required to refer all disciplinary discharges to grievance procedure before any such discharges are made effective."

Senator Ferguson said Romney's fear seemed aimed at what might happen in labor-management relations in the future, but Romney replied: "Senator, it is happening today."

"The group responsible for management functions must be free from union control just as surely as the group responsible for union functions must be free from management control," Romney said. "We believe and recommend a national labor policy should continue to protect workers from coercion on the part of management. It should protect workers from coercion by the unions. Likewise it should protect workers, unions, and management alike from governmental coercion by providing court review of administrative actions. . . . If that had been in effect during the past twelve years, this weakening of management's ability to act would not have occurred to the extent it has. We believe workers', industry's, and the nation's best interests require imposition of penalties on any union which strikes before it has exhausted the grievance procedure provided in its contract and in governmental procedures."

Romney tossed a red flag in Walter Reuther's face by pointing out that "there is no penalty applied to union representatives or to unions where they fail to exhaust the contractual and governmental grievance procedures that are provided."

"The actual practice during the war period has been that where they failed to take advantage of those grievance procedures and caused stoppage or shutdown, the government agencies expedited the giving of concessions by employers to the unions, and the actual result has been that strikes have been vastly increased during the war period," Romney testified. "The number of strikes has been increased, and the number of workers involved in strikes during 1944 was greatly increased, as pointed out in our testimony."

Romney also called for a reversal of a trend toward centralization of the administration of labor policy in Washington. He also asked for legislation that would decentralize such huge industrial unions as the UAW-CIO and permit individual industrial plants to bargain with individual local unions.

He pointed out that John L. Lewis, as head of the United Mine

Workers Union, had "perfected the industrial form of unionism to the point where he runs the coal industry, and he and the management of the coal industry have in the past asked for price-fixing and production-fixing power and obtained it from the Congress."

"That form of unionism, if left unrestrained as it is at the present time under our national labor policy, will promote and bring about the same conditions in other industries," Romney warned. "We are faced with the leader of an industrial union, with so much power that he can successfully insist that application of government restrictions be applied by the President personally, and he has done that. . . . Mr. [Philip] Murray served notice on Mr. [James] Byrnes just day before yesterday that the CIO position on wage stabilization is not going to be settled by Mr. Byrnes; it is going to be taken up to the President himself."

Romney suggested that "to further improve the equities as between workers and management, we believe the new national labor policy should give separate unions the same protection against undue concentration of power in the international unions as individual companies in the industry have in relation to their interindustry and intraindustry trade organizations."

"We believe that just as most Americans are opposed to monopolistic or cartelization practices on the part of industry, so they are opposed to the same practices on the part of unions and for the same reasons," Romney told the Mead committee. "Likewise we believe there is public agreement that the national interest requires that neither unions nor management should function in the political field."

Chairman Mead declared that under the existing national labor policy it appeared to him there were "a great many notable examples of efficient operation and friendly relations between employer and employees." He mentioned "the example of the needle trades in New York City," where labor and management "have extreme confidence and faith in each other."

"This apparent suspicion and fear that comes out in the course of your statement is entirely absent," Chairman Mead told Romney. "Where suspicion lurks or fear is evident, where there is failure to recognize progress, there is a long period of contention, sometimes leaving ruin in its wake. . . . So I am wondering if there isn't a possibility of your taking up some of the time of your council to study these notable examples and probably bring them to the splendid men in charge of this great industry out here."

"Senator," Romney replied, "we have done so, and I want to say to this committee that this industry recognizes that the biggest problem we have got in our industry is the problem of human relations. I would like to add that the War Production Board labor-management committee idea was largely conceived in the automotive industry by certain automotive companies. . . . Now, it isn't a lack of desire on the part of this industry to establish that relationship. It isn't a lack of willingness to concede the right to organize . . . and bargain collectively on wages, hours, and working conditions, but what you gentlemen need to understand if you are going to understand the manpower problem in Detroit . . . is that the primary objective of the UAW-CIO as documented in here has been, since the fall of 1940, when the Reuther Plan was announced, to obtain what was described as a voice in management."

Romney, refusing to back down in the face of questioning by Chairman Mead or Senator Ferguson, declared that the auto industry was opposed to industry-wide collective bargaining that he said would "lead to cartelization of American industry."

"England has pursued it, and now organized English employers and trade unions are asking the Government to give them jointly the power to fix production and fix prices," Romney said. "In fact, the British cotton textile industry and trade union as late as last September asked permission to fix the price of its principal competitor, rayon, as well as the prices of its own products."

Senator Ferguson asked Romney if he had not been complaining earlier that the local union stewards in various plants were taking over the functions of the foremen.

"Our position is that the steward is being used by the international to accomplish this purpose of weakening the exercise of the management function," Romney said. "We have tried to reiterate, with all our soul, that most of these workers want to do more work, and most of these workers want better discipline, and most of them want good, friendly working relationships in the plants. Ninety percent of these grievances are among five percent of the workers, and it is this minority group that is unrestrained and undisciplined that is being used to promote this problem."

Chairman Mead characterized Romney's testimony as "provocative and inciting and I think perhaps enlightening." He declared that some of the views of the automobile industry "may be helpful" but that they "may be destructive."

"In the history of the labor relations, which have been slow in reaching a point of tolerance and well-being, confidence and faith, there has been a great deal of fear and suspicion, even violence," Chairman Mead said. "The coming of the trade-union movement was always more or less unwelcome. It has been fought very bitterly. At times crusading organizations have been set up to destroy the coming of those helpful democratic industrial relations. . . . Now I wonder if you would tell the committee how long your council has been in existence."

Romney outlined the work of the Automotive Council for War Production from 1941, reviewed his work with labor-union representatives on the Detroit Victory Council and other cooperative programs, and concluded,

"My organization, Senator, has only one function and one purpose, and that is to do anything—and I mean just that, no limitation—that will promote the output of war products by the automotive industry."

The young automobile industry spokesman said he was confident that the views that he had expressed on the manpower problems and national labor policy "reflect the views of the people in this industry."

Romney declared that the automotive industry could be producing 25 to 50 percent more war goods if it were not for major problems in the utilization of labor which he blamed on the labor unions' interference with management and curbs on production.

Romney produced charts on the power load that he said demonstrated that in a Packard plant the men came in at 8 A.M., but did not get up to peak production until 9 A.M. with a sharp drop in production at 10:30 A.M. and a tapering off until at 11 A.M. the machines were idle, not working.

The charts showed that in the afternoon the plant never reached the peak production of the morning. The afternoon peak occurred at 2 P.M. and remained at this peak until about 3 P.M., when there was a fifteen-minute rest period for the purpose of increasing productivity.

"There is practically no productivity after the rest period," Romney told the committee. Almost all work was shut down about forty minutes before the 5:30 P.M. quitting time, Romney told the Mead Committee.

In answer to questions from Chairman Mead, Romney said he did not advise the automobile industry on labor policy, but did furnish certain factual information to the automobile firms that would relate to the labor picture.

"Are you personally antagonistic or are you personally in favor of the setting up of these unions in these plants?" Chairman Mead asked.

"Senator, . . . I don't believe that these plants in this industry, operating on as large a scope as they do and on as large a scale, could operate effectively and efficiently without their workers' being organized," Romney replied.

"So you favor organization?" Chairman Mead asked skeptically.

"Yes. I have tried to make that clear to the best of my ability in these hearings," Romney answered.

"Do you think that you are contributing in any way to increasing and improving the labor relations in these various plants?" Chairman Mead continued.

"Yes, sir, we do," Romney responded, "and as indicated in our statement, Senator, this industry is making these facts clear to your committee, sir, only because your committee decided to come to Detroit and get the facts. . . . We had some question in our minds as to whether your committee should come into this city at the present time to investigate this manpower problem, because we told your committee representatives that the problem your committee was undertaking to deal with was one of fundamental importance as it applies to war effort, and that failure to get to the bottom of this problem . . . would cause more harm than good as far as the war effort is concerned. Now, your committee having decided to come here, sir, we have done our best."

When Walter Reuther was called to testify, he disagreed sharply with Romney, declaring that "the manpower problems that we have are due primarily to improper production scheduling and improper utilization" of facilities and manpower by management.

"We don't think that either labor or management ought to use this committee as a sounding board to advance their particular brand of what they think labor relations ought to be," Reuther declared in a sharp personal cut at Romney's position. "I think it is regrettable that people do not realize that the sort of speeches we have heard this morning does not increase production in these plants. If you will check with the WPB [War Production Board] tonight, you will find that the production of tanks has not gone up because of Mr. Romney's speech and the production of airplanes will not have gone up."

Reuther declared that the problems of increased production could be met only "in a spirit of cooperation" which he had not found in Romney's testimony. He snapped that he believed that he could "enlighten the committee" with testimony on some of the points Romney had touched that he said "certainly ought to be clarified."

The fiery automobile union leader defended the Reuther Plan for mobilization of the automobile industry that he had first proposed in 1940, and denied Romney's contention that it was an effort to usurp management's prerogatives.

"It was put forward because at that time we had unused facilities in this industry and we were not getting the required war production materials," Reuther said. He slapped at the automobile industry and at the Automotive Council for War Production as "the wartime front of the Automobile Manufacturers Association."

"It came into being primarily to meet the public relations problems that our industry was faced with, because at that time it did not occupy a very favorable position because it was forced to convert," Reuther declared. "All of the patriotic slogans and phrases that they throw out at this late date do not change the fact that it was not until the OPA and Mr. Henderson said, 'Gentlemen, we will make no more cars with the shiny new gadgets,' did the automobile industry then begin to convert, and the testimony of the Truman Committee, which is your committee, will prove that Mr. Keller said before your committee some months ago that eighty-nine percent of their facilities that they had used in automobile production had been converted to war production; yet when we said that in August 1940, they said we were visionaries, we were impractical, we were trying to take over the industry."

Reuther rejected Romney's claim that he and the industry had accepted collective bargaining, and he added: "He [Romney] has not advanced the case of that idea [of collective bargaining] this morning by his continuous attack upon labor and its organizations."

The union leader then sought to tie Romney to the attitudes of John W. Scoville, an economist for the Chrysler Corporation, who had been quoted as telling a Detroit business group: "If you believe in economic freedom and competition, then you will be opposed to collective bargaining."

Reuther also quoted Scoville as saying: "I condemn collective bargaining as an assault on liberty."

Then Reuther lashed out at the Chrysler Corporation executives as being so unaware of the human problems of workers that they had failed to buy special double-canvas "hot mill" type gloves needed for workers at the Dodge Forge plant, a division of Chrysler.

In this instance, Reuther declared that the company had at earlier times obtained the special gloves and kept them for purchase by employees. However, several complaints by union stewards had failed to move the company to obtain the priorities necessary to make the purchases. Reuther said that he and other union officials had been forced to intervene and go to Washington to prod the automobile company into obtaining the gloves so there would be no shutdown.

Reuther related another instance of a firm which "Mr. Romney speaks for . . . here this morning," which he charged had hired a man who had served as a government hearing officer in a wage dispute to argue the War Labor Board into reversing the decision he had made as a hearing officer.

Although Romney was not linked to the case, Reuther cited it as an example of the "highly irregular" and "completely unethical procedures" engaged in by management representatives which he blamed for creating an atmosphere of "bitterness and suspicion."

Reuther said there were "direct relations between that position which he [Romney] takes here for public consumption this morning and the position that Mr. Scoville took."

"Mr. Scoville's attitude is in the factories (where it counts), and Mr. Romney's is out here, where the public can look at it," Reuther told the Mead Committee.

"Mr. Reuther," Chairman Mead said, "while you are discussing Mr. Romney—and I believe that you challenged his sincerity with reference to his talk before the committee on how his organization favors the unionization of industry and collective bargaining in all its aspect—I think that he emphasized the fact that he wasn't opposed to that part of the program, but what he was opposed to and all that he was opposed to was this usurpation on the part of labor of the management of the industry."

"That is just another windmill that they put up, hoping that we will spend our time fighting it," Reuther replied.

Senator Ferguson asked Reuther what position the union would take relative to a situation where men were found during working hours gambling with money and the cards on the table, and where the discipline was three days off work.

"We did not organize our union to give the people the right to shoot crap in the toilets," Reuther replied. "We organized our union because millions of workers who were inarticulate in a complex industry had no way of solving their problems."

"I gave you a specific grievance, and I want to know how it would be solved," Senator Ferguson insisted.

"There may be specific cases where that came up," Reuther replied. "I know a couple of cases where people were penalized for alleged gambling, and the union took the position that if the company wanted really to clean this up and go into it on a fair, intelligent basis, we were ready to help; but we know of situations where lower supervision is involved, where people are getting cuts out of it, and all that sort of thing."

"You don't claim that anybody in management gets a cut out of a card game like that?" Ferguson pressed.

"I maintain there are situations that we have had called to our attention where the boys said, 'Sure, there was a card game in the toilet. Management knew about it.' . . . I have been told that in some of the plants where there is a serious problem that it is serious because management has even been involved in it, and where we can find a grievance filed against a specific penalty, in most of the cases you will check and you will find that the attitude of the union is that the individual worker is being picked out and that they are not dealing with the whole problem."

"Well, now," Senator Ferguson asked, "does the union then defend the particular workman even though he is wrong under all rules?"

"If it is a clear-cut case and he is just guilty of gambling in the plant, as I said before, we didn't organize our union and we don't condone the use of the machinery of our union to protect gambling."

"Then no appeal should be taken in that kind of case?" Ferguson asked.

"That is correct," Reuther replied.

Reuther flatly denied Romney's claim that he was trying to take over the rights of management. "All we are trying to do is to say that we believe in a democratic society; you either have to live according to the principles of democracy and have machinery to facilitate those principles, or you have to live by the law of the jungle, and we are fighting for better machinery and that is what they call trying to usurp management prerogatives."

Reuther claimed that while Romney was asking for decentralized control of the labor unions, the auto industry was actually exerting a centralized control over labor problems in a manner that created grievances. In this connection he declared that management policies for General Motors were being made by Alfred

P. Sloan and others in New York, who were far removed from the practical plant problems.

One of these problems involved a prohibition against smoking in certain General Motors plants where the rules had no relationship to safety or productivity, Reuther said.

Reuther conceded that the union had on occasion slowed down the production lines in the automobile industry, and that one of the purposes for organizing the union "was to slow down the assembly line to a pace that was in keeping with the way a human being ought to work."

The automobile industry had worked employees to the point they were exhausted, Reuther contended. "The policy of the company during those periods was to throw people on the scrap heap when they got around forty-five because they couldn't hit the ball," Reuther claimed.

Reuther contended that the charts Romney had produced to show the lack of productivity at Packard were probably "done in a public-relations office and not in the engineering department." However, he conceded there was probably some slacking off on work under some circumstances because union members did not want to work themselves out of a job by completing a contract and "ending up on the street."

Another touchy point between labor and management involved the problems of seniority when a worker left one war plant because of a lack of work to take a job at another war plant. Reuther said that many skilled workmen refused to change plants even though underemployed because they would lose important seniority. This, Reuther said, was why some skilled forge-hammer operators would not move to other plants where they were needed, but would instead hold a job sweeping floors at a lower pay rate to retain a seniority position in a firm that did not have contracts to make full use of their skills.

Romney minimized the importance of this complaint and declared that it would only be in a small number of cases where this would be a factor. "I am not particularly concerned about the point, if you want to know the truth," he told Senator Ferguson.

William J. Cronin, secretary of the manpower committee of the Automotive Council for War Production, declared that management did not wish to make it too easy for skilled workmen to transfer from one plant to another because this could "increase turnover to the point where you disrupt production."

Romney testified that the problem of avoiding a big turnover was of less concern in 1945 than it had been in earlier years, and that he would favor some change in arrangements to provide the accumulated seniority guarantees requested by Walter Reuther and Victor Reuther, assistant director of the War Policy Division of the United Automobile Workers.

Romney cautioned that he was only one of eight on the management committee, so he could not guarantee agreement even though he said he would do his best to get an agreement.

When Reuther suggested that they meet on the next day, a Sunday, to try to work out the agreement, he met a blunt rejection. Romney declared: "Mr. Romney goes to church Sunday morning, and is going to church tomorrow morning; he is going to work all afternoon and all evening, but he is going to church tomorrow morning because that is the most fundamental thing in this country."

"We are losing, every day we delay this, workers who ought to be in another plant, that aren't there," Reuther said. "We will meet Monday or anytime."

"Will Monday be all right?" Chairman Mead asked, and both Romney and Reuther said it was agreeable.

"We will go to church tomorrow and pray that you will agree," Chairman Mead said amid laughter in the hearing room.

Those were only a few of the hundreds of problems that Romney dealt with in the course of the hearings before the Mead Committee, and those were only a few samples of the nature of his sharp criticism of the power of organized labor and of the exercise of that power by Walter Reuther and the United Automobile Workers Union.

While his comments had irritated Reuther and other representatives of organized labor, Romney won the admiration of leading officials in the automobile industry. Although he had sharp words with Chairman Mead, and occasionally had disputes with Senator Ferguson and other members of the Senate Committee, he had been articulate enough and courageous enough to hold his own in a forum that in many respects was unfavorable for such blunt criticism of union labor.

The collapse of Germany only six weeks after those Detroit hearings was followed within four months by the surrender of Japan and the end of World War II.

The problems of the automobile industry changed almost overnight, and George Romney, with six years of experience facing the toughest wartime industrial problems, was at the center of things as the automobile industry started the job of terminating war contracts and converting to peacetime production of automobiles.

SEVEN

Postwar Years

Grave concern over a national labor policy he felt was unduly balanced in favor of union labor developed from George Romney's experience in World War II. When the war ended, Romney wanted the Automobile Manufacturers Association members to continue a united front in an effort to break the monopoly power of organized labor. As managing director of the AMA, he had become convinced that Walter Reuther and the power possessed by the United Automobile Workers Union were dangerous for the nation, and he regarded Reuther as one of "the most dangerous men in America."

Although Romney was outspoken and industrious in his effort to get the automobile industry to take the lead in a fight against labor power, older heads in the big auto industry were somewhat less zealous in pursuing a philosophy so many of them shared with him. They wanted to get back to the job of manufacturing and selling automobiles with as little fuss from the United Automobile Workers Union as possible. Enough problems arose in converting from war work and getting their sales organizations moving without creating other issues.

Frustrated on one score, Romney turned his attention to promoting another idea—an Automotive Golden Jubilee. This project appealed to management, to labor, and to the public spirit of Detroit.

Instead of the feud with the UAW, which Romney would have welcomed, he found himself working arm in arm with Victor G. Reuther and other Michigan labor leaders. He generated as much enthusiasm over working with them on a community project as he would have working against them in a struggle over union power.

The Automotive Golden Jubilee celebrated the fiftieth anniversary of the first cars constructed and driven in Detroit by Charles B. King and Henry Ford. No one could argue about the importance of the automobile industry to Detroit and to the men of labor and management, so harmony and good fellowship abounded. On May 31, 1946, George Romney was the master of ceremonies at a dinner honoring more than a dozen pioneers of the automobile industry. These included Charles B. King, Henry Ford, Alfred P. Sloan, William C. Durant, Charles W. Nash, Ransom E. Olds, and Barney Oldsfield. William Knudsen received a special award for his service to the automobile industry and to the nation during the years of World War II.

The celebration was a moving tribute to the great men of the automobile industry, and a smashing personal success for George Romney. He became better acquainted with the old pioneers who were no longer active as well as the young men who were directing the operations of General Motors, Ford, Chrysler, Nash, and Hudson. His key role as managing director of the automotive-industries aspect of the Golden Jubilee put him in the spotlight, and kept him there for weeks.

"It was the first time I saw in Romney that glimpse of what I thought was an interest in politics," Victor Reuther recalled later. "He was in the middle of things, and people loved him and he liked it."

Wartime problems of the automobile industry, community problems of Detroit, and finally the Golden Jubilee had thrown Romney and Victor Reuther together for half a dozen years. A pleasant, friendly relationship developed, for they were not pitted against each other on labor problems or on political differences.

In later years, as Romney entered politics, he was to point with some pride to his pleasant working relationship with Victor Reuther as evidence that he could get along with and work with the Reuthers and the UAW. However, it was more of a convenient surface cordiality than a deep personal friendship, as later events demonstrated.

"I couldn't argue with Romney's claim that we got along," Victor Reuther said in the years after he and the UAW had voiced bitter political opposition to Romney. "We were not dealing with each other in collective bargaining. For the most part we were working on projects for the good of the community and the nation, and we had the same goals. I hardly think it would have been the same if it had been in a collective-bargaining situation."

Reuther found Romney to be "a hard worker and an evangelist on every project." But Victor and Walter Reuther both said they have always regarded Romney as "superficial" in his understanding of labor-management relations. It is certain there was no meeting of the minds on the subject.

Victor Reuther characterized Romney as "a zealous salesman and largely a promoter."

"He worked hard enough and he was enthusiastic, but I really never had the impression that George had much real depth or understanding," Victor Reuther said. "He could go out and sell the idea of bringing more Negro workers into the automobile industry, and he could do it with an enthusiasm, but I never gained the impression that he had much real comprehension of the real human problem we were trying to solve."

The viewpoint of Victor Reuther was essentially the viewpoint expressed by Walter Reuther, August Scholle, and other Michigan labor leaders as they reflected back on the career of Romney, whom they had come to regard as their archenemy when he invaded Michigan politics as a Republican.

While many did not claim early knowledge of Romney's political ambitions, Victor Reuther recalls that from some point about the time of the Automotive Golden Jubilee, he concluded that Romney had "one eye on politics" and was waiting for the opportune time to make a move.

Romney and Walter Reuther were much alike. Both were above reproach in their private lives. Neither smoked nor drank intoxicating liquor. Both were energetic, enthusiastic, and single-minded in pursuit of the goals they considered important. Both have been described by admirers and detractors as "evangelists" for the causes for which they had enlisted, though the causes were far apart.

George Romney was as dedicated to "making it possible for management to manage" as Reuther was to pushing for a maximum voice for organized labor in any policy that even remotely touched his union members. Romney was interested in making the Republican Party the major force in Michigan politics, while Reuther was obsessed with making himself a major force in national Democratic politics as well as in the Democratic Party in Michigan.

Following the Automotive Golden Jubilee, President Truman appointed Edward L. Cushman, former head of the War Manpower Commission in Michigan, as chairman of the Metal Trades Industry conference at an International Labor Organization (ILO) meeting in Toledo. Romney was named as an employer-member of the delegation, and with his usual exuberant personality made the acquaintanceship of most of the more than one hundred foreign delegates.

The 1947 meeting of the Metal Trades Industry Conference took place in Stockholm, Sweden, and again Romney was a delegate. George and Lenore made the trip together and toured postwar Europe for six weeks, viewing the results of the shattered economic conditions and retracing some of George's travels as a Mormon missionary twenty years earlier in Great Britain.

It was in August and September of 1947 that they drove through Great Britain, Sweden, Denmark, Germany, the Netherlands, Switzerland, Italy, and France. They talked with employer, labor, and government delegates to the Metal Trades Industry conference, and they talked to businessmen all across Europe.

Western Europe was still suffering from a severe drought of the previous summer. It had been followed by a harsh freezing winter which had frozen crops, and floods in the spring of 1947 again had been followed by a drought that Romney said was "unquestionably the worst since the time of Napoleon."

The normally green fields of England were parched and brown. In Denmark and other countries that were usually a major source of dairy products, they were told that dairy cattle were being slaughtered because of a lack of pasture and grain. The lush green valley meadows of France and Switzerland were now brown and inadequate for grazing purposes. In every country they visited, the Romneys found that agricultural production was off from 30 to 40 percent.

In the plight of Europe brought on by drought and economic decline, Romney saw human tragedy deeper than his own family had struggled through in the drought in Oakley or the collapse of the economy of Rexburg following World War I. George Romney was impressed with the need for United States aid in rebuilding Western Europe, and upon his return he expressed that view to Senator Arthur Vandenberg, the veteran Michigan Republican who had emerged from a background of isolationism into the major position of leadership in a new internationalist bipartisan foreign policy.

Secretary of State George Marshall had unveiled the broad concepts of his Marshall Plan for economic aid for Western Europe on June 5, 1947, and Vandenberg, as chairman of the Senate Foreign Relations Committee, had been conducting investigations and taking testimony in an effort to rally support for interim aid for Europe in the winter of 1947 as well as for a long-term program for the economic recovery of Europe. Disturbing reports of the daners of Communist efforts to seize power in France as well as in several other nations in Western Europe were brought back by John Foster Dulles, who had made a secret mission for the State Department.

In pushing for an economic-aid program, Senator Vandenberg found himself faced with objections from Senator Thomas Connally, the Texas Democrat who had been chairman of the Foreign Relations Committee, as well as from Senator Robert A. Taft, an influential conservative Republican who was reported to be maneuvering for political position for the 1948 Republican presidential nomination. Senator Vandenberg needed all the Republican support he could get, and on this issue of aid for Europe George Romney lined up with the internationalists in the Republican Party. Chairman Vandenberg asked him to testify on his experience in Europe.

On November 14, 1947, Romney appeared before the Senate Foreign Relations Committee as a supporter of the programs suggested by Senator Vandenberg and John Foster Dulles. Although he was still managing director of the Automobile Manufacturers Association, Romney did not testify in that capacity but "rather as an American citizen."

"The size of the overall European problem and its importance to us confronts us with an international undertaking second only to that of the war itself," Romney said in launching his first testimony on international matters. "Given the facts, I am sure that the same type of voluntary cooperation that played such a vital role in winning of the war will develop on the part of private organizations and private individuals.

"The facts are that the overall European problem breaks down into three basic elements: first, humanitarian; second, governmental or political and diplomatic; third, economic," the 40-year-old Automobile Manufacturers Association executive told the Senate Foreign Relations Committee. "Adverse European developments in recent years have been so cataclysmic and so frequent that few Americans understand these three elements and the basic causes of each."

He pointed out that his knowledge of European affairs before the trip was "a little above average since I spent two years abroad, mostly in Britain, in the middle 1920's. Furthermore, I had served as a tariff specialist for Senator Walsh during consideration of the Smoot-Hawley Tariff Act."

Romney told the committee he had expected to see the "disruptive effect on European economies" from the destructiveness of war. "However, I was only vaguely aware of the extent and nature of the great natural catastrophe that has occurred in Europe during the postwar period. Like most Americans, I thought the main problems in Europe were the economic rehabilitation of agriculture and industry, the political problem of working out the peace treaties, relocating displaced persons, stabilizing currencies, and reducing international trade barriers. But everywhere I went I found the most urgent problem was to arrest starvation and freezing for millions of people in Europe this winter."

Romney declared that the weather catastrophe was the primary cause for the food shortage, and that it was not understood by most Americans because it had been the result of cumulative problems piled one on top of another.

"Another important cause is the East-West division of the European continent," Romney continued. "A third is the lack of agricultural equipment, particularly in the countries overrun by the Nazis, who confiscated such equipment; and a fourth, the lack of fertilizer. A fifth is the hoarding tendencies created by unstabilized currencies. In my judgment this factor has been vastly overemphasized, leaving the impression in the minds of many Americans that elimination of hoarding would largely solve Europe's food problems. This is far from the truth."

Romney the evangelist came through in his testimony as he told the committee that a factual presentation of the European food problem "would inspire from the American people the same type of humanitarian response that has occurred following other great catastrophes."

"When Japan suffered a great earthquake, the American people did not hesitate in making their humanitarian response," Romney said. "They did not ask themselves if they liked the Japanese— if they worked hard enough, if their economic institutions were sound, or if their worship of their emperor was correct. We did not even hesitate because of growing conflict in our international aims."

Romney declared that the magnitude of the humanitarian problem abroad had to be solved in connection with abnormal food-consumption levels within the United States, and rising food prices that had become a major factor in the inflationary cycle at home.

"Supplying European subsistence needs without adequate programs to protect our own enlightened self-interest could be the cause of widespread distress at home," Romney warned. "On the other hand, unless America does help to the full limit of her capacity, human want and suffering could destroy any effective resistance to totalitarianism in those countries."

Romney declared that aid to Europe had to be considered in connection with domestic food reserves, since the wheat carry-over in 1947 was only one third of the carry-over for 1945.

"A drought of as yet incalculable proportions has occurred this fall in the Plains states area and has retarded and reduced fall wheat planting," Romney said. "After nine consecutive good crop years, we should accept the possibility—perhaps even the probability—of a bad crop year at home in making our foreign commitments and domestic plans."

He related the problem to his own experience in the automobile industry in World War II: "As in the materials-conservation field during the war, in the food field we are likely to find that substitute programs simply shift the shortages. The humanitarian and economic aspects of the international food situation are such as to merit the energetic and active participation of every economic, civic, social, and religious group is America."

He told the Senate Committee that the work of the voluntary organizations was lagging, and told of his own lack of success in organizing support for the food program in Detroit.

"As a member of the Detroit Citizens Food Committee, I can tell you that in Detroit, despite the European origin of many of our finest citizens, the people are not convinced (1) that the need is genuine, and (2) that the methods suggested will supply adequate relief where needed."

He declared that it would be unfortunate if the interim-aid program created the public impression that the appropriation of funds by Congress reduced the need for food conservation within the United States.

"In the early stages of the war there was a tendency to place too much reliance on centralization of authority and responsibility and appropriation of funds to produce the guns, tanks, and planes," Romney explained. "Now, in the discussion of the big European responsibility ahead, there again appears to be too much reliance on Government doing the entire job. This leads me to suggest that any government agency created to administer emergency European relief should be partially directed and largely staffed by people from the staffs of the existing national and international relief organizations."

Romney told the Senate Committee that over a period of years the men and women on the existing agencies had "developed effective and nonpolitical techniques and facilities for administering mass assistance on a strictly humanitarian and disaster basis."

"It would be tragic to overlook the contributions of the Red Cross, CARE, Inc., American Society of Friends, various Catholic institutions, the United Jewish Relief, the Mormon Church, and other private institutions already actively operating well-organized foreign-relief programs," Romney said. "It would be ideal if American aid could be extended primarily through such private agencies as a gift of the American people directly to the European people."

Romney said that the urgency of the interim-aid problem required reliance upon governmental agencies, but he suggested that as soon as possible it be shifted to private humanitarian agencies.

Romney declared that a report by the Truman Committee in March 1944 was applicable to the administration of the food and aid program. He quoted: "The home front will do any job that is needed of it if the facts are put squarely before the people. . . . Experience has told us that our country will flourish best when least hampered by government control. . . . Even in wartime it was the flow of private initiative that made possible the success of the war programs."

He stressed the need for working through private business organizations rather than government bureaucracy in the aid-to-European business. "No matter how earnest or sincere and experienced in other fields, men lacking economic experience, judgment, and ability are not qualified to render the type of economic assistance most required by the industries of Europe today. Making dollars, materials, and machines available through our government to their governments, under present conditions almost certainly would expedite the extension and expansion of government controls over the daily lives of Europeans."

Romney declared that most European governments were then "proceeding on the false premise that the way to prevent complete totalitarianism is to persuade or force the people to accept bigger and bigger doses of collectivism and compulsion."

"While consideration is probably being given to the need for making our assistance available under conditions that will retard this process, my experience leads to the conclusion that few such conditions laid down by our government would be either acceptable or effectively enforced," Romney said. He explained,

"While I was in Great Britain, leading businessmen and conservatives made it clear that they and other Englishmen would resent efforts on our part to meddle with present British government policies with which these particular Britishers vigorously dissent."

Romney blamed much of the problem of Europe on weaknesses that had existed before World War II in industries where there was no real competition. "At the conference I attended, and throughout Europe, businessmen as well as government and labor representatives rejected the concept of competitive cooperative capitalism which has supplied the human vigor and vision on which our technological production accomplishments and our unparalleled standards of living have been based," Romney said.

"Even before the war, Western Europe relied primarily on private monopolistic cartels," Romney explained. "The difference between such private cartels and governmentally nationalized industries is slight indeed. If European nations are to become self-supporting in terms of twentieth-century industrialism, they need the American concept of competitive capitalism, in addition to the concepts of international trade that Mr. Dulles has outlined so well."

Romney declared that there must be no repetition of the experience after World War I, when loans made to European nations became outright grants while "European industry remained monopolistic, producing high-priced products for the few and low wages for all."

Representatives of labor and management in various countries had told Romney that they could not compete with the United States on the world market because their costs were too high. They had suggested that American industry refrain from using its productive capacity to supply world needs so that they might find foreign markets.

"Most certainly we must not retard their economic reconstruction to settle differences of economic principles," Romney declared in sympathy with the problem, but he added, "At the same time, we must recognize that their ability to become self-sustaining is linked with their utilization of the competitive characteristic which is the most distinctive element in the amply demonstrated dynamics of the American economy."

He hammered at the importance of working through business firms rather than through government on the long-range aid program. "It would reduce to a minimum, as they should be reduced, political and extraneous considerations," Romney said. "The American firm would determine what was needed to make the European enterprise a going investment for American funds, including some of its own. The loan would be made providing the foreign firm was in agreement on the changes needed and was willing to make them a prerequisite to obtaining the assistance sought. This would put the problem on the sound basis of international investment that has proved so beneficial to other nations in the past, especially our own."

Romney said that the operations through private investors and industry would undoubtedly subject the United States to more charges of "dollar diplomacy" and "Wall Street imperialism." "But, let us take a square look at the alternative," he said. "If the assistance is rendered primarily by our government to their governments, the charge will be that their governments have become satellites of America. It is time for Americans to realize that, regardless of how we render the assistance needed, we will be subjected to vicious, violent, and immediate attack. The attack will

undertake to distort and twist our motives and our methods. . . .
Europeans need more knowledge about America. We cannot afford to make a mistake made repeatedly at home as well as abroad, namely, to overestimate the people's information and underestimate their intelligence."

Most of all, he warned there must be no American regimentation in the United States or of Europe. "We must avoid the fatal mistake of adopting the very methods we are fighting," Romney said. "Our record during peace and war establishes incontrovertibly that free labor, free management, and free capital in cooperation with free government can outproduce slave labor, shackled management, and governmentally confiscated capital. Freedom and voluntary cooperation are our most valuable assets in assisting a sick world."

George Romney was in tune with the humanitarian spirit and the enlightened self-interest of Senator Vandenberg and others in the internationalist wing of the Republican Party. He suggested that it was important to have some distinguished man from American business to head the long-time foreign-aid program.

President Truman first suggested Dean Acheson, then a prominent Washington lawyer, as the man for the job, but Senator Vandenberg said he did not believe that Acheson could be confirmed by the Republican Senate. Vandenberg suggested Paul G. Hoffman, president of the Studebaker Corporation and chairman of the board of the Committee for Economic Development. Hoffman, a long-time acquaintance of Romney in the automobile industry, was the kind of man Romney had in mind for the administration of the protracted aid program that was first established as the Economic Cooperation Administration.

Although there were critics of some aspects of the foreign-aid program as administered by Paul Hoffman from 1948 through September 1950, Senator Vandenberg praised him for having "performed so magnificently in your difficult assignment." Senator Vandenberg credited Hoffman with keeping politics out of the ECA, and noted that he had "flatly declined to permit anybody from the President down to dictate the choice of his associated personnel."

The Romney role in this major international problem was

slight, but his testimony and his analysis of the problem remain an indication of his genuine concern for the problems of Europe and of his much more than superficial understanding of the difficulty of administering such a program in independent nations.

EIGHT

Auto Business Executive

Many in the automobile industry were impressed with the manner in which George Romney performed as a spokesman for the Automobile Manufacturers Association and as an enthusiastic booster for the Automotive Golden Jubilee. But two men who worked closest with him as managing director of AMA believed he had the potential for executive leadership which could be important to their firms. Alvan Macauley, of the Packard Motor Company, had been president of the AMA in 1939, when Romney was first named manager of the Detroit office, and George W. Mason, president of Nash-Kelvinator, succeeded Macauley as president of the AMA in 1946.

Romney and Macauley had become close friends during the war years through their continuous contact on the problems of the automobile industry. Macauley had admired the young Mormon with his straitlaced personal principles and his industrious approach to any job confronting him. Their strong friendship and mutual admiration remained after Macauley's resignation as president of the AMA in 1946.

In February 1948, Macauley sounded Romney out in regard to joining Packard as a top executive and member of the board of directors. Romney's interest resulted in talks with George Christopher, president of Packard, who was anxious to retire to an Ohio farm.

Christopher made a firm offer to Romney to join the organization as an executive vice-president at $50,000 a year, with the additional agreement that sometime within the next two years Christopher would retire and Romney would move up to the presidency of the firm. It was an attractive offer, a firm offer, and George Romney was ready to accept when he telephoned George Mason, president of the AMA, to resign as managing director of that organization.

Mason, under pressure to groom a successor at Nash-Kelvinator, urged Romney to hold his final decision until they had an opportunity to discuss a position with Nash-Kelvinator. When Mason's offer was finally made, it was neither as prestigious nor as lucrative as the one extended by Macauley and Christopher at Packard.

The salary suggested was only $30,000, with the title of assistant to Mason, and hopes were held out that Mason would find a top executive post for him after he had spent a year or two learning the business.

On the face of it, the Packard proposal seemed much the better, but there were personnel problems in the top ranks at Packard, and Romney's friend, Macauley, was scheduled for retirement within a few months.

The uncertainty threatening top officials of Packard was sufficient reason for Romney to hesitate, and the opportunity to learn the inside of the automobile manufacturing business from Mason turned Romney in the direction of the Nash-Kelvinator job.

George Mason, a former works manager at Chrysler, had the kind of experience that George Romney lacked. He had been employed in the automobile industry since 1913, when he started with Studebaker shortly after leaving the University of Michigan, where he had studied engineering and business administration. He gained experience floating around in a wide range of jobs on the fringe of the automobile industry before being hired by Walter

Chrysler in 1921 as works manager for the Maxwell-Chalmers Company, later the Chrysler Corporation.

Moving on to a small refrigerator company for a short term, Mason was then hired by the Kelvinator company in 1927, and he proceeded to untangle production problems and develop that firm into a moneymaking operation throughout the depression.

When Charles Nash tried to hire Mason away from his job as president of Kelvinator in 1936, Mason balked at leaving Kelvinator. Because Nash was intent on acquiring Mason's services, a merger was worked out, which resulted in the Nash-Kelvinator Company in January 1937. Nash was chairman of the board, and Mason was president and operational head of the merged firm.

George Romney wanted exposure to the broad manufacturing experience of George Mason, while Mason wanted to teach the genial and hard-working Romney to direct the overall business of manufacturing Nash automobiles and Kelvinator refrigerators.

Although some officials knew Mason was grooming Romney as a successor, it was not readily apparent in the months immediately following April 1948, when he went to work at Nash-Kelvinator.

Romney's duties were difficult to equate with his executive status when he put on coveralls and went into the shop to learn the grimy and uncomfortable facts of automobiles and refrigerators from the beginning.

Romney was as much at home among the production workers and mechanics as in the executive offices. He not only tolerated a return to the overalls and work with his hands he had known as a young man, he actually enjoyed it. The skills he had acquired as a lather in Salt Lake were useful in demonstrating to upholsterers and others that he was no clumsy novice.

But George Romney learned more about the operations of the plant than mechanical details of how refrigerators and automobiles are designed, planned, and produced. Wasteful work practices that had grown up in some of the plants during the war years as a result of the cost-plus-fixed-fee contracts were revealed firsthand. Those contracts eliminated the pressure for efficiency or economy in war work, and careless, slovenly work habits developed.

Pent-up demands for refrigerators immediately following the

war did not compel management to eradicate a host of wasteful labor practices, and consequently many of them were accepted and defended by the labor unions. This was particularly true at the Kelvinator plant on Plymouth Road in Detroit, where employees were represented by the Mechanics Educational Society of America, known as MESA. This competitor of the United Automobile Workers was headed by Matthew Smith, a colorful and arrogant self-styled socialist from England.

Through his work with the Automobile Manufacturers Association and the Automotive Council for War Production, Romney was aware of many of the wasteful work practices that had developed in the war years. But his indoctrination period at Nash-Kelvinator gave him his first day-by-day encounter with a laxity he considered shocking from a standpoint of the attitude of the employees as well as from a standpoint of management.

Poor production practices were sapping the strength of the Kelvinator Division and permitting competitors to forge ahead in quality and price. Initially, Romney had no authority and was in no position to take action on the problems. Director of industrial relations was Don C. Rulo, who in line with the demands of Matt Smith insisted that management avoid direct contact with the workers and communicate only through MESA. In these policies, Rulo was backed by Ray A. De Vlieg, the vice-president in charge of manufacturing. Both Rulo and De Vlieg were resentful of any acts encroaching on their area of responsibility, and the first suggestions Romney made to improve communications were turned aside as naïve and unsophisticated moves in one of the most sophisticated aspects of big industry. Although Romney made general recommendations to Mason regarding better organization and better communications with employees and within the executive group, he did not push the issue in his first years.

As a part of learning the business, Mason assigned Romney a wide range of small tasks. When Romney went to Europe in the fall of 1949 as an employer delegate to the Metal Trades Industry Conference, he asked him to try to hire Pinin Farina, the Italian car designer whose work had impressed Mason at an automobile show in Paris. Initially, Farina was reluctant, but Romney persuaded him to sign the contract by tossing in the promise that when Farina visited the United States he would have a Nash for his personal use.

In 1950, Mason named Romney a vice-president and gave him responsibility for publicizing and testing public acceptance of a small economical car that would travel at 60 to 70 miles an hour and more than 35 miles on a gallon of gasoline. Romney was immediately enthusiastic about the car, and public response was favorable even though final cost figures were higher than Mason had estimated they would be.

Romney was one of a handful of men in Nash-Kelvinator with confidence in Mason's move to the small 1950 Nash that was to be named the Rambler. Although only 15,500 of the 190,000 cars sold in 1950 were Ramblers, the move to smaller cars had started.

Rambler sales mounted to more than 50,000 in 1951, and Romney was exuberant over the demand, although production was still far too low for it to be a successful financial venture. Many years were to elapse and many major problems had to be solved before the Rambler would prove itself successful enough for a smaller, independent automobile firm to outflank the Big Three of the automobile industry.

Mason continued what was largely a one-man show at Nash-Kelvinator while slowly yielding additional responsibility to Romney as the occasion seemed to demand it. Romney theorized there was too little communication within the Nash-Kelvinator Company. In addition to the lack of executive communication with the workers, Romney believed there was too little contact between the executives and the middle-level supervisory personnel. He established the position of director of communications and hired William H. McGaughey, an old associate from the Automobile Manufacturers Association, to head it.

Too little effort was made to develop a spirit of cooperation with the workmen in the firm, and Romney recommended that the same program designed to stimulate activity on the part of dealers be staged for plant employees in Kenosha and Milwaukee. He also proposed that employees with twenty-five years of service be given gold pins, with watches or clocks for employees who had worked for the company for thirty years.

Romney's suggestions on establishing communications with the workmen ran into immediate spirited opposition from De Vlieg, who considered this an infringement upon his responsibility as vice-president in charge of manufacturing. Romney, with five years in the firm, did not retreat from the challenge on this occasion, and Mason settled it by making Romney executive vice-president, with clear authority over all other executives except Mason.

With his authority as number-two man in the organization finally established, Romney moved aggressively to take steps he had long believed necessary to bring discipline to the work force, improve productivity, and cut manufacturing costs. The Kelvinator Division, previously a steady money-maker, was operating in the red, and decisions had to be made as to whether the company would continue to operate plants in Grand Rapids and in Detroit.

Inevitably, trouble developed between Romney and Matt Smith, who represented the union men in the Kelvinator plant in Detroit. Romney was convinced that wasteful practices had to be eradicated if the Detroit plant was to continue operations, and he believed that the union members would understand the need for a 20 percent increase in productivity if they were only given the facts on competition. The only alternative Romney saw to a substantial increase in production would be closing the Detroit plant, with the loss of about ten thousand jobs.

Matt Smith bitterly opposed Romney and his efforts to increase productivity. The sharp-tongued union leader admitted output of the Detroit Kelvinator plant was low, but he contended the workers did more than the staff in the executive suite. Matt Smith termed George Romney "a faker" who used a pious front and fine words to cover an attack on union solidarity.

When Nash-Kelvinator fired a union steward for assaulting a foreman, Matt Smith seized it as an opportunity to put Romney in his place. The fact that the steward had returned to the shop late and was intoxicated made no difference to Smith, for he was accustomed to calling the tune at Kelvinator without interference from management.

That dispute was not yet settled when Romney took the initiative to go into the plant to tell the workers that unless there was a 20 percent increase in productivity, the Kelvinator plant would be forced to close down. Romney admitted that the lack of discipline and proper productivity was probably as much the fault of management as it was of the workers themselves, but the economic facts of life were important to both labor and management.

When Matt Smith struck the plant and the workers stayed home, Romney wrote long letters to the union members, trying to answer, point by point, the arguments used by Smith and other union leaders.

While Romney tried to keep a tone of reason in his letters, there was no such effort by Matt Smith, who used his own letters to the workers to ridicule Romney and the Nash-Kelvinator management. Specific disputes were occasionally settled, but the bitter personality clash between Romney and Smith persisted throughout 1953 and 1954, as Nash-Kelvinator was merging with the Hudson Motor Car Company.

In January 1954, the merger of Hudson into Nash-Kelvinator was approved by directors of both firms, with the new firm to be known as American Motors. Book value of the stock of the largest merger in the history of the automobile industry was nearly $200,000,000. George Romney concluded the firm needed real expertise in the field of labor relations to deal with Matt Smith's MESA as well as with Walter Reuther and officials of the United Automobile Workers and recommended to Mason that Edward L. Cushman be hired as industrial-relations director.

Cushman, an economics graduate of the University of Michigan, had been Michigan director of the War Manpower Commission during the latter part of World War II. Because of their work on the manpower problems of the automobile industry, Romney knew him to have excellent relations with both labor and management—a real professional in the field of labor relations.

Cushman was only forty years of age when Romney recommended him for the job with American Motors, but he was already one of the best-known industrial arbitrators. At twenty-three, he was named deputy chairman of the Michigan War Manpower Commission after working as a research economist for the Michigan Unemployment Commission. In 1942, he became chairman of the Michigan War Manpower Commission, and following World War II he joined the faculty of Wayne State University in Detroit as a Professor of Public Administration. Cushman continued as an industrial arbitrator in dozens of major cases, and had served as a consultant for Romney at Nash-Kelvinator as well as for Reuther and the UAW.

Ed Cushman joined American Motors knowing he had a difficult job ahead of him, ironing out "a labor-management mess." The bitter personality clash between Romney and Smith was only a part of it. Cushman later described another part of his role as "interpreting Romney to Reuther and Reuther to Romney." Although the Romney-Reuther relationship had not deteriorated to the level of Romney's relationship with Matt Smith, Romney and Walter Reuther had never become acquainted under circumstances that permitted any real trust and understanding to develop.

From May 1, 1954, when Cushman joined American Motors, Romney relied upon him to untangle the accumulated patchwork labor-management agreements and bad work practices of twenty years. Hiring Ed Cushman did not result in easy solutions to the labor problems of American Motors, for difficult decisions still had to be made on how to deal with Matt Smith and MESA. Earlier strikes had settled nothing.

Cushman and Romney continued a tough policy to bring reasonable discipline into the Kelvinator plant, where men and women were operating sideline restaurant and barber businesses while on company pay, and poker games and other gambling flourished in the men's room. Management had lost the authority to manage, and obviously a tough encounter with Matt Smith was necessary to reestablish those rights.

The result was inevitable, and on August 2, 1954, Matt Smith pulled his men out of the Kelvinator plant without any discussion of a grievance with either Cushman or Romney. When Cushman called to tell him that there should have been a discussion with management on any grievance before calling a strike, Smith snapped that he had control of the workers and he would handle them as he pleased.

"Why have you gone to work for that Romney?" Smith asked Cushman contemptuously, as if he considered such association with Romney slightly indecent.

It was a question that Cushman did not feel should be answered, for no amount of discussion could have changed Matt Smith's bitterness toward George Romney at that time.

Smith suggested that he and Cushman could settle the strike with a brief discussion, but Cushman replied that it was a violation of the contract to pull the men out without prior discussions of the issues. He refused to negotiate with Smith until the workers were back on the job as they should be under the requirements of the contract.

Smith vowed to keep the men out until winter, and Cushman, with Romney's backing, declared that American Motors was not going to bend to the whims of the union. For several months prior to the strike, American Motors had been overproducing for the purpose of building up an inventory for just such a showdown with Matt Smith.

The strike continued throughout August and September. Both the union and American Motors filed damage suits in court, charging the other with breach of contract. In early October, a Labor Department official contacted Cushman to say that a settlement could probably be worked out with Matt Smith, but that Smith had worked himself into such an embarrassing position that he needed a meeting or talk prior to sending the men back to work to save face.

Cushman sent word to Smith that he would not negotiate until the men had been sent back to work, but that he would agree to an informal meeting or discussion. Such a meeting was arranged, and Cushman recalls that Matt Smith "spent most of the first thirty minutes bitterly denouncing Romney."

When Cushman shoved him a sheet of paper containing conditions that the company believed essential, Matt Smith barely scanned it while commenting that he and Cushman could have settled the matter weeks earlier and continued to castigate his favorite whipping boy, George Romney.

A settlement was reached on October 6, providing American Motors with the right to determine in which of its plants it would manufacture various products, and also providing that the company should give the union notice and the opportunity for discussions prior to any future decisions to shift production from one plant to another.

Cushman suggested that Matt Smith and George Romney sit down together for talks in connection with the settlement as a basis for better personal relations between the two men in the future. The confrontation was "fairly cordial," Cushman said later.

Although Romney and Matt Smith remained far apart in labor-management philosophy, Cushman said that before Smith died in 1958 he had come to regard Romney as "a man of integrity and sincerity," the same man he had earlier sneered at as "a pious fraud" and "a faker."

"For a man like Matt Smith it just seemed inconceivable that any big business executive could be as dedicated and sincere as George Romney appeared to be," Cushman said later. "Matt was a kind of cynic, and it took a long time before he was willing to give Romney credit for being a straightforward, honest man."

Out of that two-month strike in the fall of 1954 came a brief joint statement by Cushman and Smith: "Both the company and the union believe that a sound foundation has now been laid for constructive relationships. We are determined to make the Detroit Kelvinator plant an outstanding example of union-management cooperation."

That settlement had barely been concluded when Romney, Cushman, and other American Motors executives received a severe shock.

George Mason, president, general manager, and chairman of the board of American Motors, died following an illness of only a few days. Mason, a roly-poly, 265-pound cigar smoker, had been the spark plug of Nash-Kelvinator since 1937, had masterminded the merger with Hudson a few months earlier, and had been the initial driving force behind the idea to outflank the Big Three with a compact car.

Despite his excess weight and constant smoking, Mason had never been seriously ill prior to a hunting and fishing trip that first week of October. He developed pneumonia and his pancreas stopped functioning on October 8, 1954.

Although one major labor problem had just been settled, the recently created American Motors had dozens of other demanding problems that everyone had hoped the genius of George Mason would solve. On October 12, 1954, the day after Mason's funeral, the paramount responsibility for solving those problems became George Romney's. Named chairman, president, and general manager of American Motors by the board of directors, he was grateful for the six years he'd had the guiding hand of George Mason, but it was still an awesome responsibility.

NINE

Problems at American Motors

American Motors needed all the energy and enthusiasm George Romney could muster in the late fall of 1954. The newly formed corporation was seeking optimism in a future clouded by union labor problems, financial problems, and the competition of the giants of both the automobile and appliance industries.

Facing the competitive advantage of the Big Three of the automobile industry was a difficult task under the best circumstances, and there was serious doubt as to whether any independent automobile company could survive for many years even by getting all the breaks. A look at competition in the appliance field was no more encouraging, for formidable opposition loomed from Frigidaire, General Electric, and Westinghouse.

Settlement of some of the major problems with Matt Smith's union was helpful in planning for the Kelvinator Division, but a new problem arose when General Electric stopped buying compressors from Kelvinator and shifted its business to a new General Electric plant at Louisville, Kentucky. This necessitated a shift

110

of the Detroit Kelvinator plant functions to Grand Rapids, Michigan.

The business world and American Motors stockholders were aware of the competitive problem the firm faced under the new, and largely untried, leadership of George Romney. George Mason's ingenuity as a product planner and as a manufacturing genius had kept Nash-Kelvinator moving for years, and it had been hoped he would provide the spark and the imagination to launch American Motors. But there was a changing market with no guarantee of survival.

Unless long-range prospects for American Motors looked promising to the financial world, there was a strong possibility that plans for refinancing might fail and the entire organization collapse within eighteen months to two years. Executives of American Motors had hoped that a product reciprocity agreement with Studebaker-Packard would prove beneficial in the efforts to compete with the Big Three. In August 1954, George Mason and Romney had taken part in negotiations with James Nance, president of Studebaker-Packard, and other officials of that firm. They believed the agreement was mutually beneficial, and had announced it to the newspapers as a significant step forward in cooperation between smaller independent automobile firms.

American Motors was to buy V-8 engines from Studebaker-Packard, and in return Studebaker-Packard "would endeavor to purchase from American Motors products suitable for use by Packard . . . [and] . . . to the extent possible Packard will endeavor to make such purchase in dollar amounts at least approximately equal to dollar volume purchases from Packard by American Motors."

An escape clause in the agreement permitted Studebaker-Packard officials to be the sole judge as to whether American Motors products could be purchased "on a competitive and advantageous basis."

To Romney and George Mason, the clause had seemed fair at the time it was written, and Romney had expected Studebaker-Packard officials to buy substantial material from a bodywork plant brought into American Motors from the Hudson firm. American placed orders for the V-8 engines, but the expected business from Studebaker-Packard did not materialize.

In late October 1954, Romney was shocked to read that Studebaker-Packard had taken an option to buy a bodywork plant. Outraged, he fired off a note to James Nance at Studebaker-Packard, declaring that he considered this action "contrary to the spirit, contractual and moral obligation" of their product-reciprocity agreement. Several exchanges of correspondence with Nance and other officials of his firm revealed their position was that they were under no binding obligation to buy from American Motors. Studebaker-Packard reasoned they had performed a service in simply agreeing to sell Packard V-8 engines to American Motors.

Romney made telephone calls to various Studebaker-Packard executives in an effort to persuade them that what they were doing "is not right," and to ask them to live up to the reciprocity agreement as he interpreted it. Ed Cushman, who was present during one of the telephone conversations, relates that Romney turned from the telephone to declare: "That fellow lied to me three times in that one conversation. You just cannot do business with someone who lies."

From that moment, American Motors was determined to end its deal with Studebaker-Packard and build its own V-8 engine. Romney waited only long enough to consult with his policy board before scrapping the Studebaker-Packard contract on grounds that the other firm had broken the agreement. This meant that American Motors would have to build its own V-8 engine, and there was no money available.

One of the best properties of American Motors was Ranco, Inc., of Columbus, Ohio, then the largest manufacturer of thermostatic controls. It was a money-maker, and a source of controls for Kelvinator appliances as well as automobile heaters and air conditioners. Romney and his associates sold the majority interest in Ranco for something over $10,500,000—approximately the same amount of money needed to finance the program for production of the V-8 engine.

It was a risky venture at the time, but in the end American

Motors' V-8 was better suited for the company's purposes and substantially less costly, but it was months before Romney and his associates were certain that the gamble had been a good one.

Dozens of immediate decisions needed to be made.

Energy was as important as any other quality as George Romney went to work at the unenviable task of filling the shoes of his friend George Mason. While he had disagreed with the organizational structure under Mason, Romney had great faith in the ability and business judgment of his predecessor, and he tried to follow the general program for the future as he understood Mason had planned it.

In one of their last conversations, Mason had told Romney he believed they should try to hire Roy Abernethy, vice-president in charge of sales at Kaiser-Willys, to put some drive behind a more intensive campaign to sell the Nash Rambler. One of Romney's first moves was to retire the vice-president in charge of sales, a man vocally unenthusiastic about the entire small-car program, and to replace him with Abernethy.

The organization had to breathe confidence and enthusiasm at the executive level if it was to be a success. A team effort by a group of men as optimistic about the future of the small-car market as he was could generate that certainty. He streamlined the organization, using ideas he had first suggested to Mason as early as 1949. As a part of this he established an eleven-man policy committee to try to give the key men in the organization the real feeling of participation that Romney believed was so important.

Romney's enthusiasm was contagious within the American Motors organization. One official commented that "George exuded so much enthusiasm and confidence that we hardly realized the impossible odds we faced."

"Looking back on it now, I don't believe we had any grounds for our optimism, but George never let down, and he kept our spirits up through some pretty tough times," the American Motors official said.

Romney's bubbling exuberance was equally effective in overcoming pessimism about American Motors that had started to penetrate the New York financial community following the death of George Mason. On December 7, 1954, Romney appeared before a luncheon meeting of the New York Society of Security Analysts to explain his plans for American Motors and to answer questions. Confidence and sincerity came through in that first appearance in New York, and the lagging American Motors stock jumped from $10 to $12 a share and hung there for several months.

There was also a serious problem with the United Automobile Workers Union, which represented the workers in the automotive division. Under the labor-management contract, American Motors paid a higher wage rate than General Motors, Ford, or Chrysler. George Romney considered it an injustice for Walter Reuther and Leonard Woodcock, of the UAW, to insist upon imposing a penalty of a higher wage rate on the automobile companies least able to afford it.

While George Mason was running the company, periodic complaints were made to the UAW about the higher wages, but efforts to eliminate or reduce the differences between the wages paid by American Motors and those paid by the Big Three had met with frustrating opposition. The United Automobile Workers had the clout to cause irreparable damage to American Motors, and American Motors was not in financial condition to take a strike. The union had insisted on a "wage pattern plus" settlement from American Motors, and what the big automobile union wanted, the union had received.

It made no sense to George Romney or Ed Cushman that American Motors and other small independent firms in the automobile industry were paying higher wages than Ford and General Motors. But Leonard Woodcock, the United Automobile Workers Union vice-president and director of the American Motors Department, had been unwilling to make any concessions prior to 1955. In addition, UAW president Walter Reuther had announced that it expected the 1955 contracts with the independent companies to include a guaranteed annual wage provision.

In an appearance before the Senate Judiciary Subcommittee on Antitrust and Monopoly on June 10, 1955, Romney explained some of the factors that tended to create monopoly in the automobile industry. And he pulled no punches in relating that American Motors paid higher wages than the Big Three, and that Reuther's United Automobile Workers Union was responsible for this inequity. He expressed the hope that the union would "bargain this year on the economic facts of American Motors and not of Ford or General Motors."

Reuther, who testified later, said the questions raised by Romney would more properly be raised at the bargaining table and that they would be dealt with at the bargaining table starting the next week.

In answer to Reuther's demands that small independent firms agree to a guaranteed annual wage, Cushman asked a group of distinguished economists—all of them men who had acted as consultants for Reuther's UAW in earlier years—to study how the guaranteed annual wage would have affected the firm in the three years just passed. The conclusion was that the guaranteed annual wage would have placed such a heavy burden on the firm that it would likely have jeopardized the company's solvency.

Backed by the public-relations value of a study indicating that the guaranteed annual wage could wreck American Motors and end thousands of jobs, Romney and Cushman took a stiff-necked attitude on Woodcock's demands that American Motors grant wage increases that would retain the same "pattern plus" arrangement that had put the firm at such a disadvantage on wage rates.

American Motors would not sign a contract, and Cushman insisted that any agreement must be "tailored to smaller company's problems."

It was not until September 3, 1955, that American Motors and the UAW reached an agreement on a three-year contract covering 24,000 employees. Cushman had won a beneficial modification of the supplemental unemployment arrangement established by Ford, General Motors, and Chrysler. The union also agreed to wage increases that trimmed, but did not eliminate, the differences between the wage rates paid by American Motors and the Big Three.

Cushman declared that American Motors was pleased that the "union had recognized the economic facts and had not insisted on an application of a rigid pattern." For the first time since World War II, the labor-management contract had been modified to permit a smaller independent firm to make some progress in cutting the wage gap over the Big Three.

Although Woodcock had fought the change from the "pattern plus" of the past, he declared that the union had "recognized the company has special economic problems." That was probably the understatement of the decade.

With the labor agreement out of the way and a contract set for three years, Romney and his associates pushed ahead with the preparation for production of the 1956 Rambler, hoping it would finally win them a large-enough share of the automobile market to start to make some money. In the seven months ending July 31, 1956, American Motors had produced 117,756 cars, compared with 58,115 in the seven months ending July 31, 1955. Spectacular though the progress was, production would have to double again to get the firm out of the red.

As early as 1941, Romney had become aware of auto-travel studies at the Automobile Manufacturers Association office that showed a large percentage of car use was for short trips. Impressed with their practicality, he had become convinced that small cars could also be popular. In his first discussions with George Mason in 1948, he had agreed that American Motors could profit by getting the jump on that market before the Big Three would make a similar move.

Exploring the idea with Mason from 1950 through 1954 demonstrated there was no automatic demand for a large number of compact cars. The idea of smaller cars had to be promoted in an atmosphere dominated by Big Three advertising in which the big car had become a status symbol. Conversely, the small car was regarded as little short of a poverty symbol.

Common sense pointed to the small car for more economical transportation as well as greater convenience in driving and parking in crowded cities, but automobile buyers were more inclined toward ego builders than toward common sense. Some public reaction appeared against cars that had become too long or too wide for garages constructed in an earlier era. Gaudy ornaments and

useless fins had become the subject of jokes, and automobile writers
for newspapers in Detroit and Denver had quipped casually that
the big cars could go the way of the dinosaur.

The use of the word "dinosaur" clicked with Howard Hallas,
the American Motors public-relations director, and he suggested
that Romney give a speech titled "The Dinosaur in Our Driveway."
Romney liked it, Lenore approved, and Romney used a speech before the Motor City Traffic Club of Detroit on January 27, 1955,
to claim the title of St. George, the dinosaur slayer.

"A motor magnate splashed a little mud . . . on those big
fat cars," the *New York Times* said in reporting on Romney's attack on the "mechanized dinosaurs."

"Cars nineteen feet long and weighing two tons are used to run
a hundred-and-eighteen-pound housewife three blocks to the
drugstore for a two-ounce package of bobby pins and lipstick,"
the American Motors president told the Detroit club.

Romney contended he was unbiased in his appraisal of the big
cars because American Motors was still building the big Hudson
as well as the compact Rambler. However, he was aiming in the
direction of total small-car production.

Others had criticized the big cars, but it was a new twist when
an executive from the automobile industry said it. Although he
received wide publicity for his efforts to ridicule the "dinosaurs"
and the "gas guzzlers," he was only moderately successful in stimulating a reaction from the buying public. The red ink became
deeper and deeper in 1955 and 1956.

Economies were achieved in consolidating production, in
moving to two basic body shells, cutting executive frills, and persuading top executives to take substantial voluntary salary cuts.
Small-car sales continued to increase, but the increases were drastically lower than the break-even point.

Those operating efficiencies achieved by late 1956 were not
apparent outside the executive suite. By all usual indicators in the
financial world, American Motors was in serious trouble, with the
stock sagging to prices as low as $5.25 to $6.50 a share—half the
value in the months immediately after Romney was named president and chairman of the board. In 1956 it seemed unlikely that

all of Romney's energy and bubbling enthusiasm could make American Motors float.

As American Motors stock dropped below six dollars a share, it became a target for the talents of Louis Wolfson, a shrewd financial operator who had gained a reputation as a "raider" of corporations. Wolfson had owned a large block of Hudson stock, which had been exchanged for American Motors stock in the 1954 merger, but in the summer of 1956 he had increased his holdings and had served notice on Romney that he was a substantial stockholder and wanted to sit down and talk business.

Romney, busy struggling with refinancing at Chase Manhattan National Bank, was able to put off a meeting with Wolfson until some weeks after he had convinced the bankers that there was still life and hope in American Motors. He ended up with a $45 million revolving bank credit—a sharp cutback from the more than $70 million granted earlier—but he expected it to keep American Motors moving unless a new crisis developed.

When Romney met with Wolfson in late October to try to learn what kind of problem he faced, he was dealing from the strength of a new loan agreement, but he was dealing with one of the toughest and most able financial wolves in the business. Wolfson said bluntly that he was considering a take-over of American Motors, and he declared he had more than $8 million in cash available then, to move into the market and buy the stock he needed.

Romney opposed Wolfson's suggestion of a take-over and a partial liquidation of the assets of the corporation. He detailed his own plans for the future with enthusiasm. His frank and convincing manner disarmed Wolfson, who concluded that there was a chance for American Motors and it would be good business to go along with George Romney.

Although their personal relationship was agreeable most of the time, during a two-year period the menacing shadow of Louis Wolfson was constantly at Romney's shoulder, with questions, suggestions, and always that unspoken possibility of a proxy fight and attempted take-over.

Wolfson had the shares and the financial resources to demand a place on the board of directors, but Romney convinced him it would be a mistake for Wolfson to be associated in active management. American Motors was in a crucial period, and Romney said bluntly that Wolfson's reputation as a corporation raider could cause a lack of confidence in the future of the company. The realistic Wolfson accepted that fact.

When it became necessary in March 1957 for Romney to confirm that Wolfson had become the largest stockholder, the American Motors president tried to turn it to the advantage of the firm.

"Based upon my information, Mr. Wolfson has proved to be a successful investor in other enterprises and has strengthened the companies in which he was involved," Romney said. "His [Wolfson's] purchase of American Motors stock, which probably makes him the largest single stockholder, evidences belief on his part that he can capitalize on this investment because of the company's future possibilities. We share this viewpoint."

Wolfson made a public statement that he was not conducting a proxy fight for control of American Motors, expressed his confidence in Romney's leadership, and said he had the impression that Romney had the stockholders' interests very much at heart. He suggested some trimming, paring, and pruning of the overhead cost to make American Motors more efficient.

Romney's associates had been concerned that naïve George might be outmaneuvered by the wily Wolfson, but before it was over, Romney established that he had kept the top hand and won in the end through the simple exercise of a disarming frankness that was difficult for Wolfson to overcome.

Throughout most of their association Romney and Wolfson enjoyed a genial relationship. Romney answered Wolfson's questions, and accorded him the same respect he would have displayed with any other large stockholder. There were a few tense scenes generated by Romney's belief that someone in Wolfson's group had leaked information to a financial columnist, and they disputed the manner in which Wolfson sold out his interest in early 1958 to take a profit of about $2 million on the basis of rising American Motors fortunes.

As it turned out, it was an unwise sale, for although American Motors had risen to more than $12 when Wolfson sold, sensational sales later sent the stock above the $95 mark in 1959.

The ominous figure of Wolfson lurking in the background drastically complicated Romney's planning through the severe financial crisis in 1956. Romney later revealed to Ed Cushman that during this period "there were a couple of times when I looked at Elmer Bernitt's work sheets and I figured that we'd probably had it."

Cushman, one of those who lived closest to Romney during those days of crisis, said he had never seen "any indication at any time that Romney had anything but the greatest confidence that we were going to be successful in the end."

American Motors was in the red by nearly $7,000,000 in 1955. As the loss soared to $19,746,243 in 1956, dreary forecasts for the firm made it apparent that under the best circumstances more red ink would flow before Romney could get into the black. In December 1956, at the end of the most disastrous year, Romney was asked to head a Detroit Citizens Advisory Committee on School Needs.

The Detroit schools were in serious financial trouble. A long-range building program was needed, and the immediate need was for extension of a special school tax so that teachers' salaries and other expenses could be paid.

Romney and Ed Cushman sensed the general purpose when Romney received and granted a request for an appointment by Dr. Samuel Miller Brownell, the former United States Commissioner of Education who had become Detroit Superintendent of Schools, and William D. Merrifield, a Chrysler personnel executive who was president of the Detroit Board of Education.

"You just can't do it, George," Cushman told Romney as they speculated that he would probably be asked to take some role in connection with the pressing Detroit school problems.

Romney agreed with Cushman's assessment. American Motors was under fire from creditors who had become concerned over the fact that the firm had never been out of the red since it came into existence in 1954 and Romney had taken the helm. Also, Romney's family and church responsibilities were always accorded first priority on his time. As a devoted family man, Romney insisted on time for his two daughters, Jane, 21, and Lynn, 18, and his two sons, George Scott, 15, and Willard Mitt, 9. Since 1944, Romney had been president of the Detroit Stake of the Church of Jesus Christ of the Latter-Day Saints, and in that capacity had headed building drives and a wide range of other church activities.

When Dr. Brownell and Mr. Merrifield arrived for their appointment, Romney was certain that he was going to decline to serve. But as they explained the serious condition of the Detroit school system and told him he was needed to head the drive, his resolve weakened.

"You couldn't have come to me at a worse time," Romney commented, but agreed to think it over for a week. He told Dr. Brownell and Mr. Merrifield that if he accepted the chairmanship, he would like to have Ed Cushman as vice-chairman.

"The way they explained the situation, I just couldn't help but respond," Romney apologized to Cushman a short time later. Romney also admitted he had indicated that he wanted Cushman for his vice-chairman if he finally accepted the chairmanship.

"I knew we were in it then," Cushman said later, although it was several days before Romney made a formal acceptance of chairmanship. "Some men could accept the chairmanship and glide along while someone took the responsibility and did the work, but George Romney could not be nominal head of anything. He threw himself into it with the same drive he put into everything else, and it was successful."

Romney chaired breakfast meetings and luncheons, presided at a Thursday afternoon meeting every two weeks, gave hundreds of speeches, and was credited by the newspapers, Dr. Brownell, and others closely associated with the program as being the actual leader as well as titular head of the group in the two-year struggle to overcome current financial problems and outline plans for a revitalization of the Detroit school system.

"I was afraid it was going to take too much time away from American Motors," Cushman said. "Somehow we managed all of the jobs at American Motors as well as the Citizens Advisory Committee. It was actually good for the company in the long run to have that record of active participation in an important civic program. I don't mind saying now that at the outset I had my doubts about whether we were doing the right thing."

Romney and Cushman worked under a back-breaking schedule, but by May and June of 1957 all their burdens seemed lighter. Rambler sales were rolling. Although American Motors was still in the red, Romney could finally see some light at the end of the long tunnel of troubles. He hoped to get the company in the black by the last quarter of 1957, and barely managed it, but it seemed certain that American Motors was going to be a substantial money-maker in 1958.

With business success just ahead, George Romney was in high spirits enough to go out and pick a fight with Ford or General Motors. In essence, he did just that at the next opportunity in a national forum.

TEN

The Fresh Breeze

Senator Estes Kefauver, of Tennessee, launched an investigation early in 1957 into the soaring cost of living, with special emphasis on the price boosts in the steel, petroleum, and automobile industries. Hearings on the automobile industry got under way in late January 1958, shortly after American Motors Corporation had posted a profit of $4.9 million for the last three months of calendar year 1957.

Business antagonism to the probe by Senator Kefauver's Subcommittee on Antitrust and Monopoly was countered by enthusiasm for the investigation by such labor leaders as Walter P. Reuther, president of the United Automobile, Aircraft, and Agricultural Implement Workers, and vice-president of the AFL-CIO.

Reuther charged management with the problems of rising prices in basic industries, and told the Senate Subcommittee: "We are very much concerned with the impact of the administered price policy of the automotive industry upon the general economic well-being of the nation. We are very much concerned about the growing and serious imbalance in the American economy, the increase

123

in unemployment, and the forces of recessions which have set in in many aspects of the American economy."

Much that was wrong with the economy the loquacious Reuther blamed on American industry, and he had special criticism for "the Big Three: General Motors, Ford, and Chrysler, who dominate this industry and who represent ninety-seven percent of the production of the passenger-car industry."

"We believe that the impact of their administered prices, the fact that they can in the exercise of their monopoly position in this industry set aside the laws of supply and demand and rig their prices at a level which . . . short-changes the American consumer, American farmers, and American workers," the auto union president declared.

Reuther wanted the investigation to put the spotlight on the pricing practices in industry in a manner which he said would "enlighten public opinion" to force restraint on prices.

The fiery union president declared himself opposed to "any kind of totalitarianism" and said he was "irrevocably committed to a free economy." He denied specifically that he or any others in organized labor wanted to take over the direction of American industry.

Reuther denied being in league with the Big Three of the auto industry, and declared that auto union executives "have given a great deal of time and careful thought trying to figure out what we can do to try to check the growing concentration of economic power and control in the hands of the Big Three."

"We think it would be a sad thing for America and a bad thing for our union if the small companies get pushed out, and we are trying to help them," Reuther said. "You will find that we have specifically tried to devise a wage-policy approach that will tend to maintain the smaller companies in business rather than squeeze them out."

Reuther's tendency to place blame for economic problems on the back of big business was matched a few days later by testimony from the highest officials of the Big Three, who tended to blame high automobile prices and other economic ills on the high wage demands of labor. Harlow Curtice, president of General Motors Corporation, T. O. Yntema, a vice-president of Ford Motor Company, and L. L. Colbert, president of Chrysler Corporation, appeared in succession to defend administered prices and to explain that they believed the large automobile manufacturing organizations are needed for economy.

"You cannot make automobiles on a small scale and make them efficiently," Yntema testified. He said that "by and large, the industry has served the country very well."

Chairman Kefauver, Committee Counsel Paul Rand Dixon, Dr. John M. Blair, the committee's chief economist, and others expected George Romney, president of American Motors Corporation, to be just another defender of the bigness of the automobile industry.

George W. Romney seated himself in the witness chair at 10:15 A.M. on February 7, 1958, and the whole atmosphere of the hearing changed. Romney was accompanied by Edward L. Cushman, vice-president in charge of industrial relations, J. J. Timpy, vice-president, Richard L. Cross, director and counsel, William McGaughey, vice-president in charge of communications, and Howard Hallas, director of public relations.

But from the time Senator Alexander Wiley, a Wisconsin Republican, introduced Romney, it was essentially a one-man show. Flushed with the success of profits of $4.9 million in the last three months of 1957, Romney prophetically told the Senate Subcommittee that American Motors had "turned the corner" and was "well on the road to what I think is going to prove to be a very historic success in the automobile business."

As contrasted to some of the other automobile company executives, George Romney said he was glad to be there to testify because "your committee is dealing with the most important question concerning the economic future of America, and we feel we are in a unique position to assist you."

Romney declared that he and other officials of American Motors had "decided to stick our necks out here this morning and make a very frank and full statement." All that Friday and the following

Monday, February 10, Romney rolled out the most candid views on the evils of concentrated power in labor, government, or business.

Chairman Kefauver and members of his committee were amazed when Romney declared there was too much concentration of power in the Big Three in the automobile industry and suggested that for the good of the country the laws should be changed to try to break up the automobile industry into several smaller firms.

"I do not appear as a special interest pleader," he told Senator Kefauver. "I am not here for the purpose of asking for any special help for American Motors. . . . I am not here to goose-step with the Big Three and I am not here as a labor baiter, but I am here to discuss the problems of the industry as I think they affect the consumer and the public interest and as they affect employment, as they affect inflation and deflation, and also as they affect smaller businesses throughout our economy."

Romney was then serving as president of the Automobile Manufacturers Association, but he declared that he wanted it "understood that anything I say here has no reference to that capacity."

He stressed the need for strengthening laws to avoid "excess concentration of power in any form, whether in industry or unions." Romney said there was a need for revision of the antitrust laws "to encourage economic birth without interfering with the process of economic death in our mature basic industries."

"Present companies should give birth through division to new and separate automobile manufacturers to maintain the auto industry's dynamic progress and national benefits," Romney explained.

He declared that there was "a need for labor-law revisions to disperse the excess power of unions and create needed practical balance in collective-bargaining relationships."

"I would like to emphasize that I consider both the births in industry and the dispersion of union power equally necessary," Romney said. "I am not here to advocate one versus the other. I think it will be a great misfortune if action should be taken on one without considering the other and dealing with them jointly and simultaneously."

As George Romney viewed it, the UAW's "combined bargaining demands and the joint use of economic power accelerate the concentration of industry, shrink automobile employment, and prevent adequate labor-management cooperation."

"My basic approach," Romney told the subcommittee, "is that what is good for the goose is good for the gander, and what is good for labor is good for industry, and vice versa, and what is good for one American is good for another American as far as public policy is concerned."

Romney told the committee that while American Motors was a small company when compared with the Big Three, the firm ranked as the eighty-seventh-largest manufacturing company in 1956 on the basis of total volume of sales from the automotive division, Kelvinator appliances, and national-defense contracts.

He characterized American Motors as one of the "comparatively small elephants" in relation to the "full-scale mastodons" that were the Big Three and a few others. But Romney told the committee that size alone had been overrated, and that when he took over at American Motors in 1954, one of the biggest problems facing him was "the widespread idea that had been built up . . . through the country that a smaller company could not succeed in the automobile business."

"The second-biggest problem we had to deal with was a frozen big-car mentality . . . which had been built up as a result . . . of the concentration of the big companies on the perpetuation of the big-car mentality," Romney said.

The third problem, in Romney's view, was the propaganda that resulted in a widespread misconception of the importance of size in manufacturing, and engineering and research.

He placed some blame for erroneous impressions on Walter Reuther: "In his testimony, Mr. Reuther said that a smaller automobile company would have enough customers in an eight-million-car year, but not in a five-million-car year. Here again the illusion of size is substituted for logic. Even Mr. Reuther furthers this idea because of his lack of knowledge of the competitive facts in the automobile business."

Romney told the subcommittee that at that time the automobile industry was not doing much better than a five-million-car year, but that "American Motors is doing very well."

"In 1955, when more than 7.1 million cars were sold, we lost heavily," Romney said. "The truth is that success is not only related to the size of the total market, but to the effectiveness of the individual producer, and . . . what customers think about the product and what customers think about these ideas of size and continuity."

To dramatize that smaller companies can compete, Romney told the Senate Subcommittee how he and his associates had embarked upon a three-year program to move American Motors into the compact-car market. "This was accomplished last fall," Romney said proudly. "The soundness of our program is indicated in the soaring sales of Ramblers, the only cars which we produce other than the Metropolitan, which is a small car we import from England.

"Our Rambler sales are up forty-nine percent for the model year as against a year ago," Romney said. "We are the only company in the industry that is really moving up in sales and production as compared to a year ago, and this improvement is rather substantial."

In answer to questions by Senator Kefauver, Romney said that American Motors had reduced the automotive break-even point to 120,000 cars a year.

"We shift from loss to profit at that point," Romney declared. He pointed out that this was a pretty small percentage of the more than five million cars a year sold and demonstrated that "you do not have to have the volume of the Big Three manufacturers to be efficient."

Studies done for American Motors showed a company can build between 180,000 and 220,000 cars a year on a one-shift basis and make a very good profit, and "not take a back seat to anyone in the industry in production efficiency."

The American Motors president told the subcommittee that on

a two-shift basis "annual production of 360,000 to 440,000 cars will achieve additional small economies, but beyond that volume only theoretical and insignificant reductions in manufacturing costs are possible."

"It is possible to be one of the best without being the biggest," Romney said.

He explained that in weighing the cost problem, the subcommittee should remember that the 1.5 million Chevrolets and the 1.5 million Fords being produced each year were not produced in centralized plants. The assembly operations were scattered, and this resulted in "terrific material-handling costs that an integrated operation in one spot does not get into."

"You have exploded one idea right there that I think has brought some light into the picture," Senator Wiley said, "because everyone always thinks that every time you increase your volume, you decrease the rate-per-unit cost."

"Which is not so," Romney responded. He added that while General Motors and Ford beat them on cost on some things, in other areas American Motors could beat any of the Big Three.

"We have got more modern facilities than they have got in many areas," Romney said. "Our material-handling costs are less. Our overhead costs are less. We assemble the car more efficiently than they do, in the main."

"Do they agree with that?" Senator Wiley asked.

"I will say this to you," Romney responded. "They have been over in our plant studying those methods, because one thing about the automobile business is that you do not refuse to permit a competitor to come in your plant and take a look at how you are doing things. . . . We have had Big Three companies in our plants in the last two or three years studying some of these methods that we use that are more modern than theirs."

Senator Wiley praised the American Motors executive for demonstrating "the effectiveness of a right idea." Senator John Carroll, a Colorado Democrat, asked Romney if it was not true that the Big Three, and specifically General Motors, didn't have some significant advantage in volume purchases.

"Senator," Romney replied, "in the procurement area there

is not any question that some of the car companies that bit the dust in the past resulted from better prices extended to the large companies by the major sources of raw materials and parts."

Romney declared that the Robinson-Patman Act stopped the advantage from a standpoint of purchase of material and parts "as far as we have been able to ascertain."

The American Motors president declared that in the post-World War II period, other automobile companies were paying a premium for steel that was "greatly in excess of what the Big Three were paying."

"I sat in meetings at the start of the Korean War when the Big Three took the position that there should be no controls of materials because, after all, one of the competitive advantages they had built up was the relationship they had with their suppliers," Romney testified. "Well, actually, that is simply saying that in a period of shortage your volume and therefore your preferential standing with the suppliers ought to be the primary consideration rather than equitable distribution of available supply."

Senator Kefauver commented that his subcommittee had taken testimony that "at least two of the Big Three did loan money to steel companies in order to get preferred treatment during a time of shortage."

"I think what you are referring to is the fact that General Motors, for example, has invested in McLouth Steel, and invested in Republic, and invested in Jones and Laughlin, and that obviously gives them a preferential situation in periods of possible shortage," Romney replied, ". . . after all, they are part owner of the business."

"I think it also evidences the degree to which concentration is reaching in this country," Romney said. He pointed out that Ford had become "relatively integrated in this respect, because they have their own steel mills." Also, Chrysler had invested in Pittsburg Steel, Romney said.

"That does give them some advantage over you, which is not related to efficiency," Chairman Kefauver commented.

"That is correct," Romney replied. "There are very definite advantages in the financial area that flow simply out of financial strength and have nothing to do with the particular ability of management or the efficiency of manufacturing or tooling."

Chairman Kefauver and other subcommittee members had hardly expected such a frank discussion of the automobile industry from one of the top executives, and the committee chairman referred to Romney as "a fresh breeze" in management.

But Romney did not confine his criticism to the management side of the automobile industry. He told the subcommittee members that there had been "wholly misleading" testimony from UAW president Walter Reuther to the effect that "there has only been a one-dollar increase in wages for every four-dollar increase in prices" in the automobile industry in recent years. He explained that a relatively small portion of the cost of an automobile is paid out by the automobile companies for hiring employees.

"The vast bulk of the labor and cost of building an automobile is paid out to others in the form of things purchased from them," Romney testified. "So to take the increase in price resulting from the increase in costs of the automobile, the materials you buy, plus all the things you do yourself, and compare that with the increase in the wage level, is to compare completely irrelevant things, and to give this committee a distorted picture and an unfair picture."

While Romney expressed admiration for some aspects of the Big Three operations, he told the subcommittee that such big firms as Ford and General Motors "become muscle-bound" and that this keeps them from changing to meet public demands.

"You get so darned much invested in the way you are doing things today that it takes a heck of a lot more to change and do things differently than it does somebody else who hasn't quite reached that point," Romney explained. He cited the Big Three's heavy fixed investments and equipment costs, which had increased to the point where it would require hundreds of millions of dollars to modernize methods that cost no more than forty million dollars prior to World War II.

This was one of the factors that kept the Big Three making bigger and bigger cars even after nationwide surveys showed that ahe pattern of automobile use was changing.

Romney pointed out that the Model T Ford had been successful because it was "a dependable means of transportation" at a time when income was low and people wanted the lowest-cost transportation.

At a later period the car was wanted for group mobility on family trips and vacations, but later surveys showed that more than 85 percent of all car trips were short trips for shopping.

"That use of the car for personal mobility makes it utterly ridiculous to use a four-thousand dollar car for the wife to go down to the grocery store and get a loaf of bread." Romney explained the appeal of the compact cars that were the strength of American Motors.

Romney declared that even as of that time in February 1958, the Big Three were continuing to build cars "bigger and bulkier and more powerful."

"As far as I am concerned, I hope they keep doing it for a while," Romney said. "We are confident of our success. We are in league with the future huge market for our type car."

Romney told the subcommittee that he did not believe any automobile company should be seeking special or preferential help from Washington, and that "if American Motors cannot make it on the basis of selling and producing products that people want to buy, why, we are going out of business. It is just that simple."

"I think this country is in danger of being sunk by special-interest groups and groups coming down here [to Washington for help] including business," Romney said.

While Romney was bubbling enthusiastically about the success American Motors was enjoying, and the prospects for even greater success in the years ahead, he said he was "gravely concerned about critical trends in the automotive industry and the country as a whole."

"This is a critical point in our history," Romney said. "Either our wage, price, inflation, and monopoly problems must be wisely solved, or America will be surpassed by others. I refer to the recent failure of domestic automobile sales to keep pace with growth in national income. Historically, the automobile business, automobile sales, have kept pretty close pace with the growth in the national income, and even though we are now moving into a multiple-car era, that is not happening."

"That is an alarming fact, because more families are using more units, and we should be selling more cars in relationship to gross national product and income than was true previously," Romney said.

He told the committee that between 1950 and 1955 car sales were nearly $5.8 million annually, and the sales of imported cars in the United States "were insignificant." Although the population increased from 152 million to 172 million, and licensed drivers increased from 65 million to 81 million, the annual sales of domestic cars averaged only about 8.5 million in the 1956-58 period. In 1956 and 1957, imports of foreign cars exceeded export of American cars for the first time.

"We have not kept pace, and that is a very alarming fact," Romney said, "because the automobile business is the generator of more employment in the national economy than any other single industry. One out of every seven people in the United States is employed through the manufacture, distribution, or use of automobiles, and the very source of that employment is drying up."

Romney declared that the wage and price trend on American cars was such that they were pricing themselves out of international competition. He explained that Ford and General Motors were going abroad with large plants to take advantage of more favorable conditions, and that Ford executives at that time were predicting that "the export of American automobiles will be extinct by 1970."

"I think it is going to happen sooner than that," Romney gave his own view. He said that General Motors and Ford had recognized the demand for smaller cars in their production outside of the United States, but that the lack of competition within the United States had caused them to disregard the demand here.

"When you get an inadequate number of companies in an industry, the customer ceases to be king," Romney said. "He begins to be dictated to by the concepts that a few have as to what he ought to have, and that is what I am here talking about . . . because there is inadequate and deficient product competition in the automobile business."

Romney called for a full evaluation of "current wage-price trends" and their influence on the position of America in the world. He listed what he considered to be "the significant factors that produced America's miraculous industrial accomplishment."

They were:

"1. American economic development has been achieved largely as a result of the American political principles of individual rights and the limitation of governmental power. I would go one step back of that and say that that is based on our concept of man and our trust in God and our belief in God, and the most basic aspect of America, both politically and economically, is religious faith and conviction, and based on that we divided up political power.

"2. This system has encouraged individual initiative by providing opportunity to sell products or services to customers who are free to make their selection from a number of separately competing firms or individuals. Where there is no competition, the customer has no choice and has no control over the industry or the economy. Or, where it is inadequate, it begins to diminish his influence in the marketplace.

"3. American economic progress has been greatly stimulated by relating profits, salaries, and wages to contribution and risk. While I do not get into that subject particularly in this memorandum, that is one of the principles that is under fire here before this committee, and has been attacked with great skill and adroitness in testimony previously given, and it gets into the heart of some of the problems we are confronted with in America economically. The Russians are getting around that. The Russians have got more incentive in their economy now than we have got in most sectors, and have got more motivation in it, and that ought to make us sit up and wonder about some things we are doing economically.

"4. Voluntary cooperation in noncompetitive areas has played a vital role in meeting community and public needs on an industrial and national basis. Unfortunately, we are all so familiar with competition that we do not know too much about what cooperation has done, and that there would be no automobile industry as we know it today if there had not been a high degree of cooperation outside of those areas prohibited by law and by the economics of competition.

"5. The antitrust laws have served a useful purpose in developing our economy and prohibiting unfair methods of competition and unreasonable restraints on trade.

"6. The various segments of the American economy have benefited from large-scale economic advances, and I am not here arguing for small industry. I am not here arguing against big enterprise. I am concerned about supercolossal giants that we have got that go way beyond the range of efficiencies that can benefit the consumer, and way beyond what is desirable for this country if we are going to remain free.

"7. Genuine and effective economic collective bargaining between an employer and the representatives of his employees has provided a sound and desirable means of achieving a reasonably equitable and balanced distribution between labor and capital of the value added by industrial and business activity."

While Romney generally praised past operations of collective bargaining, he was critical of developments in the four or five years prior to 1958. But he declared that some of the factors which had created the strengths of the American economic system "are in serious jeopardy" because of a lack of balance in collective bargaining that gave too much power to labor unions.

"These developments have created internal stresses and strains in the American economy that could prove more disastrous to human freedom than the external threats of collective tyrants," Romney said. "And I believe that utterly. We will be licked from within and not from without, because the only weakness that is real is internal weakness and not external weakness."

Romney pointed out widely recognized evidences of serious internal weakness:

1. A periodic repetition of the wage-price spiral after World War II.

2. A continuing increase in industrial prices and decline in agricultural prices enlarging the disparity between the prices received and paid by the farmer.

3. An increase in business mergers resulting in a decline in the number of separate firms in most basic industries. This had increased economic concentration of industrial power.

4. The merger of the AFL and CIO has increased collaboration between affiliated international unions on collective bargaining, thus further concentrating union power.

5. A mounting attack on the profit-and-loss system resulting from lack of public understanding and use of excessive union power to squeeze profits down to a dangerous level.

6. Tax and defense procurement policies that encouraged greater economic concentration.

7. The use of monetary controls to fight inflation and deflation in a manner that was ineffective in meeting the basic problem.

Romney's points were a surprise to committee members. Many committee members with special interests in large farm constituencies were surprised to have Romney express his concern over prices paid to farmers.

"In recent years agricultural prices have gone down 11 percent at the same time that industrial prices have been going up 29 percent," Romney said. "That is as of November 15, 1957. In other words, the disparity is in the area of 40 percent here in the last few years, just to give you some idea of the magnitude."

Comparing 1957 agriculture prices with base prices in the 1947-49 period, Romney said that agriculture prices were only 89 percent of the base while "the prices paid by farmers for all commodities, services, interest, taxes, and wage rates, the whole ball of wax, is now 119 percent."

Then, with no regard for the sensitivity of the Eisenhower Administration or a fellow Mormon, Agriculture Secretary Ezra Taft Benson, Romney explained that the drop in farm prices had started in 1953—the first year of the Eisenhower Administration.

"In 1953 it was 97 percent," he said. "In 1954 it was 95.6, in

1955 it was 89.6, in 1956 it was 88.4, and in 1957 it was 91.9 that was November 12, but as of November 15, it had dropped to 89."

Romney declared that it would be impossible to subsidize agriculture up to 100 percent of parity on farm products as long as the wage-price spiral was continuing on other products.

"We cannot subsidize agriculture back into parity as long as we permit the forces that are operating here to continue to operate," Romney said. "And agriculture has already priced itself, as a result of subsidies, out of world markets."

He declared that the world markets were gone because "we have got the prices of our agricultural products up here on stilts."

"One of the colossal economic blunders made in this country was one made while I served up here as part of a Senator's office, and that was the colossal blunder of hiking industrial tariffs and giving the farmers a subsidy to stop them from asking for the elimination of industrial tariffs," Romney said.

"It sounds like you must have been an administrative assistant to Senator Cordell Hull," Chairman Kefauver quipped.

"As a matter of fact, I worked for Senator David I. Walsh, of Massachusetts, and the result was I got quite an exposure to particularly the industrial problem, and the tariff problem——"

"I have never heard many manufacturers give such a strong argument for farmers as you have," Senator Kefauver interrupted. "Do you feel it very vital to your company that farmers do well and have purchasing power, Mr. Romney?"

"Yes, sir," Romney answered. "As a matter of fact, Senator Kefauver, I think that it is essential to the economic health of America that we see that the economic progress that we make is spread as widely as we can do it. . . . Now you never do that perfectly, but when any big segment like agriculture gets out of line with the rest of the economy, that hurts the whole economy, and one of the things causing some of the unemployment in the automobile industry today is the fact that farmers cannot buy new cars the way they used to buy new cars."

Romney hit a responsive note with both Senator Kefauver and Senator Wiley when he spoke with the greatest sympathy for the farmer and with some knowledge of the cost squeeze that they had discussed so often on the Senate floor.

"I really feel very sorry for my good friend Mr. [Secretary of Agriculture Ezra Taft] Benson, because I do not think the problem is going to be licked in the areas that are being dealt with," Romney said. "In 1955 ownership of motor vehicles among farmers was 74 percent, that is, ownership of passenger cars, and 13 percent of them owned trucks. Then nearly half of the United States farmers had models five years old or older. Only 13 percent were driving current models, and that has declined more recently, I am confident on the basis of my feel of the situation."

Senator Wiley interrupted to comment: "If you can do for our milk farmers in Wisconsin what you have done for your industry, won't you please give us the remedy?"

"I don't say I have the complete remedy, Senator," Romney replied. "I say that I am prepared to discuss what I consider to be the principal factor in that disparity, and a factor which must be dealt with if we are going to put agriculture back on a healthy basis. Because it is important that we not just keep it alive, keep agriculture alive; it is important we keep it healthy."

Romney pointed out that William McChesney Martin, chairman of the Federal Reserve Board, and Marriner Eccles, former chairman of the Federal Reserve Board, had warned as early as 1956 that as a result of labor contracts "an alarming wage-price spiral is developing."

Romney quoted Eccles as stating on October 11, 1956, that "if the present situation is permitted to go unchecked, further price inflation is inevitable. Under these conditions the difficulty of stopping inflation by the use of monetary and fiscal policy should be apparent. To stop the growth of the money supply would stop the growth of the economy. This would soon stop the growth of production and employment."

"To permit the money supply to grow so as to finance the wage-price spiral would be feeding inflation," Romney continued to quote Eccles. "This is the present dilemma that confronts us."

Romney quoted Harvard economist Sumner Slichter as stating

that some conditions that make for upward pressure of prices "are politically popular."

"Full employment and strong trade unions are examples," Slichter said. "Upward pressure on prices is aggravated by the farm policy, which causes the Government to spend billions each year trying to keep up the price of foods and fibers, and by the tax system, which leads the Government to subsidize heavily wage concessions by employers. . . . Hence, although the United States has not adopted gradual inflation as a way of life, the country is not prepared to remove the conditions that produce gradual inflation."

Slichter suggested that the United States could stop inflation by insisting "that no employer, except in unusual circumstances, grant wage- and fringe-benefit increases of more than 2½ percent a year, about half the wage increase of the last year."

Romney slapped hard at wage increases in the automobile industry by pointing out that the 2½-percent increase suggested by Slichter was "only one fourth the wage increase granted by the automobile industry in 1955."

Senator Wiley asked Romney if American Motors was forced to pay the same wage increase as the Big Three in the auto industry.

"Over the years we have had to pay more," Romney replied. "It happens that in 1955, as a result of very aggressive programs, we succeeded in getting the union to wipe out some of the inequity that we were carrying in relationship to our competitors, but we are still paying more than our competitors, both in the automobile business and the appliance industry.

"We have now reached the point in this country where in our large basic industries—and the automobile industry is one of the major ones—the wage increases now exceed the level of national productivity increase and exceed the level of the industry productivity increase," Romney said. "Wage increases to workers that completely absorb productivity improvements, or even exceed them, deny to all but those workers many of the benefits of economic advance. Industrial progress results more from reinvestment of owners' earnings and management ingenuity than from increased employee effort and skill."

Romney had praise for early General Motors management in adopting a product philosophy that was "in keeping with the then existing economic and social trends," based on making cars "bigger, more powerful, and better styled."

"However, the smaller companies historically have been the principal innovators," Romney explained. "As a matter of fact, the philosophy of the large, more successful companies has been to be not the first to try the new and not the last to drop the old. . . . That has been the philosophy which permits the really radical innovating to be undertaken by a smaller company and if it succeeds, pick it up."

Romney declared that "during the postwar period, the few surviving smaller companies have contributed relatively more basic product pioneering than their bigger competitors. However, their competitive positions have not compelled Big Three adoption of the most important innovations involving the greatest capital cost."

For specifics, Romney cited "Studebaker-Packard pioneered torsion-bar suspension, separate rear-wheel traction, greater driver vision front and rear, as well as other functional and styling advances."

"American Motors pioneered modern car heating and ventilating, low-cost air conditioning, improved body painting and rust prevention including full body dip, smaller and more economical cars, and, most fundamental of all, the application to automobile design of latest engineering principles developed in aircraft construction," Romney said.

Senator Joseph C. O'Mahoney commented on the power of Congress "to regulate all trade and commerce that affects national commerce" and tossed a challenge to the auto-company executive:

"It is not anti-American, it is not socialism."

"That is right," Romney replied.

"It is not an invasion of fundamental American principles for the Congress to regulate commerce in the public interest," Senator O'Mahoney continued. "The refrain we hear from the lips of big business managers in defense of free enterprise I interpret to mean only that these enterprises desire to be free from all regulation in the public interest so that they may write their own ticket, which they are doing now."

"I am not appearing here as a special pleader," Romney tried to square things with the Wyoming Democrat. "I am not asking for any special help for my company. . . . We can make it on our own, but also let me say this: that I never use the term 'free enterprises' because it does not mean anything in my book. It does not describe the economic system that we have and one of the fundamental points I am leading up to . . . I believe that our economic development has gone far beyond the stage it was in when we wrote the present laws that relate both to industry and to labor, and I emphasize the labor part of it as much as the industry part of it because both were intended for very laudable purposes, but our economic development has been so rapid here in the last two or three decades that they (the laws) are now inadequate."

Senator O'Mahoney commented that he had introduced legislation twenty years earlier "to provide that all corporations which engage in commerce affecting national and international commerce, all labor unions which are employed in that commerce and affect that commerce, and all trade associations which operate likewise, should receive their authority setting for their powers, their duties, and their responsibilities from the Congress of the United States, instead of writing their own tickets . . . as they do now."

Continually Romney minimized the innovation brought to the automobile business by the Big Three. He said that "power steering was developed by a supplier company, not by a vehicle company."

"You take improvements in the application of steel to automobiles; the steel industry does more of that improvement than the automobile companies themselves," Romney said.

"The automobile industry actually draws on the technical organization and research of all these industries that feed into the automobile industry and uses those advances to build better automobiles. We have as much access to that improvement as the large companies, and actually as a smaller company we are able to move faster. . . . A big company becomes muscle-bound . . . and they become resistant to change if the change involves tremendous capital expenditure."

Romney agreed with Senator John Carroll that the huge advertising campaigns of the Big Three shaped public thinking on "the big-car mentality."

"The availability of large sums of money for advertising can perpetuate an archaic and old-fashioned product concept if it is drummed home sufficiently," Romney testified.

"It is true that the Big Three introduced modern V-8 engines, automatic transmissions, and promoted the horsepower race as an advance," Romney continued. "They introduced wraparound windshields that do not significantly improve vision and made them a hallmark of design. A small company could not have made the wraparound windshield a successful thing because when you get right down to the guts of it, it has no basic advantages over the straight windshield."

Romney also commented critically that the Big Three introduced power steering and power brakes made necessary by the constant increase in car length, weight, and speed, but their primary emphasis has been on greater car size, horsepower, and angular style obsolescence.

"This is because in the adoption of a common product philosophy, their basic product competition has ended," Romney said. "This was not a result of agreement. Rather, it was due to the fact that all were advertising, promoting, and selling basically identical product ideas, and this dominated customer thinking about product."

Romney told the committee that there would have been only three automobile companies in business in the United States at that time "if American Motors had not pioneered the design, engineering, and marketing of a new type of automobile," and if Studebaker-Packard "had not obtained government help" by being "indirectly subsidized through defense contracts granted to Curtiss-Wright."

In connection with the government contract to Curtiss-Wright that subsidized Studebaker-Packard, Romney complained that this "had an adverse effect on other companies . . . that were entitled to the defense work received by Curtiss-Wright."

"How has American Motors fared on these government contracts?" Chairman Kefauver asked.

"Well, our judgment is that we have not received fair treatment in the placement of defense work since the formation of American Motors," Romney replied. "We have sought it very vigorously. Actually, we spent a great deal of our own money in doing research and development work for defense agencies in the hope that . . . we could prove to them our ability and could qualify for contracts."

The American Motors president said he had personally had "the ironical experience . . . of having top procurement people in the Army tell me that they placed research and development contracts with the Ford Motor Company to apply this type of construction to lightweight military vehicles, because they did not consider us qualified."

"I told them we had pioneered in this type of construction, and they knew that because we had applied it to a lightweight military vehicle that we were developing in conjunction with the Marine Corps, where we have spent our money to develop it," Romney said.

Romney said the procurement officials then "had to back up" and take recourse in saying that they were from Ordnance and that American Motors was an Air Force contractor.

"One of the most discriminatory defense situations that I know of is in this lightweight military-vehicle field, where the Ford Motor Company has been paid to do research and development work in applying single-unit construction, a thing we pioneered," Romney declared.

Romney declared that Ford had to hire some American Motors personnel to help on the lightweight construction project, and he added that Ford was paid more for just research and development work than American Motors paid out of its own pocket on the original pioneering and development on the lightweight construction concept.

"I have been battling, Senator, for two years to get that contract consummated, and it is still not consummated, although the Marine Corps has been very anxious to proceed with it," Romney said. "The Ordnance Department is proceeding with the other vehicle despite the fact that top research and development people in the Defense Department have assured me at various stages . . . that the vehicle of our development is superior."

"In other words," Chairman Kefauver said, "they have been paying Ford for research and development on the very subject that you have been . . . specializing in . . . and spending your own money."

"That is correct," Romney replied. "I think it is one of the most discriminatory situations I have encountered in military procurement, and I think there is absolutely no foundation for it."

Romney declared that American Motors had "a discouraging experience" in dealing with the Defense Department, and that he had been advised on one occasion to "get smart, do not spend your own money" on research, but to wait until government funds were available.

"One of the principal pieces of business we had reason to expect [to win] was actually turned over to Curtiss-Wright as a result of this subsidization of Studebaker-Packard," Romney said. "Our experience has been such that we are literally pulling out of the defense procurement field."

"This is a situation about which something ought to be done," Chairman Kefauver told Romney. "We are going to send our findings to the Secretary of Defense and the procurement agencies."

Romney recalled how the power of military procurement was used in World War II to create competitors for the Aluminum Company of America, with the birth of several competitors being subsidized with taxpayers' money.

The American Motors Company president declared that this was the wrong way to create competition, and he told the Senate Antitrust and Monopoly Subcommittee members that new firms could be created by providing legislation to force the splitting of giants of industry into several firms. He urged that laws be passed to make it possible to break up General Motors and Ford in the manner that the Standard Oil Company was broken up and thirty-four oil companies created from the earlier monopoly.

"What a tremendous contribution for a company to grow to a point where it could sire thirty-four vigorous companies that have since contributed to the well-being of the country," Romney said in praise of Standard Oil. "As a former employee of Alcoa and as a citizen, I think that if our competitive economy is to maintain the vigor needed to support the total strength America's future requires, we must find a better way of providing needed industrial births than by resorting to governmental subsidization."

He warned that the economy which "loses the discipline of competition exposes itself to the discipline of absolute authority," either public or private.

Romney pointed out that "in the lushest market the [auto] industry has ever known, Kaiser-Frazer failed to survive."

"It has been thirty-four years since a new United States manufacturer has successfully entered the automobile industry," he continued. "The fact is that some of the ablest men in industry doubt the possibility of establishing a new automobile company without taking over an existing organization including its essential dealer structure."

Faced with this problem, Romney argued that new laws were needed to force the big firms to split up, and to provide relief from the heavy tax penalties that would follow such splits under the law as it existed.

Turning to inadequacies in the Sherman Antitrust Act, Romney declared that the "procedures are too slow."

"It took twenty years in the courts to terminate the proceedings against the Aluminum Company of America," Romney said. "It took fourteen years between the filing and conclusion of the cases against General Motors Acceptance Corporation. It took more than ten years in the courts to try and settle the problem of monoply in the motion-picture industry. In the meantime, the advent of television had completely changed industry patterns."

"Do you mean by that some fellow who is trying to be able to compete by virtue of the antitrust laws, if he has to wait eight, ten, twelve, sixteen years for a decision, he is gone and forgotten about by that time?" Chairman Kefauver asked.

"He just isn't there," Romney answered.

"I think that is a very justified criticism of the enforcement of the antitrust laws," Chairman Kefauver commented. "Justice so long delayed is justice denied."

Romney declared that under the law then on the books it was not only necessary to prove a monopoly existed, but to also prove that the dominant firm had the desire and the intent to exclude his competitors from business.

"Even in the Aluminum Company [of America] case, where they were doing 100 percent of the business, it took them twenty years to decide that the Aluminum Company was a monopoly," Romney said.

Romney explained his ideas for getting around the "excessive imbalance," of economic power:

"To achieve the desired ends, the antitrust laws should provide that when any one firm in a basic industry . . . such as the automobile industry exceeds a specific percentage of total industry sales over a specified period of time, it shall be required by law to propose to an administrative agency a plan of divestiture that will bring its percentage of sales below the specified level."

"Where a firm is engaged in more than one basic industry, the maximum percentage of total industry sales should be fixed by law at a point lower than the percentage to be fixed for companies operating in only a single basic industry," Romney said. He explained that "where a company is engaged in more than one basic industry, its competitive position is strengthened and it is able to dominate a single market with a lower percentage in any given industry. This results from its ability to concentrate its resources on a single industry or product at any time and to expand its market position by relying on earnings from its other activities."

Romney said his proposed changes in the antitrust laws would have these advantages:

1. It would promote and preserve adequate competition.

2. The companies affected, not the Government, would have the opportunity to originate the method of compliance.

3. Achievement of the sales percentage requiring a split-off or "birth" of a new firm would become evidence of economic success.

4. Competitive effort and growth would be encouraged, not restrained.

"What I mean by that is," Romney explained, "if you take General Motors, for example, and General Motors becomes the sire of more than one company, then those companies can grow and expand and the net result is that General Motors winds up being in effect a bigger and more beneficial part of our economy than if they stay in a single lump that has to be concerned about whether it is going to get too big or not."

"Instead of making mere size itself an offense, the test under the law would be based on the size of a company in relation to that of its competitors," Romney said. "My proposal is not an effort to eliminate big business. In the automobile business you have to have big business, as it is a big industry."

"We are dealing with economic collectivism," Senator O'Mahoney commented.

Romney said he did not like to use the term "collectivist" with regard to industry because of the meaning of centralization of absolute authority that goes with it, although they were in agreement on the general problem of monopolies.

The American Motors president declared that his proposal would "assure an adequate number of companies for adequate competition" in the automobile industry and other industries.

"Frankly, this proposal, if adopted, would make several new companies out of the Big Three," Romney said. "I believe this would be in the interest of stockholders, employees, dealers, customers, competitors, communities, states, and the nation. Creating new automobile companies would increase competition in the automobile industry. It would remove the need for future subsidization of any automobile company in the interest of providing an adequate number of firms. Let me emphasize, I am not seeking, nor is American Motors seeking, to reduce competition. We are seeking to increase it, and to make sure that it will continue."

Romney declared that "competition" was "the fundamental objective and purpose" of his suggestion for amending the law.

"I don't think we can retain economic freedom in this country if we don't retain competition and keep a division of economic power in industry and labor. It has to be divided in both places or we are going to lose it."

Romney suggested tax-law changes to make it easier for such large firms as General Motors to split without unreasonable tax burdens.

Romney noted that Sumner Slichter, noted Harvard economist, had proposed that "voluntary split-offs should be encouraged by forgiving all liability for the capital-gains tax up to the date of dissolution."

"This is a broader approach than I would take," Romney said. "I would recommend that merely by postponing capital-gains tax, there would be created a real incentive to business to cooperate with government in working out a sensible plan of divestiture. By making divestiture free from immediate capital-gains tax, the achievement of the sales percentage requiring divestiture could become evidence of economic success rather than branded a crime."

Romney said that under the law existing at the time, the "unfortunate tax consequences of court-imposed divestiture, even a civil Sherman Act case is regarded as an action to impose a penalty for success."

As Romney declared that "it is not in the public interest" for one firm to dominate an industry, or for two or three companies to control almost all industry sales, he urged the antitrust and monopoly subcommittee to note that Big Labor represented just as great a threat to freedom in America as did the business monopoly.

He said it was vital that the Congress apply the same principles to the concentration of union power that they were considering applying to concentrated business power.

Romney volunteered to review "the circumstances which gave rise to excessive union power" and to analyze the bargaining strategy of Walter Reuther's United Automobile Workers Union, and examine the impact of union activity on the automobile industry.

When Senator Wiley said that the subcommittee would probably want to have Reuther back for testimony, Romney declared that if they were going to have Reuther back, he wanted to appear at the same time "to protect myself" and to see that the subcommittee got "an accurate picture."

Senator John Carroll commented that Reuther "is not as big as the Big Three nor American Motors itself," and he was interrupted by an impatient Romney:

"Walter Reuther is bigger than any of us."

Romney declared that it was "one of the unfortunate misconceptions in this country" that the automobile industrial giants are more powerful than the UAW.

"I understand in his field he is pretty large," Senator Carroll said.

"He is a lot bigger than anybody in the automobile business," Romney declared again for emphasis.

"Certainly Reuther does not have the staff——" Senator Carroll did not complete his observation when Romney broke in again: "He has got a lot more staff than I have got."

Senator Carroll suggested that perhaps Romney and Reuther might appear together before the Senate Subcommittee, and Romney declared this would be agreeable to him "with one provision, and that is that the committee would insist that we both talk to the question and keep our discussion germane to the point under discussion."

"You mean not get into labor bargaining?" Chairman Kefauver asked.

"I do not care what the question is, Senator," Romney replied. "I am not saying limit the questions. But I am saying that when the committee asks us a question, if the committee will see to it that both of us keep our answer germane . . . and not raise a lot of extraneous things that have got nothing to do with it."

Romney said he was perfectly willing to discuss American Motors and his own salary, but "I do not want to deal with Mr. Curtice's salary and General Motors profits and anything else that can be thrown on the table to create the impression that I am trying to defend a lot of things that I am not responsible for."

Exhibiting a keen awareness of the problem of debating the glib UAW president, Romney told the committee there are two ways to have a discussion: "One is to say things that are pertinent to the question being discussed, and the other is to throw so many things on the table and make so many charges that the other fellow can never catch up with all those charges."

Romney said he would face Reuther only if they could come and "discuss the issues and not begin to talk about the Hottentots not having milk out in Africa as being pertinent."

Senator Carroll complimented Romney on "your courageous presentation" of the operations of the Big Three in the auto industry, and added, "There are many things that Walter Reuther states that agree with our statements."

"Sure," Romney replied.

"He [Reuther] thinks there ought to be greater production, he thinks there ought to be wider competition," Senator Carroll said.

"Many principles are the same," Romney agreed.

Chairman Kefauver said he felt that Reuther and Romney might submit written statements to clarify any differences in views, and that while "it might not be as dramatic or as interesting as joint discussions," that it would achieve the subcommittee's objective.

Romney declared that he would comply with the subcommittee requests whether it was to answer questions in writing or meet on a face-to-face basis. He related that Reuther had been proposing meetings with all of the automobile companies for years, and Romney said he had replied that many of the suggested meetings might be violations of the antitrust laws. He said he had written Reuther saying American Motors "would be very happy to discuss with him individually the problems he wanted to discuss as they relate to American Motors."

"We have written letters of that type going clear back to 1954, and we still have not had answers to them, so we are not ducking the opportunity to discuss these matters with Mr. Reuther," Romney said. "The record will show that Mr. Reuther has not been interested in discussing them with us. He has been interested in precipitating a meeting with the Big Three."

Romney told the subcommittee that the underlying policy of labor aims in the United States is that a union must be allowed to acquire a power sufficient to equal that of the employer at the bargaining table.

"I subscribe fully to that in principle," Romney said. "It was the obvious underdog position of the workingman in our big business economy that resulted in passage of laws that remove virtually all limitation on the concentration of union power."

Romney said there were "terrible abuses" of power by management, and there was need for giving union labor more power.

However, in the process of correcting one power problem, the Congress and the courts through interpretation of laws gave the unions the power "to stifle and eliminate competition and to create monopoly."

"Now, as the result of legislation that removed any limitation from the concentration of union power . . . we have no federal legislation that in any significant way prevents a union or unions from concentrating their economic, political, and social power in whatever way they want to do it, as long as they do it as unions, or as long as they do it in conjunction with one employer at a time," Romney said. "The result of this has been to shift the imbalance of the power . . . so that the scale has now been tipped dangerously and excessively on the side of union power."

Romney declared that "labor leaders still pay lip service to preserving competition among employers," but that the result was to "aggravate seriously the competitive problems of smaller companies."

Romney said that Reuther had only a few days earlier criticized the "concentration of economic power in the hands of the Big Three" and also commented, "We think it would be a sad thing for America, and a bad thing for our union, if the small companies get pushed out, and we are trying to help those."

Romney declared that "actions speak louder than words" and that a review of the record showed that Reuther was following policies that "were against the interests of the smaller companies."

"Through their power advantage, the union has succeeded in making smaller vehicle companies as well as many automotive parts and tool-and-die manufacturers meet the GM-Ford pattern on a plus basis," Romney said. "What I mean by that is that until 1955 in our settlements with the auto union we had to give more than General Motors had to give, so it was a pattern-plus basis, and the same thing is true of many smaller companies. . . . If you take the small tool-and-die plants around the city of Detroit, they are paying fifty cents an hour higher wages than [are paid] the men doing the same work in General Motors, Ford, and Chrysler."

In a direct challenge to Reuther's claim that the union helped smaller companies to survive, Romney asked the subcommittee members, "What economic basis is there, what ethical basis is there, what social basis is there for using the collective bargaining power to compel smaller companies to pay more than the richest companies in the land, and pay higher wages and higher fringe benefits?"

Romney said it was true that Reuther and the UAW had "modified the degree of our penalty in our automotive plants in 1955." He added, "But that inequity was not eliminated, and we are still paying higher wages than General Motors, Ford, and Chrysler in our automotive operations, and we are still paying higher fringe benefits, and they represent a very significant competitive disadvantage for American Motors."

Romney explained that some concessions made in the 1955 agreement did not wipe out accumulated inequities.

"Our automotive plants still remain with higher wages and more costly economic benefits and plant practices than our major competitors," Romney said, "and I want to say this to you: When you take an agreement reached with a company like GM and you apply it to another company without relating it to the economic facts of that company, you can create higher costs just by insisting on that pattern."

He gave the example of the large number of seniority employees at American Motors, and said that in the Kenosha plant the average seniority is about twenty years.

"You take the same fringe benefit based on seniority and apply it to us on the same basis and our costs are higher . . . than General Motors," Romney said. He said this was only one example of many of the economic facts through which "distortions and inequity" are created "that affect the competitive position of the company."

"The insistence by the UAW on applying the automotive pattern of wages, benefits, and practices to our main Kelvinator appliance plant at Grand Rapids has put the rates there substantially out of line with our competitors, who deal with international unions other than the UAW," Romney said. "Our rates at those plants are out of line as much as fifty cents an hour as compared to our major competitors, General Electric and Westinghouse, and companies of that type."

He went on to say that American Motors had tried to remain firm in 1955 and demand a contract under which they would pay only the same wages as General Motors, but that they had to buckle "to the greatly excessive power" of the UAW. He said American Motors remained firm "right down to the point where the union actually began to pull the men out of the plants. . . . We had men on the streets by the time that we agreed to settle for less than the elimination of the inequities that we had. Now the reason was that we were in no position to engage in a long strike. We did not have the resources to do it."

The American Motors president said, "It is nice to talk about 'the power of persuasion,' but the hard, cold, brutal facts are that the 'persuasion of power' is the thing that is settling collective bargaining in the automobile industry."

Romney declared that when Reuther was before the committee he had been asked several times if he felt the Big Three should be broken up and that "Reuther never even suggested that the Big Three be broken up, and I think there are reasons for that."

As the UAW has tightened its power over the automobile industry, it has been demanding "a voice in an ever-widening area of the management of business," Romney told the committee. "No activity affecting a worker in his capacity of worker or citizen is considered by the UAW to be outside its sphere. Americans who still think collective bargaining is limited to early union goals of recognition, wages, hours, and working conditions must be awakened to the new economic and political role of unions."

Romney declared that because of the union's tremendous power organized on an industrywide basis as compared with that of the individual company, that share in the management and ownership would inevitably lead to union domination of the entire management function.

"If the concentration of union power on an industrywide basis is not divided, unions could secure domination of all companies in an industry and through the union structure accomplish the joint control of prices, production, and distribution that the antitrust laws are designed to prevent," Romney warned.

Romney told the Senate Subcommittee that if the members took action to curb the large industries without taking equally stringent action to curb the large unions, "it will be a great mistake."

"You say that big concentrations of business power and of labor power should be broken up," Chairman Kefauver said. "Which would you start with first?"

"Both," Romney snapped. "The most misunderstood area of public interest in the United States is the lack of knowledge as to the change that has occurred in the status of collective bargaining and the power of unions, and the people generally do not realize what has happened. We also haven't thought through the degree of growth and concentration in our basic industries. Senator, I don't think a politician can be very successful who does not take a solid position on the good old American principle that he is opposed to excess power in any form, wherever it exists.

"That is what the great Presidents of this country have done, as they have had to do it, and that is what the statesmen of this country have done, and we have got to have some of that if we are going to save this country. I think it is both [big industry and big labor] and . . . I don't want to see new imbalance created by just dealing with one and not both. You have got to deal with both."

Romney felt at that time the "major economic and political issues that would make or break America" were as follows:

1. Monopoly or competition.

2. A centralized planned economy or voluntary cooperation under minimum government regulation and public policy.

3. Collective bargaining based on conflict or collective bargaining based on cooperation.

4. Excess concentration of industrial, union, and government power, or adequate dispersion of industrial, union, and government power.

The American Motors president declared that the United States should consider the experience of other nations, and he noted specifically "England's decline and her experience with a planned economy."

"Failure to apply our American principles to growing industrial and union power could soon confront us with the only alternatives apparently available to the English people during the debate over the nationalization of the steel industry," Romney told the subcommittee.

Romney quoted Sir Stafford Cripps as saying that England's "only choice is between private monopoly and public monopoly."

Romney continued, "One of the primary reasons for that is because they have had industrywide bargaining in England, they have had the cartel system on the part of employers, and literally it was a case of private monopoly or public monopoly, and we are drifting in that direction as a result of this concentration of employer power to try to offset this union power and labor laws that promote the full concentration of union power."

Romney told Chairman Kefauver that "the economic power concentration in the auto industry has assumed such proportions that even testifying as I have done could be dangerous."

"I know I have taken real risks in submitting this testimony," Romney said.

"Mr. Romney, you have been very frank in your statement," Chairman Kefauver said. "You have said exactly what you believed. We know that you have told us what you think of conditions from the viewpoint of industry as well as labor. You spoke from your heart, as a person interested in the welfare of his country. You have been critical of both big business and big labor. . . ."

"I do not contemplate that there will be any retaliation or attempted retaliation toward you and your company," Senator Kefauver said. "We would have reached a bad place in the state of things if that should occur, but we would, of course, expect you to let us know if there is anything of that kind. We may not have any power to prevent it, but we would at least do our best to see that public opinion afford the remedy."

When the hearings on "administered prices" in the automobile industry were started it was doubtful that any representative of management would emerge with good relations with the more liberal subcommittee members. Yet, George W. Romney managed to win the praise of Chairman Kefauver, Senator Carroll, and Senator Wiley of Wisconsin.

"Your presentation has been forthright, intelligent, and courageous," Senator Carroll said. "I think the record will show, Mr. Romney, you are the first witness who, as a manufacturer, was willing to offer productive suggestions."

To other committee members, Senator Carroll declared, "Mr. Romney is . . . a fresh breeze from the West; he brings new thinking, creative thinking, and it has been very helpful to me, as I am sure it has been helpful to all members of this committee."

The liberal Colorado Democrat declared that if anybody from either industry or labor should "attempt any punishment because of your forthright presentation, it would merely serve to prove the statements that you have been asserting here."

Senator Wiley lauded Romney for his "great contribution" to an understanding of the problems of monopoly in the automobile industry, and he declared that he hoped that the American people got the message as well as both labor and management.

"I think I'm in the doghouse of both [management and labor] right now, Senator," Romney replied. "That probably indicates that it has some degree of balance in it."

Senator Wiley said he believed that the American people "appreciate courage and they appreciate folks who will appear as you have before your Government and lay it on the line."

Senator O'Mahoney added that he wanted to compliment Mr. Romney for his outspoken testimony.

"It has been a very remarkable demonstration of comprehension of what is happening to the free economy which the framers of our Constitution thought we were establishing," Senator O'Mahoney said. "I am glad to have you mention just a moment ago that in the old cartel system in Europe, when business leaders spoke about free enterprise, they were talking about enterprise that was free from government regulation."

Senator O'Mahoney said he had "seen the same disposition upon the part of leaders of some of the giant corporations in this country" to speak of free enterprise as European cartel leaders did.

"Now what is happening, however, is that while we represent ourselves to be the defenders of free government in the world, the leaders of the fight to maintain free government against political totalitarianism, we find that we are drifting toward economic totalitarianism," Senator O'Mahoney commented.

"Yes, sir," Romney agreed. "Economic totalitarianism that will bring about political totalitarianism. And, Senator, we are making the terrific mistake of moving in the direction of trying to lick our possible enemy with his weapons, playing his game."

Romney declared that to maintain freedom it is necessary "to develop greater individual strength and capacity through dispersion of power and responsibility and authority."

"In World War II, Senator, the automotive industry reached a degree of voluntary cooperation in producing guns, tanks, and planes that Hitler was still trying to get out of German industry by edict and order," Romney said. "Now why? Because the essence of teamwork, effective teamwork, is a group of individuals or organizations that have got such individual capacity that, when they join together, they have great combined capacity, and this direction we are moving in is taking us completely away from that."

Senator O'Mahoney stressed that he was particularly happy that Romney came, because he came from the management camp, and he spoke for the American system.

"Too many times those of us who offer what we consider, or

may think we consider, to be remedies for the preservation of a
free economy, are regarded—and perhaps we give some grounds
for this opinion—as enemies of big business."

"We do not attack business," the Wyoming Senator continued.
"We are trying to protect business against government control,
against the merger of economic and political totalitarianism which
would close the door of opportunity to every capitalist in America,
if it ever happens here."

"I agree with that," Romney replied.

"In other words, you adhere to the basic theory of the American
system of government that the power of government should be
divided and should not be concentrated?" O'Mahoney asked.

"Yes, sir," Romney responded.

"And you adhere to that same principle with respect to the
economy, do you not?" Senator O'Mahoney asked.

"With respect to labor and capital, with respect to industry and
unions, yes, sir," Romney answered.

"I am glad you had the courage to come before the committee,"
Senator O'Mahoney said. "I hope the leaders of your industry and
other companies will carefully read your testimony."

Members of the professional staff of the Senate Antitrust and
Monopoly Subcommittee were as impressed as the various Senators
over the Romney performance. He knew American Motors, and the
entire automobile industry. What was more important was that
he understood how the problems of the automobile industry related to the general problems of industry and government. He was
not afraid to face the wrath of business associates by saying what
he believed was wrong with the industry.

Unlike other top corporation executives, Romney did not consult with his aides before every answer while trying to avoid approval of any legislation. He was frank and direct, drawing on
his experience as a legislative assistant to Senator Walsh of Massachusetts, his activities as a Washington lobbyist for Alcoa, and his
experiences as a wartime spokesman for the entire automobile
industry.

His former employment as lobbyist for big business would
have made him suspect in many eyes, but to many others on the

Washington scene their first impression of George W. Romney was of a man with thorough knowledge of his field and the courage to make specific suggestions to cut the power of big labor and big business.

ELEVEN

Romney's Brainchild

The national attention Romney received as a result of his testimony before the Senate Antitrust and Monopoly Subcommittee was only a warm-up for what was ahead. The year 1958 was George Romney's year. American Motors had sales of $470,349,420—up $112,000,000 over 1957. Profits in 1958 were $26,085,134, compared with a loss of more than $11,000,000 in 1957. He was the Associated Press "Man of the Year" in industry, and the National Management Association also voted him "Management Man of the Year." Although his career in active politics was several years away, there were suggestions that the 51-year-old Michigan industrialist just might make a winning candidate for state or national office.

In early 1958, Louis Wolfson unloaded his American Motors holdings in a grab for profits when the stock first started to surge upward. It proved an unwise move on Wolfson's part because stock was selling at from $12 to $15 a share, and the really prosperous era for American Motors had barely started. Although the manner in which the sales of stock were made caused some criti-

160

cism of Wolfson by the Securities and Exchange Commission, Romney was able to state frankly that Wolfson had never been a part of management of American Motors and that he had no knowledge of the tactics that Wolfson or others might have used to influence the market at the time of the sales. It was a relief to Romney to be rid of the Wolfson shadow with the constant threat of some unorthodox financial maneuver that could upset his planning. Holding Wolfson in check for two years had been a difficult and wearing ordeal in the face of other major problems.

A new three-year contract was signed between American Motors and the United Automobile Workers, roughly paralleling agreements the union had reached with General Motors, Ford, and Chrysler. At Romney's suggestion, Ed Cushman had arranged a series of secret meetings for Romney and Reuther at a Detroit hotel. Romney wanted to become better acquainted with Reuther under circumstances not involving the tensions of collective bargaining or public debate on controversial issues. The meetings stressed rambling philosophical discussions along with practical problems of business and government, and it had seemed to Cushman that it did improve the personal relationship between the two men in a manner that would be helpful in later labor-management negotiations.

It had set the stage for the discussions that resulted in American Motors' making in 1961 an unprecedented profit-sharing agreement that was to, at least temporarily, make Romney the darling of organized labor. Reuther on that occasion hailed Romney's actions as "the most significant and historic collective-bargaining agreement ever signed in the United States." In return, Romney and Cushman won concessions from the union that wiped out waste and pay for workless time—concessions worth millions of dollars to American Motors. Reuther also agreed to modification of seniority rules that gave management a greater flexibility.

Even as the new UAW contract was signed on October 17, 1958, Romney reported that orders for 1959 Ramblers already totaled 72,400—almost double the figure of a year earlier. These orders were the first solid indicators that American Motors car sales were to climb to 401,446 for 1959, out of a total of 5,593,707 cars produced by the entire United States automobile industry for that year. Net sales for American Motors totaled $869,849,704 that year, with profits of more than $60,000,000.

The crisis period at American Motors was over in late 1958, and George Romney headed a well-coordinated management team which permitted him time needed to carry the major burden of work for the Citizens Advisory Committee on School Needs. The continued success of American Motors in 1959 and 1960 was to free him for even greater involvement in public service, with the attendant public exposure and inevitable suggestions that he be a candidate for public office.

In November, Romney and his Citizens Advisory Committee on School Needs completed eighteen months of study and prepared a six-inch-thick, fifteen-pound report detailing two hundred recommendations and urging that the Detroit schools raise a total of $198,500,000 over a period of ten years. On November 26, 1958, Romney and sixty-four members of his committee delivered the report to Dr. Remus G. Robinson, then president of the Detroit Board of Education, and Dr. Samuel M. Brownell, superintendent of Detroit schools.

As he handed the report to Dr. Robinson, Romney stressed that it represented substantial unanimity of opinion on how to handle the school problems. He declared that it was an effort to unite rather than divide the community, and he urged that the Detroit Board of Education strive for early action on the things it agreed with.

"It takes only one issue to divide and confuse a community on a subject as fundamental as education," Romney warned. "We know hundreds of things affect education. The most sensitive part of the program is the pocketbook area, around which the greatest concern will focus." He urged that in the future it be kept in mind that "it is necessary to have a two-way communication so that the Board of Education can benefit from the viewpoint of parents, teachers, and citizens."

Although the report completed the official work of the Citizens Advisory Committee on School Needs, Romney went back to work when defeat seemed possible for the sixty-million-dollar-school-bond issue and an increased special school tax.

Surveys indicated that the bond issue and school tax might not be approved in April 1959 because of a lack of understanding of the issues, and Romney volunteered for further service. He teamed with Walter Reuther on the eve of the school election in a broadcast over WJBK-TV in Detroit.

Romney explained that, if both proposals passed, it would cost the average Detroit property owner only about fifteen dollars a year. Romney declared that even if the bond issue and tax increase passed, the money available would only take care of about a quarter of the schools' needs in Detroit.

"Usually, I am on the other side of the bargaining table from Mr. Romney, but in regard to the school issues I am on the same side, and I think everybody ought to be on the same side," Reuther told the television audience.

The bond issue and tax increase, both apparently slated for rejection only a few weeks earlier, were passed on April 6, 1959, by overwhelming votes. The bond issue carried by nearly 60 percent of the vote, and the school-tax increase was approved by more than 64 percent.

George Romney was free to look for new community projects, for American Motors was selling Ramblers at a pace that was to push profits to more than $60,000,000. The crusading American Motors president did not have to look far, for the chaotic fiscal affairs of the state of Michigan had become a national disgrace.

Even before he had made the formal presentation of the Detroit school report in November 1958, Romney had engaged in conversations with Ed Cushman on the idea of using the voluntary citizens-committee approach to focus attention on financial problems of Michigan. In the spring of 1959, Romney arranged a meeting with others who were equally concerned about the crisis developing in Michigan finances. Romney said he saw no reason why there could not be a duplication of the successful undertaking in getting the community moving behind additional financing for the Detroit school system.

Some of the troubles could be traced to the 1958 recession, which had been a severe blow to the automobile industry, but other equally important factors included an outmoded state constitution and feuding between the Republican-controlled Michigan legislature and Democratic Governor G. Mennen Williams.

There was little possibility of agreement between Governor Williams and the Republican legislature on any kind of solution, and by April the State General Fund was so depleted that several hundred workers went without pay. There was still no money to pay more than 26,000 state employees in early May.

Following a series of meetings with other public-spirited men, Romney announced in mid-June that he was organizing a statewide committee to be called Citizens for Michigan, which would undertake to arouse public opinion and direct public action toward achieving a more mature and responsible political climate.

Among the men present in some of the earliest discussions of Citizens for Michigan were Martin Hayden, editor of the *Detroit News*; Robert S. McNamara, then a vice-president of Ford and later to be named Secretary of Defense; Edward Cushman, vice-president and director of industrial relations at American Motors; Dr. Samuel M. Brownell, the Detroit superintendent of schools; Dr. William E. Stirton, vice-president of the University of Michigan; Ronald W. Haughton, a codirector of the Institute of Industrial Relations at Wayne State University; Mrs. Berrien C. Ketchum, formerly a president of the Michigan League of Women Voters; Circuit Judge Wade H. McCree, Jr.; Dr. Charles Killingsworth, professor of economics at Michigan State University; and Leonard Simons, president of Simons-Michelson Company.

McNamara was to be particularly active in connection with a special subcommittee of the tax-study committee of Citizens for Michigan. McNamara was initially adamant in his opposition to a state income tax on grounds that the Federal Government had already preempted the field. He later gave his support to a state income tax after extensive studies indicated that there was no practical alternative to such a tax.

The "payless paydays" for employees of the state of Michigan had dramatized the pressing need for reform of the Michigan constitution to meet the needs of an urbanized industrial society. Some changes were made in the constitution in 1909, but in a larger measure it was the same constitution adopted in 1850 for an agricultural society. About 75 percent of the people in Michigan were classed as rural in 1909, but by 1959 about 80 percent of the population had been urbanized.

The League of Women Voters and the Michigan Junior Chamber of Commerce had worked for more than ten years to revise and reform the constitution, trying to swing away from rural control of the legislature, so cities would have a greater voice in state affairs. As long as rural thinking controlled the Michigan legislature, it was useless to think in terms of the progressive legislation that the League and the Junior Chamber believed essential to the future of Michigan.

The League and the Junior Chamber wanted fiscal reform which would take the financial operations of the state out of a taxing and spending straitjacket. Although the views of the League and the Junior Chamber had the backing of newspapers in the major cities, efforts to obtain constitutional reform failed. This failure could be attributed to the resistance of the agricultural areas and to the political posturing of Democratic and Republican politicians.

George Romney said he believed the nonpolitical approach used to rescue the Detroit schools could be adapted to a statewide effort to get Michigan out of its financial mess. He surmised that the time was ripe after the payless paydays for Michigan employees, and that the Citizens for Michigan could be a powerful third force overcoming selfish and partisan appeals that had blocked progress and had created chaos which was making Michigan the laughingstock of the nation.

The *Detroit Free Press* on June 13, 1959, declared:

. . . the situation in Michigan is such that some sort of grass-roots revolution has become almost inevitable.

It could take a number of forms and directions, some of which might be highly undesirable. It is fortunate, we believe, that someone of Mr. Romney's stature has recognized the need and has assumed the leadership. No one would accuse the Detroit industrialist of being a wild-eyed, radical social reformer. On the contrary, he is a man of great acumen and broad experience in human relationships.

He has admitted that his tendencies are toward the conservative. Therefore, the movement he is sponsoring is likely to proceed along moderate lines.

The *Free Press* editorialized its endorsement of Romney's general views:

It should be, as he has promised, nonpolitical, and it should be concerned, not with the quick palliatives which have produced much of our present governmental confusion, but rather with getting at basic conditions which must be corrected.

As Mr. Romney pointed out, the conditions which have produced the present situation in Michigan—financial confusion and an aura of doubt about the State's economic prospects—are not new ones. Nor, as he stated, can they be blamed on any one political party or leader.

Mr. Romney says he has noted a deterioration of public responsibility over the past thirty years. It may have been going on longer than that, ever since, in fact, Michigan began to change from a primarily agricultural to an urban-industrial society.

The *Free Press* praised Mr. Romney's magnetism and drive and added:

We hope he is successful, because if he is not, the next movement may be of a nature which we do not care to contemplate. Citizens for Michigan, under the Romney leadership, can be a powerful force which this State needs to lead us out of our present doldrums into a bright progressive future. The movement merits the support of every thoughtful citizen, for there is much at stake.

It is not often that public figures or men of industry receive such praise as the *Free Press* heaped on Romney. The highly competitive *Detroit News* was equally laudatory in commenting on Romney and the project they headlined "Romney's Brainchild." The *News* said editorially:

If anyone can shape and lead a citizens organization to the rescue of Michigan from its political wilderness, it is George Romney. They said it couldn't be done of Romney's struggle to rejuvenate two tired old auto companies wedded in death-bed desperation. They said it of the "compact car" concept which was the cornerstone of that struggle.

They will say it now of Romney's proposal that citizens "free from political affiliation and economic self-interest" band together for objective study of Michigan's basic political problems.

They were wrong about American Motors. There is reason to hope that they will be just as wrong about Romney's proposed Citizens Committee for Michigan. Not that the task he has set for himself and others of goodwill is easy. It is difficult for men to insulate themselves from political predilections and economic interests as they deal with complex political and economic problems. It is difficult—even more so—for them to convince others that they have in fact succeeded in doing so.

And most difficult of all will be the task of persuading people now convinced that compromise and objectivity are impossible . . . that they must prevail or be crushed . . . into believing that one-sided and narrowly partisan victory is hollow.

Both the *Detroit News* and the *Detroit Free Press* agreed that Michigan was going down a chaotic road, and that the Democratic and Republican political parties were engaged in shortsighted political posturing that created more problems than solutions.

Newspapers were hopeful but skeptical of the chances for success of the Citizens Committee, for it was obvious that there would be political efforts to take over the movement if it appeared likely to upset the *status quo*. Although regular political leaders were not barred from participation in the Citizens for Michigan Committee, Romney was wary of any move by the Democratic or Republican organizations to try to dominate his brainchild. He was equally wary of any moves by big labor or big business to obtain undue leverage over the Citizens for Michigan. Dozens of times, Romney had complained that the United Automobile Workers Union had an unhealthy influence over the Democratic Party through financial contributions as well as through the ties of the leadership. He regarded the Democratic Party organization in some areas to be little more than an extension of the United Automobile Workers. Romney was equally concerned over the role of Ford and General Motors in Republican politics in Michigan.

To avoid financial domination by any group, Romney and his associates barred contributions of more than a hundred dollars from any one person in any year. In addition to reducing the possibility of financial domination, this policy forced the Citizens for Michigan to keep its appeal broadly based, which was the only manner for it to become the strong third force Romney had planned.

As further insulation against partisan political involvement, Romney announced that the Citizens for Michigan would not support any candidate for political office. He also said he would not be a candidate for political office while serving on the Citizens for Michigan committee.

In the first months, the Citizens for Michigan were absorbed in the hard work of setting out the areas of study and doing the background research necessary to determine precisely what they expected to accomplish. By May 1960, committee members had concluded that the calling of a constitutional convention was the priority project upon which most reforms hinged. The committee gave its full support to a drive to obtain signatures for a petition for the constitutional convention and in this effort cooperated with the League of Women Voters and the Michigan Junior Chamber of Commerce.

In November 1960, the voters gave approval to the proposal for a constitutional convention, and there was a subsequent election in early 1961 of the delegates for the long-awaited Michigan constitutional convention.

In September Romney was elected from Oakland County as one of the 144 delegates to the constitutional convention, and on October 14, 1961, he was elected as one of the three vice-presidents of the convention. Being one of the most influential figures at the convention as well as one of the most publicized, there was some controversy over his role. Most outspoken among his critics was August (Gus) Scholle, president of the AFL-CIO in Michigan. Scholle accused Romney of using the Citizens for Michigan Committee as well as his office in the constitutional convention as political stepping-stones, and the *Michigan AFL-CIO News* claimed Romney had a poor attendance record at the convention.

The major work of the Citizens for Michigan was completed when the constitutional convention was convened, in October 1961, and Romney felt free to listen to those who were urging him to become a candidate for Governor of Michigan. Within a few weeks of the time the constitutional convention started work, it was apparent that Romney was giving serious consideration to an active political career.

By the time the 144 convention delegates had finished their general draft of the new constitution on May 10, 1962, there were two major campaigns in full swing against Romney. One was the campaign by the AFL-CIO and Gus Scholle in cooperation with the Democrats. The other was an assault by the conservative Republicans in the Michigan legislature, who wanted no part of Romney's independent and suspect "progressive" thinking. The long-time personal antagonism between Romney and Scholle, resulting in part from a deep philosophical difference on labor-management matters, now focused on the proposed constitution. Democratic Governor John B. Swainson and his supporters in the AFL-CIO banded together to attack the proposed constitution as creating a "seriously weakened" executive branch.

The pattern of the proposed Michigan constitution was along so-called progressive lines approved by the League of Women Voters and comparable civic groups. It seemed likely that it would be supported by organized labor. The term of office of the Governor and other major elected officials were changed from two to four years, in keeping with most reform suggestions from political-science organizations. Although the Attorney General and the Secretary of State continued to be elective offices, the new constitution provided for the appointment of department heads by the Governor with the approval of the Senate. The purpose was to provide for technical experts in areas where expertise was needed rather than political popularity. It contained a strong antidiscrimination section that had great appeal to most liberal groups.

The proposals for a reapportionment of the seats of the Senate and the House to provide more voice for urban areas were also a move that in many areas would have won the support of organized labor, but the Romney identification with the proposed constitution was enough to turn Gus Scholle and many Democratic organization leaders against it.

Governor Swainson complained that the new constitution would interfere with the people's right to elect state officials, and he contended that the requirement for Senate approval on appointments would give the Senate the tools for obstruction of executive decisions.

The political fight that developed over the proposed constitution became highly partisan, with the major opposition centering in the AFL-CIO and in the Democratic Party. In an unusual development for Michigan, the Republicans and business interests backed the "progressive" new constitution in an amazing alliance with the League of Women Voters, the Parent-Teachers' Association, and dozens of other nonpartisan civic organizations.

The Democratic administration of Governor Swainson and the AFL-CIO engaged in a series of successful legal maneuvers that took the issue of procedures into the courts and made it impractical, if not impossible, to get the new Michigan constitution before the voters on the ballot in the November 1962 election. The initial planning schedule had to be abandoned, and the vote on the new constitution was delayed until April 1963.

Neither the arrows of the Democrats and the AFL-CIO nor the cuts from conservatives in the Republican Party were to interfere with George Romney's decision to present himself as a candidate for Governor of Michigan in November 1962.

TWELVE

The Candidate Emerges

In 1960, efforts were made to persuade George Romney to become the Republican candidate for the United States Senate against the Democratic incumbent, Senator Patrick V. McNamara. Although it appeared for a time that Romney might agree to run for the Senate, he announced that he would not consider running for political office until he had completed the work he had set for himself in establishing the Citizens for Michigan. Reportedly Romney had the additional reason that he did not believe American Motors had yet reached the point that he could leave active management.

On February 9, 1962, after twenty-four hours of prayer and fasting, Romney made his decision to seek the Republican gubernatorial nomination. The basic work of Citizens for Michigan was completed, the constitutional convention was half through its work, and American Motors had held a steady production and profit level for four years.

American Motors sales reached 217,332 cars in 1958, the first successful year, jumped to 401,446 in 1959, soared to 485,745 in 1960, dropped slightly to 372,485 in 1961, and were off at a pace that reached 454,664 in 1962.

On Saturday, February 10, Romney called a press conference to announce he had made the decision to become a candidate for Governor. He told the press that he had informed the board of directors of American Motors that he would resign but insisted he would take no active part in campaigning until his work as a delegate to the constitutional convention was completed.

The board had urged him to take only a leave of absence, Romney told the reporters. "It is inconsistent with my convictions that I become a candidate for public office and maintain my business responsibilities," he explained. "I will request an immediate leave of absence as soon as I get to work on Monday morning. I will receive no salary or bonus compensation from the company during my leave of absence."

The confident Romney declared that his leave of absence would extend indefinitely, and that he was proceeding on the assumption that he would be elected Governor of Michigan. Although he pictured himself in an underdog role, he felt confident he could defeat Governor John Swainson, or he would not have made the decision to become a candidate.

In consistent Romney fashion, he lashed out at the domination of the Democratic Party by labor and the domination of the Republican Party by big business.

"For some considerable period of time, it has been my conviction that any government bearing the brand of any single clique or class, and thus deriving its strength primarily from one faction or special-interest group, is doomed to eventual failure," Romney explained. "Such a government tends to become subservient to a single faction or special-interest group for guidance, if not control, in the policy it makes and the actions it takes."

Romney declared that "such actions and policies, designed for the benefit of the dominating group, must—of sheer necessity— bring harm and hardship to those members of the community who live and have their being outside the border of the privileged circle."

He engaged in a furious attack on the "sorry and tangled mess" that Michigan finances had become, and added, "The responsibility for that must be laid in part at least at the doors of too many partisan politicians of both parties acting like narrow partisans first and Michigan citizens last."

"I believe we can achieve our full potential," he said, "and it would be my purpose in the active political campaign ahead to expose for citizen consideration the reasons why we have failed to use to the fullest here in Michigan the talents a gracious God has given us."

Former President Dwight D. Eisenhower and former Vice President Richard M. Nixon had mentioned Romney as a possible dark-horse presidential nominee for 1964, which had already caused considerable speculation about his future ambitions. In announcing his decision to run, Romney felt compelled to deny that his quest for office in Michigan was tied to any higher ambitions. "As a gubernatorial candidate I will have no interest in any other position in the state or nation—elective, appointive, or otherwise," he said. "My first concern is to be of assistance in the creation of a new constitution that will furnish the needs of our state and all its citizens and the citizens of some generations to come. That accomplished, my second concern will be to gain the Republican nomination for Governor."

"When elected, my only concern will be to conduct myself and the affairs of state with which I would be charged so that at the end of my term of office, Republicans, Democrats, and independents alike would be able to look at the facts and at the record and agree that the best job possible had been done in the best interest of all and that we in Michigan were rolling ahead once more," Romney said.

Romney was accompanied by his wife, Lenore, and his youngest son, Mitt, then age fourteen, when he made the announcement of his candidacy. Mitt created a minor problem by telling reporters that his father had confided to the family that he had awakened at his hotel room at Lansing at 3:30 A.M. on Friday and had made his decision. Romney was at Lansing attending the constitutional convention.

When reporters asked Romney about this early-morning de-

cision, he explained his son's story in one detail. He said he had
not made his "final decision" until he was driving from Lansing to
his home in Bloomfield Hills on Friday.

Even as he announced his candidacy, Romney reviewed his record as chairman of Citizens for Michigan and as a vice-president
of the constitutional convention. He emphasized the importance of a new Michigan constitution "under which this state
can stride forward at a pace in step, on all fronts, with the progress
of our day."

"This new constitution must be a document that our people
can adopt, with its primary provisions cutting sharply across the
lines of partisan politics and providing the charter base on which
the functions and services of all our people can be built efficiently,"
he explained his general philosophy. "Because such a document is
the very heart and core of good government for all, because without such a document no first step along the road to good government can be taken, and because I was elected to the Con-Con [con-
stitutional convention] for the purpose of assisting the creation of
that document, I feel that every effort of mine must be dedicated
to that purpose until the job is done."

Romney's comments met with sneers from Gus Scholle and from
the *Michigan AFL-CIO News.*

"The big clown," Scholle said scornfully "This business of trying to put on an act of having a pipeline to God in order to become
Governor of Michigan is about the greatest anticlimax to a phony
stunt that I've ever seen."

New Jersey Governor Richard J. Hughes, a Democrat, joked
about the fact that former President Eisenhower and former Vice
President Nixon were "trying to bring in a new model—the compact candidate—since their last candidate [Nixon] ran out of gas
and had a hard time finding a place to park."

The *Michigan AFL-CIO News* criticized Romney for "his many
absences from Con-Con sessions" and tossed out statistics the editors claimed showed that Romney had missed 50 percent of the
roll-call votes. The editors of the labor newspaper said that from
early October until January 31, 1962, Romney had missed 43 percent of the Education Committee's meetings and 20 percent of the

general sessions. The *AFL-CIO News* claimed that Romney was often present at the convention "just long enough to answer the attendance roll call."

The labor newspaper made the specific charge that Romney was playing politics when he should have been tending to business as a Con-Con delegate, and cited one instance when it was claimed that he did not attend an Education Committee meeting on the Upper Peninsula on December 1 and 2, 1961, but instead "was closeted with Republican leaders in the Botsford Inn, near Detroit, talking about his political ambitions."

Romney answered the labor newspaper's charges with a claim that "the figures on my attendance are misleading and incomplete."

"For example, a number of absences from convention sessions were because of official convention business, including the visit of President Dwight D. Eisenhower," Romney said. "The same thing was true with committee absences. Again, only half the members of the Education Committee were invited to go to the Upper Peninsula. Because I had been there several times and visited Educational institutions, I did not feel I should prevent a committee member from going who had not enjoyed this privilege."

Although Romney wasn't officially carrying on an active political campaign, even the writing of the new Michigan constitution became an issue. Democrats contended that the Republicans, instead of seeking a truly progressive constitution, were simply trying to write a campaign document for Romney's run for the governorship. While Romney and the Republicans were dedicated to giving the urban areas a greater voice in Michigan politics under a formula that took area and population into consideration, the Democrats and labor were pushing for a one-man, one-vote principle.

Not content to be in a major fuss with labor leaders and the Democratic leadership, Romney had seemed to go out of his way to create problems for himself within the Republican Party. Initially suspicious, the most conservative elements of the Republican Party in the Michigan legislature were irritated by Romney's constant attacks on the "partisan Republicans" whom he blamed as much as the Democrats for the "financial mess" in Michigan fiscal affairs. He had further widened the breach in early 1962 by praising the Republican moderates who had joined with Senate Democrats in a bitter fight for a state income tax.

In his tribute to the Republican moderates, Romney lauded "those senators who courageously put the state's interests above lesser interest." He said they "evidenced that type of courage and leadership needed to find solutions to our problems."

"While the proposals that have been under consideration in the Senate may not be entirely right, nevertheless we must overcome the petty bickering and economic conflict that has divided our state and created a tangled mess," Romney said in a pointed jab at all the Republicans who had failed to cooperate on a compromise tax-legislation matter.

In the words of one of his long-time business and political associates, "Romney's chance for political success in 1962 looked about as bleak as American Motors' chances for financial success in 1955 and 1956. For most men it would have been impossible, but George Romney is a fellow you can never count out."

Even in that confused political climate, Romney had no trouble recruiting able and independent people who were willing to back him on the basis of his record with the Detroit schools, the Citizens for Michigan, and the constitutional convention.

Romney selected Arthur George Elliott, Jr., dynamic little Oakland County Republican chairman, as his campaign manager. Romney had viewed at close hand Elliott's participation in politics from 1952 and in the period from 1957 to 1962 had seen the Royal Oak insurance and real-estate man build a political organization envied by other county chairmen. Elliott swung the county into the Republican ranks, and held it there with a firm hand. In 1961 and early 1962, when Elliott and Romney were among the seven Oakland County delegates to the constitutional convention, Elliott had served as chairman of the Local Government Committee.

"He was responsible for making the Oakland party organization a model of political organizations, responsive as they should be to the wishes of citizens," Romney said in introducing Elliott as his campaign manager. "He showed the state, as chairman of the

Local Government Committee at Con-Con, that all forms of government can be strengthened if given this type of responsiveness."

Others on the Romney team included Dr. John T. Dempsey, a Democrat who had served as a legislative assistant to the late Senator Thomas Hennings of Missouri before becoming a professor of political science at the University of Michigan; Max Fisher, a wealthy Detroit industrialist and long-time personal friend; Albert B. Chennault, a Negro builder; Dr. Walter DeVries, a professor of political science at Calvin College; Charles M. Tucker, Jr., a young Negro business executive and business graduate from Wayne State University who had been active in civil-rights work.

Dr. Dempsey served as state chairman of the Romney Volunteers, Dr. DeVries was research director, Albert Chennault was treasurer, and Max Fisher, with extensive background in local fund-raising drives, was finance chairman. Tucker was in charge of publicity in the race-relations and civil-rights area.

They were a few of the men of ability who believed that George Romney might succeed at the almost impossible feat of winning despite the long string of Democratic victories, despite the money and manpower of organized labor, and despite the sniping from his own party. These men felt a change was essential to rescue Michigan, and, like many newspaper editors, they believed the change was long overdue.

The *State Journal* of Lansing, Michigan, was one of a number of newspapers seeing Romney's candidacy as "a chance that state house control may be wrested from the Democrats after a long fourteen years."

"Not since [former] Governor Willliams' early years has the view been quite so optimistic," the *State Journal* said. "The GOP provided a succession of willing and able candidates, but they could do nothing with the combination of Williams' magic and labor's organization, a combination which carried over to elect Governor Swainson."

The *State Journal* saw Romney as "a man who not only has made a habit of success but who has picked up a bit of a reputation for magic himself.

"Too, he apparently has the ability to cross the myriad factional lines within the Michigan Republican structure."

Noting that Michigan labor's political bosses were certain to oppose him, the *State Journal* reminded readers that "Romney has been somewhat of a champion of the laboring man in his meteoric career at American Motors, and some of them may remember this fact at the polls."

The *State Journal* reaction was that the Democratic fear of Romney was proved in the "instant and critical responses to his announcement" by labor and organization Democrats.

It took notice of the fact that Romney was already being mentioned as a possible dark horse for the Republican presidential nomination in 1964, and added: "The national spotlight is being focused on Michigan's November general election and, if Romney should ride off with victory, its probing beam could be pinpointing a prime presidential candidate."

Optimistic in the light of the hazards Romney faced at that time, the editorial concluded: "Romney's projection onto the political scene has provided new zest to a campaign year and a healthy boost for the minority party, both in Michigan and nationally."

As the active campaign began, the *Ann Arbor News* (June 21, 1962) declared there was "no doubting Romney's sincerity, integrity and personal dynamism.

At times his platform manner is almost evangelistic. Here, obviously, is a man with tremendous capacity for leadership, a man of supreme self-confidence coupled with a realistic appreciation of the problems confronting the next Governor of Michigan.

But the Ann Arbor newspaper also found another side of Romney that was not so appealing.

It revealed itself in Romney's insistence on speaking in glittering generalities, his substitution of slogans for specifics, and, most of all, in leaving the impression that he doesn't fully understand the difference between running a large business corporation and presiding over a state government.

Perhaps Romney does appreciate the fundamental differences be-

tween the sweeping authority of a corporation president and the limited
powers of a Michigan Governor. Perhaps he realizes that a Governor
can't simply issue orders from his executive desk and have them auto-
matically carried out. If he does understand these subtleties of government, he didn't make it clear. Romney probably can't be elected Governor if he continues to speak only in generalities and slogans. And he
certainly cannot be a successful Governor if he insists on the authori-
tarian approach.

An editor for the *Wyoming* (Michigan) *Advocate* was impressed with an entirely different Romney, who "preferred to talk
with people, rather than to them." That editor commented on Romney's "casual manner of greeting" and the "unassumed humility
of an outstanding industrial leader who has already taken a business empire out of financial doldrums, to the amazement of his
colleagues and competitors."

"What he did for American Motors he might well do for Michigan," the *Wyoming Advocate* said, "and it is quite likely that Michigan is in no greater trouble today than his company was some
years ago."

As Romney moved into the active campaign in May, his immediate target was Gus Scholle. No one questioned where Scholle
stood on George Romney, for he had tossed every insult possible
at Romney from the time Citizens for Michigan was formed. He
had questioned both the sincerity and integrity of Romney's involvement in citizens' movements. It was all "a front," Scholle said,
for clever political scheming to launch Romney in Republican politics.

Romney had nothing to lose and everything to gain by meeting Gus Scholle on the same basis, for Scholle was the archenemy
of the Republican Party, and a feud with Scholle was recommended
as a method of unifying Republicans. Romney charged that Scholle
had "perverted the principles" of the Democratic Party and declared that "the inherent character of the Gus Scholle Democratic
Party structure is politically corrupt, morally wrong, economically
unsound, and socially indefensible."

His attack on Scholle was consistent enough, but contrary to the
predictions of Romney's advisers, it did little to unify the mem-

bers of the conservative veto bloc which had registered bitter opposition to a compromise tax plan supported by Democrats and some moderate Republicans. The so-called veto bloc defeated the plan, and they were not about to forgive George Romney for his criticism of them, nor his praise of the Republican moderates, whom they regarded as little less than traitorous.

Senator John P. Smeekens, one of the Republican Party leaders in the legislature, belittled the accomplishments of Romney and his Citizens for Michigan. "When the Citizens for Michigan was launched by George Romney, it flopped on its face," Smeekens declared. Senator Carlton H. Morris, another leader in the veto bloc, characterized the Citizens for Michigan as no more than a purveyor of "myths that have been repeated." Still other conservative Republicans were trying to find a conservative opponent of stature to run against Romney in the August primary.

Romney was not intimidated by the conservative efforts, and, to prove it, broke Michigan Republican tradition by declaring that Richard Durant, the key leader in the Fourteenth District, had made a mistake in affiliating with the John Birch Society and should be replaced in the party.

As soon as the June deadline for filing was past and no primary opponent had qualified against him, Romney started making plans for a head-on clash with Durant and any other Republicans who were active in what Romney considered to be "extremist" organizations.

The afternoon of July 26 Romney met with Durant, then vice-chairman of the Fourteenth District Republican organization, and bluntly told him that his activity in the John Birch Society was giving the Republican Party a bad public image. Although only vice-chairman, Durant was undisputed boss of the district Republican organization, with more influence than Stanley J. Baldwin, who held the title of district chairman. Durant refused to step down unless he was promised a voice in the selection of new officials for the district organization, but his compromise was rejected.

An evening meeting lasting until 1:30 A.M. was equally unsuccessful, but the firm public stand Romney took against the John

Birch Society won him the acclaim of the *Detroit News*. "George Romney suddenly has grown ten feet tall as the Republican candidate for Governor of Michigan," the *News* bubbled. "His unconditional demand that Richard Durant get out of the Republican Party . . . has the ring of leadership for which his party has been waiting."

"Romney, in his ultimatum to Durant, has said clearly and decisively that the GOP now can have only one face in Michigan," the *News* said. "Too many faces have been the party's weakness, as so many of Romney's predecessors learned when they counted the returns after November elections."

The *News* declared that "the Republican leadership, from President Eisenhower to Paul D. Bagwell, twice Republican nominee for Governor, has been forced to listen to Durant's dulcet song about party harmony while feeling the knife in their backs."

"It matters little whether Durant surrenders or is thrown out or is preserved by his coterie of party againsters," the *News* said. "What does matter is that Romney has cleared his party image for the voters."

In earlier periods, the Republicans who tried to project a responsible image with progressive principles had found attention was focused on reactionary Republicans in the Michigan legislature or on Durant and the John Birchites in his district, the *News* related.

"What Romney proved by his refusal to compromise an inch in the Fourteenth District is that he can match words with action," the *News* said. "This is what will catch the unbelieving in his own party and the hecklers in the opposition party by surprise."

The *News* urged Republican voters in the Fourteenth District to cast their ballots only for delegates clearly pledged to clean out the influence of Durant and the John Birch Society in the Fourteenth District.

Although he had strong editorial backing, the storm that Romney was brewing for himself could destroy his campaign for Governor. He placed his personal prestige and his chances for the governorship on the line in a meeting before nearly four hundred candidates for precinct delegates in the Fourteenth District. Romney told them bluntly that if the delegates reelect this man (Durant) to a position of leadership, then "you will have repudiated me."

He told the candidates for delegates that he wished to make it clear "that I do not question the right of any individual to believe in what he wants to believe in," but he warned that the Republican Party would fail at a crucial time if it "can become identified and tainted with the narrow views of one group."

Mixed reaction from the audience was evident when Romney completed his plea displaying more than a touch of anger at the heckling from the Durant supporters, and declaring forcefully, "George Romney is not prepared in any way to become identified with Welchism."

When Durant took the microphone, he did not strike back at Romney. He said he was "distressed by the spectacle of Republicans quarreling among themselves" and his plea was for unity.

Instead of criticizing Romney, Durant spoke of his respect for the Republican gubernatorial candidate and described Romney as "a man whose policies and actions tend constantly to increase the importance of the individual."

"His personal life reflects this; his personal beliefs; his business success; his constant attack against monopoly; his gallant leadership in the Con-Con," Durant said. He urged the delegates to "put aside any thoughts of distrust, or suspicion, or divisiveness."

Whether those were his genuine views of George Romney or flattery to serve the moment, it was a futile gesture. Romney had made up his mind, and the firmness of his decision was apparent to the Republican delegates who saw in him the first real hope for a Republican Governor.

Although Romney's resolve was obvious, Durant was confident of his own ability to win reelection despite anything the Republican gubernatorial candidate might do. Asked if he might change his position before the district party convention, Durant replied, "The delegates will elect the district officers. Even Mr. Romney conceded that."

Much to Durant's surprise, he was defeated in his bid for reelection at the August 15 convention. It was a dramatic Romney victory in the week following the August 7 primary when his vote total of 446,398 was substantially higher than the 318,396 votes received by Governor Swainson. Both were unopposed, and the primary was no more than an indication of the tremendous Romney strength in the area outside of Wayne County and Detroit.

Even before the primary, the Republican organization had found Mrs. Lenore Romney to be as effective a campaigner as her husband. Some even said she was more effective. In the beginning, she had no intention of taking an active part as a speaker. She planned to remain at home and provide him with a bit of tranquillity away from the din of the campaign trail. Her participation started as a simple effort to fill in the gaps on the schedule when Romney couldn't find the time, but her appeal was quickly apparent to Mrs. Elly Peterson, Republican state vice-chairman, and local leaders.

Lenore Romney's message was simply a plea for "standards of excellence in government, courage, integrity, honesty." There was conviction in the way she spoke of these virtues, and of her confidence that the man she had known since she was a fifteen-year-old high-school student could create the proper climate for reform of the state government in Michigan. When she finished the last of seventeen speeches on a five-day tour of the Upper Peninsula, an elderly man reportedly rose and seriously asked: "Mrs. Romney, is it too late to run you for Governor?"

In the final months of the campaign, George Romney needed Lenore's two hundred speeches and every other bit of help he could find to fight the leadership of the United Automobile Workers and the AFL-CIO. Romney knew he had to reach into the ranks of labor or he was finished, and Gus Scholle and Walter Reuther were determined to make it as difficult as possible for him to speak before labor groups.

Scholle, Reuther, and Al Barbour, president of the Wayne County AFL-CIO, disregarded Romney's complaints that the labor leaders would not give him a hearing and were afraid to permit union members to listen to him. Governor Swainson and other Democratic candidates were invited to address large labor meetings, and it was no secret that organized labor was providing most of the money and most of the organization for the Democratic Party. By contrast, Romney was snubbed.

The snub was dramatized when the Republican gubernatorial candidate asked for an opportunity to take part in the Detroit Labor Day celebration slated for Monday, September 3. The AFL-CIO rejected Romney's bid, and Barbour told labor union members that Romney's request to speak at the rally was a "shocking and shabby attempt to make political hay out of your day."

The irrepressible Romney disregarded the flat rejection of his bid for a spot on the speaker's platform, but when the Labor Day parade started, he was there as an uninvited guest. While Governor Swainson rode in a car as a guest of honor, the 55-year-old Romney strode down the parade route with the same confident immunity to jeers and insults that he had exhibited thirty years earlier in England to audiences hostile to his Mormon missionary preaching.

Hatless and coatless, and beaming with his best political smile, Romney walked near the front of the parade, shaking hands with spectators, exchanging jocular comments with rank-and-file union members, and in general acting as if it were his parade. Some distance behind were the cars carrying the Democratic hierarchy and the leaders of labor—Governor Swainson, former Governor G. Mennen Williams, then serving as Assistant Secretary of State in charge of African Affairs, Senator Pat McNamara, Senator Phil Hart, Walter Reuther, Gus Scholle, and Al Barbour.

When the parade ended at the State Fair Grounds, Romney took a place in the rear of the audience as one speaker after another criticized and ridiculed him for his intrusion into the parade and rally. Gus Scholle told the crowd he regarded Romney's uninvited appearance as "disgraceful" and "his strategy repugnant." Scholle predicted that the Romney march would not be successful: "Such tactics will get Romney as many votes as Swainson would get if he sent people into Republican meetings to seek votes."

Barbour explained the refusal to extend an invitation to Romney: "Labor Day is a day when we invite our friends to share in the glory and celebration. And we have yardsticks by which we determine who our friends are and where they are. We know the working people of this state will give their answer November 6 to those who intrude themselves on our affairs and our programs."

There was no restraint in the Scholle attacks on Romney, but Walter Reuther kept most of his criticism on a reasonably high level for Michigan political campaigns. Rather than direct his criticism at Romney, Reuther aimed his blasts at the conservative nature of the Republican Party in Michigan and declared that if Romney were elected he would be the "prisoner of a bunch of eighteenth-century politicians."

"GOP reactionary diehards will make hamburger out of Romney's white horse before he gets the saddle off," Reuther predicted in a typical bit of sniping at Romney's image as a crusader.

"I haven't asked the endorsement of any unions in this campaign," Romney declared. "I haven't asked any union for support as a union or any corporation for support as a corporation. I have only asked individual citizens to support me."

Following his spectacular intrusion into Labor Day celebrations in Detroit and later at Muskegon, Romney received invitations to speak before a number of labor unions. It started with Detroit Carpenters' Local Union 938 and UAW Local 155 and spread to other unions.

These invitations were the break in the wall that the Democratic organization did not believe he could penetrate. Romney, intent on making inroads in Wayne County, accepted every speaking engagement before union groups and showed up at the plant gates of Detroit industries to shake hands with the men who were going on or off duty and to ask for their support.

Although he was plagued with organized union hecklers, the energetic and smiling onetime missionary seemed to enjoy it.

"You're parrots, you're stooges," he told the hecklers. "You should start thinking for yourselves."

"It appears that these few union leaders are making desperate and frantic last-ditch attempts to repair the crumbling political wall they have built around the rank-and-file members," Romney declared. "They are afraid to let their membership even look at a candidate except the one they favor."

When the hecklers fired loaded questions, Romney retorted, "You don't really want to hear my answers, you just want to ridicule me."

When there were serious questions, Romney tried to answer them. A Ford employee, concerned over the condition of Michigan finances, asked: "Why don't you legalize gambling? That would give Michigan a good income."

"I don't believe in gambling," Romney replied frankly, and added: "I don't want Michigan to become another Nevada."

The power of organized labor was the major problem, but other issues had to be dealt with. The substantial Negro vote by tradition went to the Democratic Party. The Church of Jesus Christ of Latter-Day Saints denied the priesthood to Negroes, and it seemed likely to create a problem for Romney, despite the fact that he and Governor Swainson, a former member of the Reorganized Church of Jesus Christ of Latter-Day Saints, had made public statements that religion would not be permitted to be a campaign issue.

In the heat of a campaign, such pledges are often forgotten, or are disregarded by supporters who conclude that the use of such an issue has become expedient. The few comments on Romney's religion and the Negro backfired against the minor candidates who made them, and they were repudiated by their own party.

When the question of the Mormon and the Negro were raised with Romney, he simply asked that the questioner examine his personal record with regard to civil rights. He and his supporters pointed to his work for integration in the Detroit schools, his support of a Fair Employment Practices Act in Michigan as early as 1955, and his work on what he called "model civil-rights provisions" in the proposed new Michigan constitution.

In the late stages of the campaign, Romney took the initiative in seeking Negro support. He declared that new laws might be needed to assure the Negroes equal opportunity for apprenticeship training in the labor unions.

Making this thrust at one of the most sensitive points in labor's record of liberalism, Romney told a Negro audience that they "ought to get away from the practice of permitting anyone to take you for granted."

From the time the first public-opinion poll was published by the *Detroit News* on September 5, both the Democrats and Republicans knew it was a nip-and-tuck race. The poll conducted for the *News* by the Market Opinion Research Company had been remarkably accurate in predicting winners, and it showed Romney with 50 percent of the vote, as compared with 48.8 percent for Swainson.

Although Romney dipped to 49.5 percent in the September 30 poll, compared with 49.5 percent for Swainson, it was apparent that the Democratic Party would need all the push possible if Swainson was to survive.

President John F. Kennedy's help was solicited, and on October 5, the attractive young President went to Michigan for a self-styled political trip. The purpose, he told the voters, was to support men who "have stood up for progress." He invoked the name of former Governor G. Mennen Williams, called Swainson "a distinguished Governor," and told the voters that Michigan was enjoying almost full employment as a result of Democratic leadership.

President Kennedy pulled large audiences, but unionists complained that the President had unwittingly switched their campaign strategy from the need for Democrats to fight unemployment to a questionable claim of full employment.

Romney wasted no time in a counterattack. He charged that Swainson was trying to ride into the White House on the coattails of the Kennedy Administration, and then he declared that President Kennedy was painting a false picture of prosperity.

Fewer people were working in Michigan in 1962 than in 1960, when Governor Swainson took office, Romney declared. Many were obliged to leave the work force and Michigan because of a lack of jobs. Romney's comments were substantiated by figures from the Michigan Employment Security Commission showing that the labor force had decreased by 114,200 from 1960 to 1962, and revealing that 300,000 workers had left the state's labor force between 1956 and 1962.

Still more Democratic figures with national reputations poured into Michigan to give Swainson a boost—Vice President Lyndon B. Johnson, Secretary of Commerce Luther Hodges, Democratic National Chairman John M. Bailey, and former President Harry S Truman.

"We'd better get leadership in this state that doesn't need to rely on a dozen coattails in order to get reelected," Romney commented caustically.

The Democrats were even more concerned when the *News* poll published on October 21 indicated that Romney was forging ahead despite the help from national figures. That poll gave Romney 52 percent of the vote and Swainson only 47.3 percent. The Cuba missile crisis made it impossible for President Kennedy to make a last-minute rescue effort.

Other tricks were in the Democratic bag, including the announcement by Governor Swainson on November 2, the Friday before the election, that a $102,000,000 missile contract had been awarded to Michigan, and he declared that this would make "a significant dent in Michigan's problems."

Republican State Chairman George M. Van Peursem characterized the announcement as "political." "Why does the announcement come five days before the election?" he asked. "Why is this announcement made by the Governor, when traditionally, these announcements are made by U. S. senators?"

Romney declared that he would "hesitate to classify this as a campaign contract, but the timing of the announcement is very interesting."

"We still have 149,000 people out of work," he said. "We still have 275,000 fewer people working or looking for work than in 1956."

The missile-contract award, the full-scale attacks by labor, and the major invasion by nationally known Democratic figures were not enough to save Swainson. The final *Detroit News* poll published on November 4 gave Romney 50.9 percent of the votes compared with 48.4 percent for Governor Swainson. Although Romney's lead appeared to have been halved in the last two weeks, he emerged the winner on November 6 by 78,497 votes—about the same margin as the *Detroit News* poll had predicted. Romney received 1,419, 046 votes and Swainson 1,340,549.

When Swainson conceded defeat at 4 A.M. on November 7, it

marked the end of fourteen years of Democratic rule in Michigan. No one doubted that it was a George Romney victory, carved out of the most unfavorable circumstances and against what had seemed unsurmountable odds.

Ballot splitting by Democrats elected Romney, with the former industrialist biting just a little deeper into the labor vote and the Negro vote than any Republican candidate had been able to do in more than a dozen years. His unorthodox intrusion into the Detroit Labor Day parade was one of the important points in the campaign, for it gave him wide public exposure with the labor-union members. Also, it dramatized the tight rein of labor officials over their members in political matters, a point which tended to irritate a good many of the more independent-minded members.

The *Detroit News* said that some union critics of the Democratic Party strategy contended that the visit President Kennedy made to Michigan had been the turning point, for it had fouled the entire party strategy built on the theme that Democrats were needed to combat unemployment.

Romney's margin of victory was too small to carry any other Republican candidates for state office with him, but he had both the blessing and the curse of Republican majorities in both the House and the Senate. Many Republican legislative leaders were as far to the right of Romney as some Democrats were to the left. There was also resentment among some regular Republicans of the fact that he had avoided any more than casual mention that he was a Republican and that he did not carry the Republican label on most of his campaign literature.

The Republicans of Michigan were reminded that it was a Romney victory, rather than a Republican victory, in an editorial carrying the caption: "Remember who won!"

"George Romney defeated the Democratic Party in yesterday's election," the *News* said on November 7. "For jubilant Republicans that day is a fact of political life worth remembering. Much though they may yearn to cheer a Republican triumph over fourteen years of Democratic rule, election statistics—and specifically the picture of more conventional Republicans left far behind the Romney coattails—deny them that particular satisfaction."

The *News* commented that Romney's victory was made possible by "trusting and hopeful people, not by partisans." "And having some acquaintance with Mr. Romney's philosophy of life, we know his desire to pay such debts and to thwart those in both parties who give their allegiance to the cliques of the self-interested, not to Michigan as a whole."

Romney was reminded of the goals he had announced in the campaign: governmental reorganization under a new constitution, tax revision, state financial stability, a recouping of Michigan's prestige abroad, and a buttressing of her economic strength at home.

"Everybody in Michigan has a stake in Romney's success," the *News* said. "What we seek is a better state and a better life for all of us. In that effort he deserves the backing of Republicans, Democrats, and independents—the same coalition that forged his initial victory at the polls."

George Romney had a slim victory, but he had important support as he cut his last executive ties with American Motors and launched a new crusade to try to put a bankrupt state on its feet. It was a job that would have overwhelmed most political figures, and it was to tax Romney's energy and ability before it was accomplished.

THIRTEEN

Governor Romney

The week after he was elected Governor of Michigan, George Romney bowed out as vice-chairman and a director of American Motors. "Resignation is an emotional hurdle," he told reporters, "when you have been as intimately connected with the company and its people as I have in the last fourteen years." He had resigned as president, chairman of the board, and general manager when he had announced his candidacy, and after the election he cut the last ties to management in the firm he had lived with for fourteen years and for eight years had guided as the chief executive officer.

Romney had brought prosperity to the firm, and the prosperity of American Motors had made Romney a wealthy man. His salary and bonuses had run more than $200,000 a year. He owned 104,324 shares of American Motors stock worth more than $1,877,000 on the market at that time, and had passed up the opportunity to pick up options on 27,000 more shares of stock at prices as low as $9.91 when American Motors was selling at more than $18 a share. He announced that he was putting his stock in a trust account for as long as he remained in public office.

On Tuesday, January 1, 1963, Romney stood on the steps of the State Capitol in Lansing and was sworn into office as Michigan's forty-first Governor. The 55-year-old Republican appealed for a "coalition of concerned citizens" to make a nonpartisan effort to straighten out the financial mess in state government.

It was the same George Romney who had rescued the Detroit schools and had fought the battles of the Citizens for Michigan and the constitutional convention. "I shall encourage, support, and recognize coalitions of concerned citizens skilled in the unequaled tool of voluntary cooperation as the mainspring of Michigan's future progress," he said, adhering to his consistent theme. "I appeal to all citizens to join in the use and recognition of this unequaled source of power and growth."

There were practical reasons why Governor Romney should continue his appeal to nonpartisanship, for he was caught in a difficult political squeeze likely to create more problems than solutions. Two programs were high on Governor Romney's agenda as he started his term in office. First, he wanted the voters to approve the new constitution in the April election. Second, he wanted an income tax and other tax legislation to give Michigan a stable income base.

Under the old constitution, overbalanced in favor of the rural areas, the voters of Michigan had given Romney a Republican legislature. However, it was a highly partisan conservative legislature likely to balk at any state income-tax measures. Romney's margin of victory over former Governor Swainson had been so small that he had not carried the rest of the Republican ticket with him, and he found himself surrounded by Democrats. Even the new Lieutenant Governor, T. John Lesinski, was a Democrat. Others were Secretary of State James M. Hare, Auditor General Billie S. Farnum, Attorney General Frank J. Kelley, Treasurer Sanford A. Brown, and Superintendent of Public Instruction Lynn M. Bartlett.

As he had campaigned for office, the state's deficit had climbed to $85,000,000, and it had seemed the "Romney luck" or the "Romney magic" would have to outdo itself if even greater financial catastrophe was to be avoided. First, he needed that new constitution, and then he needed new tax legislation.

Fortunately, business boomed in the first months Romney was in office, with sales tax receipts soaring and the money pouring into the state treasury. It relieved the budgetary pressure.

For Romney, his first big drive was largely an extension of his work with Citizens for Michigan and the constitutional convention. The vote on the new constitution was slated for April 1, and as the time for voting drew near, the Democratic Party and the AFL-CIO intensified their opposition.

Although most Republicans stayed in line to back the new constitution, the election was what the *Detroit Free Press* called "a close and nerve-shattering thing."

"For several hours Monday night the statewide vote on Michigan's new constitution looked like as big an upset as the Truman-Dewey returns of fifteen years ago," the *Free Press* said on April 3.

The new constitution was adopted by a margin of only 9,567 votes when it had been expected to carry by an overwhelming margin. It was so close that the mistake of a key-punch operator at the Associated Press tabulation headquarters resulted in a 20,000-vote error, and news stories and headlines initially indicated that Governor Romney had lost his first major test as a public officeholder.

Romney had warned that "defeat would mean a great setback for the fundamental process of democratic society." In Wayne County he had been able to bring 45.5 percent of the voters around to support of the new constitution despite the bitter opposition by Gus Scholle, and Democratic leaders. Romney had won only 39 percent of the votes cast in Wayne County in his successful election the preceding November.

It was in the areas outside of Detroit and Wayne County that Romney lost ground between November and the April vote on the new constitution. The Republicans in the rural areas were willing to give Romney a margin of victory of almost 80,000 votes, but were cool to a constitution which would shift more power in the legislature to the urban areas, where the seats were almost certain to be filled by Democrats.

But even as the new constitution was adopted, Gus Scholle announced plans to contest the reapportionment as violative of the Fourteenth Amendment to the United States Constitution. Scholle and the AFL-CIO leaders contended that the shift toward more power for urban areas did not go far enough because Senate districts were to be based on a formula that gave 80 percent credit for population and 20 percent credit for land area. Scholle and other top labor organizers insisted on a one-man, one-vote apportionment of the Michigan legislature.

Governor Romney declared that the adoption of the new constitution made it "the most significant week in Michigan history." That might have been a bit of an overstatement, but it was certainly one of the most significant weeks in the career of George Romney. The *Detroit Free Press* referred to it as a personal triumph for Romney, and again recalled his role in leading Citizens for Michigan, in the constitutional convention, and in the weeks before the election, when "it was he who fought hardest on behalf of the document."

"He insists he is not interested," the *Free Press* said, "but his national stature is increased as a result of Monday's vote of confidence in him and his administration. Though the document is not perfect, as we have said before, it is a great improvement over the ancient model we are now using. The main point is that Michigan has taken another major stride on the way back. The future looks good."

In addition to the reapportionment of the legislature, the new constitution provided for greater borrowing authority for the state and cut the number of state agencies from an unmanageable 120 to 20 coordinated departments. The number of elected state officials was reduced to the Governor, Lieutenant Governor, Secretary of State, and Attorney General. The term of office of the Governor, other state officers, and the state senators was to be lengthened from two years to four years, with election in off-years from the presidential election.

Although the new constitution was to become effective on

January 1, 1964, the new four-year term could not apply until the 1966 election because of the presidential election in 1964. This was ideal if Romney's planning was aimed at the 1968 presidential election. Election to a four-year term in 1966 would leave him free to campaign hard in 1967 and 1968 with complete assurance that he would remain a political power in Michigan until 1970.

The legislature was given until January 1, 1966, to revamp the state bureaus, commissions, and agencies by the new constitution. If the legislature failed to act, the Governor was then empowered to carry out any reorganization he deemed necessary under executive order until January 1967.

The new constitution established a bipartisan Civil Rights Commission, consisting of eight members to be named by the Governor. The constitution provided that the Civil Rights Commission would start to function on January 1, 1964.

According to the *Detroit Free Press,* the next important business was "the special session (of the legislature) to be called this fall on tax reform." The newspaper noted that without the new constitution the scheduled special session for tax reform "might well have been little more than a bad joke."

When he took office, Romney pledged himself "to the job at hand . . . without an eye to greener pastures somewhere else." That statement might have seemed to bar any immediate presidential ambitions, but most politicians reserve the right to change their minds because of changing circumstances.

The divorce and remarriage of New York Governor Nelson Rockefeller made it appear that he had destroyed his chances for the 1964 Republican nomination. Rocky's marital mix-up had caused many political figures to reassess earlier decisions. Those prominent in the more liberal wing of the Republican Party were musing over the field of possible condidates to sidetrack the conservatives and Senator Barry Goldwater.

When Governor Romney traveled to Washington in May 1963 to speak before the United States Chamber of Commerce, some columnists interpreted it as the first move in a bid for the Republican nomination in 1964. *The New York Times* reported that a number of the key supporters of former President Eisenhower and

Vice President Nixon were pushing Romney for the nomination. When the Michigan Governor made a routine call on Senator Goldwater to invite him to speak in Michigan, political antennas of some writers sensed a strategy conference between two major contenders for the Republican nomination.

"I am not a candidate and I am not going to become a candidate," Romney said. It was really doubtful if anyone believed him in the Washington rumor mill, where denials are so often regarded as the first confirmation of the truth.

One denial was not enough for the editors of the *Detroit News*, for it appeared to them that the man they had supported for Governor was more than a little fascinated with the national attention he was receiving. The trained eyes of their editors looked for a flat and unequivocal assertion from Romney that he would stay in Michigan and run that state, and would refuse the 1964 Republican presidential nomination even if it were offered to him. The *News* declared that he should make just such a statement to kill speculation immediately.

The Romney denials seemed to leave the presidential door more than slightly ajar, and his national reputation continued to rise. A boom in automobile sales poured sales-tax receipts into the Michigan treasury, and the deficit dropped to $35,000,000 by July 1963.

The improved financial picture in Michigan was not the result of any "Romney magic." Romney stressed that the prosperity could vanish as quickly as it had come, and the only way to avoid future crises was to reform the archaic tax structure. Michigan relied upon a patchwork of taxes including a 4 percent sales tax, a business activities tax based on a firm's gross volume rather than on net profits, and a wide range of excise taxes on such items as cigarettes and liquor.

Romney believed it necessary for Michigan to have an individual income tax and a corporate income tax if finances were to be put on a sound footing. He avoided bringing the highly controversial issue before the regular session of the Michigan legislature in 1963, for he feared that it would interfere with other important legislation and would also go down to defeat. Before he pushed the issue on an individual income tax and a corporate income tax, Romney wanted to do some further groundwork with the voters as well as with the members of the legislature.

The prosperity that had temporarily solved Michigan's tax problem had also changed the attitude of many legislators who might have been willing to face up to an individual income tax and a corporate income tax if there were an emergency. Now that the sun of prosperity was shining on the Michigan treasury, there was little inclination to take on the distasteful chore of climbing out on the roof to make much-needed repairs. Romney was hopeful that he might argue and cajole Republican and Democratic leaders into a more receptive mood when entertaining them at the Governor's summer home at Mackinac Island.

He tried his persuasive powers on Republican and Democratic leaders, he took his message to the voters, he called the special session, but it didn't work. The legislature refused to approve his tax-reform program.

Governor Romney paid a heavy price for his bitter and unsuccessful fight for tax reform in 1963. In one acrimonious night session in November, the Republicans in the Michigan legislature did more damage to Romney's reputation than the AFL-CIO and the Democrats had been able to do in the first ten months he was in office. The Senate, dominated by Republicans 23 to 11, refused to vote two income tax bills out of the committee. In the House, where the Republican margin was 58 to 52, the Republican supporters of Romney's controversial income-tax measures felt compelled to hold the tax legislation in the committee because they faced the embarrassment of having no more than 30 votes for any House floor fight.

Typical of the reaction of the legislative opponents of income-tax legislation was Lloyd Stephens, a member of the Senate Appropriations Committee. "I voted against an income tax under the Democratic governors," Stephens said, "and I'm not going to go for an income tax just because a Republican proposed it."

Losing the tax-reform battle was an embarrassment to Romney as a political leader in Michigan. He was saved further embarrassment by the booming economic condition that sent total car production to 7,637,173 in fiscal 1963 and brought sales-tax dollars pouring in at an unprecedented rate. Favorable economic conditions cushioned the political impact of the losing tax-reform struggle, but it did not eliminate the serious damage to the winner image Romney was trying to project. Nor did it hide the political feuding taking place within the Republican Party.

The hectic tax-reform battle with leaders of the Republican Party was not forgotten quickly. A veteran Republican State Senator, Claude Geerlings, resigned from the Republican Party with a blast at Romney for supporting a $663,000,000 budget—the largest budget in state history. Geerlings, who served as chairman of the Senate Tax Committee, accused Romney of "twisting the arms of Republican legislators."

Geerlings was as vociferous as Gus Scholle in denouncing Romney, questioning his motives, and generally accusing the Republican Governor of acting like a prima donna. He declared that Romney had "kicked farmers in the teeth," and "thrown small business into a tailspin." But what bothered him more than any other point was the manner in which Romney either claimed, or was given, political credit for almost anything the legislature did that was regarded as laudatory.

"I am tired of the front office taking credit for going from payless paydays to a sixty-million-dollar surplus," Geerlings said. "The payless payday, as everybody knows, was a hoax. And the surplus is due to legislation passed in 1962 by a previous Republican legislature and by an expanding Michigan economy."

Romney was irritated at Geerlings' bitter criticism, and despite his own feuding with Richard Durant and other conservative Republicans, he said disdainfully, "This is not the sort of thing to expect from someone loyal to the Republican Party."

George Higgins, a former Republican State Senator, announced that he planned to challenge Romney in the Republican gubernatorial primary in 1964 because Romney, who "calls himself a Republican, is an impostor."

"He used the Republican Party to get himself elected and has abused the Republican Party ever since," Higgins complained. He claimed other members of the Michigan legislature would vouch for him as a man of his word, and declared that those same legislators know "you can't depend on anything Romney says."

Every political figure who takes a strong stand makes political enemies, but it appeared that Governor Romney was faced with more than his share within his own party and among men who had been influential for years. Not the least of these was Dick Durant. Ridiculed and ousted from party office by Romney for his activity in the John Birch Society, Durant was to be an irritating anti-Romney factor for years.

As the only real winner the Republicans had found in fourteen years, Romney had an aura of political wizardry around him permitting him to ride out Republican storms of 1963 and 1964. But problems the vigorously aggressive Republican Governor faced in Michigan were only symptoms of bigger and more nagging difficulties developing with conservative Republicans on the national scene.

Senator Barry Goldwater and George Romney had become acquainted when Romney was running American Motors. A friendship developed as Romney emerged symbolic of the best virtues of the hard-working American businessman. In many respects Goldwater and Romney seemed to be cut from the same block. Both were rugged and amiable men from the West, and each said just about what he thought on even the most controversial issues of the day. Although sharp philosophic differences were to emerge, Romney's slashing attacks on the power of organized labor and big government were little different from the attacks Senator Goldwater made before the Senate and in hundreds of speeches before business groups from coast to coast.

Barry Goldwater recalled that he was "probably among the first to suggest to George Romney that he run for Governor of Michigan." Eisenhower and Nixon were also among those who made early suggestions that Romney should run for political office in Michigan. While these suggestions may have stimulated Romney, it is likely that the dynamic self-starter had given the matter more than casual thought before any national Republican figures mentioned it.

In early 1963, any reason for rivalry between Governor Romney

and Senator Goldwater was unthought of. New York Governor
Nelson Rockefeller was the front runner for the 1964 presidential
nomination, showing as much as 49 percent of the vote in the
Gallup Poll in February, and seeming to be certain of winning.
Senator Goldwater was trailing with 17 percent, and seemed to
have little serious interest in the presidential nomination. He appeared content to make speeches at Republican rallies and bask
in the good fellowship of other conservatives. Governor Romney
registered 13 percent in the Gallup Poll at that time, but he had
pledged to the voters of Michigan to do "the job at hand . . .
without an eye to greener pastures somewhere else."

The next few months were to bring a series of events upsetting
the Republican picture completely, and resulting in a pattern of
activity by Governor Romney which caused the editors of the *Detroit News* to sound a warning to remember his pledge to stay in
Michigan and clean up problems there.

On April 1, Michigan voters approved the new Michigan constitution, and Romney's political stock rose. He accepted an invitation to speak at the National Press Club, and J. Willard Marriott, his old friend, used the visit to arrange a large reception for
the Michigan Governor in Washington.

To a large number of political observers, including Martin Hayden, editor of the *Detroit News*, the Romney moves had many of
the familiar earmarks of a budding campaign for a presidential
nomination. This became even more likely when Nixon announced on the same day that he was moving from California to
New York to enter the private practice of law, and in giving up his
residency in California seemed to be abandoning any hope for a
political future.

Nixon's stunning defeat by Edmund G. "Pat" Brown in the
1962 California gubernatorial race, followed by an undiplomatic
assault on the press, had appeared to have eliminated him earlier.
He made no mark in the early 1963 polls, but as the Republican
standard-bearer in 1960 he had many ties and had to be considered
in any assessment.

The political bombshell came on May 4. Governor Rockefeller
married Mrs. Margaretta "Happy" Murphy, who only a month

earlier had divorced her first husband, Dr. James S. Murphy. The impact on the polls was immediate. The Gallup Poll showed Rockefeller dropped from 43 percent to 29 percent, while Senator Goldwater's jumped from 26 percent to 40 percent and then higher.

Governor Romney, who had registered consistent strength of 13 percent, suddenly jumped up to 16 percent, and those who knew him best were seriously concerned that he would be so bitten by the presidential bug that he would abandon much unfinished business back in Lansing.

While he was in Washington on May 3 and 4, Romney took the initiative to call on Senator Goldwater at his office at the Capitol for a general discussion of politics. He later said that these private discussions were limited largely to three points: First, Romney assured Goldwater he had a commitment to the people of Michigan, and would not be a candidate for national office in 1964. Second, he extended an invitation to Goldwater to appear in Michigan in the same manner he was extending such invitations to other leading Republican candidates for the presidential nomination. Third, Governor Romney expressed his concern that the Goldwater campaign in Michigan might involve some "extremists" who would upset party unity and harmony, and he uged Goldwater to avoid involvement with this type of political figure.

As Romney remembered it later, he was at that time inclined to support Goldwater's candidacy because the civil-rights issues "that subsequently became of grave concern to me were not then particularly apparent." He could not remember that problems connected with civil rights were even mentioned at that meeting.

Others have viewed Romney's activities in that period as indicating serious interest in the presidential or vice-presidential nomination in 1964, but if any such ideas of a Romney boom entered his head, they were quickly banished. Martin Hayden of the *Detroit News* was concerned about the way Romney was acting.

Hayden, who had been present at the first discussions of Citizens for Michigan, was an enthusiastic supporter of Romney as the man to clean up the financial mess in Michigan. In an editorial entitled COME HOME, GEORGE, the *News* declared that Romney should disregard the lure of national politics and Washington headlines and "get on with the chores" in Lansing. F. Clifton White, a key figure in the Goldwater campaign in 1964, has credited that editorial with killing any Romney boom before it could get started.

Criticism by the most influential newspaper in Michigan was sufficient cause for Romney to become cautious about presidential hopes, for his 1962 victory had been a slim one and he needed all editorial support in Michigan he could garner in his rematch with the AFL-CIO and the Democratic Party.

Romney became so concerned about criticism of his political aspirations that a week later he created a minor political blunder by being too cautious. He refused to be photographed with Senator Goldwater when he returned to Washington for a testimonial dinner at the Sheraton-Park Hotel for the purpose of honoring the Arizona Republican. When he realized he had stumbled, Romney quickly reversed himself and was photographed with Goldwater. But in politically sensitive Washington, it created much speculation about Romney's attitude toward Goldwater and the political implications.

In fact, no substantial problem existed between Goldwater and Romney at that time, for civil rights was barely emerging as an issue.

Civil-rights turmoil burst forth in Birmingham, Alabama, in April 1963 as the Reverend Dr. Martin Luther King opened a campaign against segregation. Violence involving police and demonstrators erupted periodically throughout April and May, but it had seemed to be largely a problem caused by the attitude and repressive measures of Alabama Governor George C. Wallace, an outspoken foe of integration. On June 12, 1963, Medgar W. Evers, a 37-year-old field secretary for the National Association for the Advancement of Colored People, was murdered by a sniper, and his case became a great rallying point for civil-rights advocates.

By late June, the civil-rights demonstration fever had moved to Michigan. On Saturday, June 22, demonstrators were met by a jeering, shouting crowd of about two thousand at Dearborn, and on Sunday, June 23, a massive Freedom Walk was held in downtown Detroit.

Governor Romney declined an invitation to the demonstration in Dearborn because of other commitments. He also declined an invitation to the Freedom Walk because he said he had religious scruples against such activities on Sunday. Civil-rights leaders had started to comment critically that Romney was not with them in their demands for equal rights.

On Saturday, June 29, Romney showed up without an invitation for a civil-rights demonstration against discrimination in housing in fashionable Grosse Pointe, an all-white suburb of Detroit. Governor Romney was accompanied by his 25-year-old daughter Jane, Mrs. Bruce H. Robinson, of Boston, as he walked up to the starting point and took his place in the front ranks next to Edward M. Turner, president of the Detroit chapter of the National Association for Advancement of Colored People.

Turner introduced Romney to the crowd with the comment that he was pleasantly surprised at the Governor's appearance. "This is where we've been trying to get him for a long time," Turner continued. "And with all due deference, he's going to tell you that he has been out in front of us all along." When the march was concluded, the Governor quipped that his swift pace in leading the marchers resulted in "the only time Ed Turner has ever criticized me for going too fast."

After speaking Romney received a standing ovation from the demonstrators. He declared that the "elimination of injustice and discrimination is the most critical and urgent problem" in the nation, and added: "Until we eliminate this discrimination, our words will have a hollow sound in the world."

The Governor pointed out that "the Negroes in the North and South . . . are showing the nation the way through these nonviolent marches." He spoke with pride of the new Michigan constitution, which was to become effective the next January, which represented a demand by "the people of Michigan . . . that . . . all forms of discrimination . . . are to end."

The major point of protest was the denial of equal opportunity in housing in Grosse Pointe, Turner told the crowd. Real-estate men in Grosse Pointe had used a point system that involved salary, education, position, and race to determine whether a prospective homeowner was eligible to purchase a home in the exclusive suburb.

"Grosse Pointe represents the epitome of the sophisticated kind of discrimination, the kind practiced by every man, woman, and child who lives in the community," Turner said. "Their contribution is silence, and we're here to break that silence."

Abraham Ulmer, chairman of the Detroit NAACP Housing Committee, declared that his Negro action group was then and there "calling on the Governor . . . to call a meeting of all the mayors and city managers of all these suburban communities around Detroit, so that we can iron out and clean out all these problems of integration and segregation."

In his answer, Governor Romney avoided a direct commitment. He said he would be "happy to respond favorably if this would serve a useful purpose." When questioned later by reporters, the Governor said he had no specific plans to follow Ulmer's suggestion, but would be involved in many events, including the appointment of an eight-member Civil Rights Commission provided in the new constitution.

Although most of the 500 to 700 marchers were pleased at the Governor's role, one spectator took a personal cut at Romney, who owns a home in Bloomfield Hills, by shouting, "Hey, Governor. Bloomfield Hills tomorrow."

The problem of making meaningful civil-rights progress required a difficult balancing act, and Governor Romney was only one of dozens of public officials in northern states who were to face much more serious problems in the months ahead. Racial clashes in Cambridge, Maryland, in mid-July were followed by demonstrations and rioting in New York City a few days later over discrimination on jobs in the construction industry.

The problem of racial discrimination and violent demonstrations had emerged as a national issue a few weeks later as civil-rights leaders, Negro and white, organized a massive March on Washington to dramatize their demands for immediate action on more civil-rights legislation, integrated schools, and open housing.

More than 200,000 demonstrators marched in Washington on August 28, 1963, and conducted impressive ceremonies at the Lincoln Memorial. This march convinced Democrats and Republicans in Congress of the political need for swift action on a new civil-rights bill. President Kennedy declared, "The cause of twenty million Negroes has been advanced by the program conducted so appropriately before the naton's shrine to the Great Emancipator, but even more significant is the contribution to all mankind." Civil-rights legislation and the general problem of integration had become a flaming issue.

In September 1963, Governor Romney requested an opportunity to meet with Senator Goldwater and to discuss the whole civil-rights issue "privately and in depth."

Romney's meeting with Goldwater did not materialize, but Goldwater aide F. Clifton White went to Mackinac Island in mid-September for a state Republican meeting. In his book *Suite 3505: The Story of the Draft Goldwater Movement,* White related that he went to Michigan to stimulate Goldwater support rather than to attack Romney, as some political observers had expected.

White explained his mission as simply to sit down with Governor Romney and explain that he would urge all Goldwater supporters to get behind Romney's reelection in 1964. He said he did it with the hope that the Governor would eventually come around to supporting Goldwater for the Republican presidential nomination.

Certainly, Creighton Holden, then head of the Michigan Goldwater Committee, tried to support Goldwater's presidential hopes and Romney's hopes for reelection with equal vigor. Although Romney did not endorse Senator Goldwater in 1964, Holden remained a firm Romney supporter in 1964 and 1966. In 1967, he was an ardent advocate of Governor Romney for the Republican presidential nomination in 1968.

"It doesn't represent any switch for me to be for Romney, for I've been for Romney all along," Holden said. "I saw nothing inconsistent in being for Goldwater for President and Romney for

Governor, and I don't hold it against Romney that he didn't endorse Goldwater. There are some who do."

One of those very much for Goldwater and very much against
Romney in 1963 and 1964 was Richard Durant, and his relationship with Romney saw no significant change in late fall of 1967.

Durant was very much on Romney's mind in September 1963,
for the outspoken former John Birch Society leader represented
a serious threat to Romney's control of the Michigan delegation
to the Republican convention in 1968. Romney had already denounced Durant a year earlier as an extremist and had led the
fight to toss him out of party office, but in the fall of 1963 he
wanted help from White in denouncing Durant. White refused at
that time in what he described in *Suite 3505* as a shouting match in
which "Romney kept repeating that Durant was a cancer in the
Republican Party."

Later, after Durant had filed a libel suit against Romney, White
said he concluded that Durant had gone too far, so he did repudiate him publicly.

Goldwater's fortunes continued to soar in the fall of 1963. In
the South he moved ahead of President Kennedy by a margin of
54 to 34 in the Gallup Poll, and Goldwater's supporters were
confident that with more than a year to go, they could push their
candidate ahead of Kennedy on a coast-to-coast basis.

The assassination of President Kennedy on November 22,
1963, shocked the political world. There was the sense of out-
rage at the act that had ended his life, sympathy for the family
and the man who stepped into his place as President, and be-
wilderment about what this all meant in relation to the election
that loomed ahead in November 1964. It was to be months before
the Republican candidates and their advisers were to be able to
make any reasonable judgments on the impact of the assassination
and the elevation of Lyndon B. Johnson to the nation's highest
office. Final judgment had to await the election itself. While
awaiting that judgment, the Republicans did everything possible
to destroy themselves as an effective opposition party.

FOURTEEN

A Matter
of Survival—1964

Senator Barry Goldwater announced on January 3 that he would seek the Republican nomination for President. The Arizona Republican declared he was taking the step because he had not heard from any possible Republican candidate "a declaration of conscience or of political position that could possibly offer to the American people a clear choice in the next presidential election."

For a noncandidate, Governor Romney started making strange noises in early 1964. Before a National Press Club audience in Washington, D. C., Governor Romney said he felt he would have a duty to accept a genuine draft to be the Republican presidential nominee. Romney made it clear that he wanted to play a larger role in national politics, and some writers viewed his announcement as an effort to gain sufficient strength to be a key figure in the event a Goldwater-Rockefeller deadlock developed.

The *Detroit News* on January 8, 1964, tossed a wet blanket on any aspiration that Romney might have had with a stinging editorial captioned "Count Us Out." Martin Hayden, editor of the *Detroit News,* put an end to Romney's presidential fever with the flat statement that "the *News* will not support him in that contest" for the Republican presidential nomination. The editorial stated:

This newspaper supported George Romney for the governorship of Michigan even before he made up his mind to run for it. But if Governor Romney places his obligation to the people who elected him here second to what he may believe is his obligation to make himself available as a candidate for the Republican presidential nomination this year, the *News* will not support him in that contest.

The *News* editors said they were startled that he would be available as a presidential candidate through a genuine draft. The *News* commented:

. . . That's the standard form of presidential race entry, and no one using it in the past ever has waited for a draft. . . .

We hope and trust that Governor Romney made his statement . . . unaware of its implications among the professionals and out of political innocence. We have firmly and unalterably credited his oft-repeated protests that he would not seek the presidential nomination in 1964; that he recognized a longer term commitment to those who elected him governor. We want to believe in that continued commitment.

Romney's "ability and integrity are great," the *News* editors declared, adding that as far as his work in Michigan was concerned "he is well begun on that assignment—but well begun only."

The *News* said bluntly:

His claim to political stature sufficient to make him a worthy contender for the presidency can be based only on political integrity, experience, and accomplishment. For him to run for the nomination now would bring the first quality into question and fall short on the other two qualifications.

The *News* went on to say that there was no trained political leadership in the Republican Party in Michigan to take his place, and that to step out of the Michigan picture would

. . . return his party to feudism which paralyzed its statewide efforts prior to his appearance.

We will support Governor Romney in his announced objectives for the people of Michigan. We will continue to do so as long as he remains pledged to those objectives with all his heart and splendid ability.

If he abandons those sworn objectives for a chance at the presidential nomination in 1964, with the Michigan governor's office as a launching pad, count us out.

Martin Hayden had pulled the rug out from under Romney's presidential boom for the second time, and Romney pulled in his horns almost immediately. He kept them in until just prior to the Republican convention when it appeared to a few liberal Republicans that a stop Goldwater move might be successful and could throw the nomination up for grabs.

Governor George Romney, chastened by the *Detroit News,* stayed in Michigan and dealt largely with Michigan problems as Senator Goldwater and New York Governor Rockefeller launched primary campaigns designed to grab delegates as well as provide the psychological lift necessary to win the Republican nomination.

Under Oregon law, the Secretary of State is required to list on the ballot the names of all persons mentioned as possible candidates for their party's nomination. The only manner in which a man mentioned prominently as a possible candidate can stay out of the Oregon primary is by signing an affidavit stating that he does not intend to become a candidate. George Romney was the only prominent Republican to sign this affidavit, taking himself out of the Oregon race as well as out of the campaign before the March 9, 1964, deadline.

Senator Goldwater, Governor Rockefeller, and Senator Margaret Chase Smith of Maine were the announced candidates. The Oregon Secretary of State also listed former Vice President Nixon, Ambassador Henry Cabot Lodge, and Pennsylvania Governor onstrating an interest in the nomination if it should start to fall William Scranton, since they declined to sign affidavits thus dem- in their direction, although they were not announced candidates.

Ambassador Lodge was the big winner in the New Hampshire primary on March 10. The handsome former Massachusetts Senator received 33,459 write-in votes to lead the field despite the fact that he was in South Vietnam and did not campaign. He was trailed by Senator Goldwater, with 21,748 votes, and Rockefeller with 19,475 votes. Both Goldwater and Rockefeller were listed candidates who had campaigned vigorously. Former Vice President Nixon finished fourth, with 15,736 write-in votes, and there was only a scattering of votes for Senator Smith and former Minnesota Governor Harold Stassen.

Despite a mediocre showing in New Hampshire, Goldwater won the Illinois primary on April 14 with 65 percent of the votes, or more than 512,000. Senator Smith, the only other listed candidate, received 205,700 votes, and Ambassador Lodge as a write-in candidate received 46,500 votes.

As expected, Governor Scranton was an easy winner in the Pennsylvania primary on April 21, with 220,000 write-in votes, or 53 percent, and he was trailed by Ambassador Lodge with 21 percent of the votes. Nixon received only 9.7 percent, and there was a surprisingly poor showing by both Senator Goldwater and Governor Rockefeller. Goldwater received only 8.5 percent of the votes and Rockefeller an insignificant 1.9 percent.

It was no surprise that Lodge was the winner in the Massachusetts primary on April 28, with 63,688 votes—approximately 79 percent of the total. Senator Goldwater received only 10 percent of the vote, Nixon 6 percent, Rockefeller nearly 3 percent, and Scranton less than 1 percent.

Although Goldwater had pinned down several hundred delegates, he was far short of the 655 votes needed to win nomination on the first ballot. Early primary races had presented a confusing picture, with little spontaneous support for Rockefeller but a surprising write-in strength for Ambassador Lodge.

Goldwater piled up impressive victories in the primaries in May. The Arizona Senator received more than 75 percent of the votes in the Texas Republican presidential primary on May 2. Ambassador Henry Cabot Lodge was in the number-two spot as a write-in candidate. He received more than 8 percent of the votes, which was quite remarkable. By contrast, New York Governor Nelson Rockefeller, whose name was on the ballot, ran third, with less than 5 percent of the votes, after an unsuccessful effort to force election officials to remove his name from the ballot. He and his supporters contended it was a "phony" primary, completely dominated by Goldwater people.

On May 5, Goldwater won easily in Indiana, and on May 12 the Arizona Republican won the Nebraska primary with more than 49 percent of the votes. Goldwater was the only declared candidate, but a substantial write-in for former Vice President Richard Nixon totaled 31.5 percent of the votes. Ambassador Lodge had 16.2 percent on a write-in, and Rockefeller trailed with an inconsequential 1.7 percent.

On the same day that Goldwater was posting a primary victory in Nebraska, Rockefeller, who was unopposed, was winning the West Virginia primary, which did not permit write-ins.

The Oregon primary on May 15 provided the only significant good news that Rockefeller was to receive. Governor Romney had taken himself out of the Oregon primary fight, but even so it was a six-way contest.

Governor Mark Hatfield was an outspoken champion of Governor Rockefeller, and the New York Republican had an upset victory of more than 93,000 votes. Ambassador Lodge was second with 78,227 votes, and Senator Goldwater was a poor third with 49,784 votes. Former Vice President Nixon was fourth with 47,621 votes. Senator Smith was fifth with 8,268 votes, and Governor William Scranton trailed the pack with only 5,716 votes.

The Rockefeller victory in Oregon gave new life to his campaign after many disappointments, and with renewed vigor the Rockefeller organization approached the California Republican primary on June 2. Governor Rockefeller poured money and teamwork into California in what he hoped would be a crucial victory over Goldwater. He had the open support of Ambassador Lodge, Oregon Governor Mark Hatfield, and Senator Thomas Kuchel, the liberal California Republican.

However, in a desperate move for wide support, Rockefeller's campaign strategists distributed literature that Rockefeller was a kind of a stand-in candidate for all the moderates or liberals in the Republican camp—former Vice President Nixon, Ambassador Lodge, Governor Romney, Governor Scranton, and former Minnesota Governor Harold Stassen.

The campaign literature carried a large picture of Rockefeller, with smaller pictures of Nixon, Lodge, Romney, and Scranton under the caption: "These Men Stand Together on the Party's Principles." There was also a large picture of Senator Goldwater with the label: "This Man Stands Outside—by Himself."

The Rockefeller camp had not sought approval from Romney, Nixon, or Scranton, and the whole idea backfired. Governor Romney remained true to earlier indications that he would be a favorite-son candidate from Michigan, but would not enter into an agreement to throw the delegation to anyone.

In a telegram to former Senator William Knowland, one of the Goldwater champions in California, Governor Romney declared: I AM NEITHER SUPPORTING NOR OPPOSING ANY CANDIDATE.

Former Vice President Nixon issued a press statement denying any connection with the Rockefeller campaign.

Senator Goldwater then wrote to Scranton, enclosing one of Rockefeller's pamphlets, and bluntly demanded to know if Rockefeller "does in fact represent you in California."

Governor Scranton replied that no one had asked permission to use his picture or his name in the Rockefeller literature, and he added: "Since I am not a candidate, no one 'represents' me in California or anywhere else." Scranton declared that his one overriding interest was for unity within the Republican Party.

"I have refused to join 'Stop Goldwater, Stop Rockefeller, or Stop Anybody' movements," he said in a letter that was most interesting in the light of later developments.

The Republican presidential primary race in California was a two-way struggle between Goldwater and Rockefeller, admitted by all parties to be a nip-and-tuck affair that would be crucial. For Goldwater, it meant a chance to pin down those last delegates necessary to put him over the 655 votes needed for a first-ballot win at the San Francisco convention. For Rockefeller, it was a last chance to stop Goldwater, a last chance to pin down some important delegates, and a last chance to demonstrate that he could be a winner despite his divorce and remarriage the year before.

A new crisis developed on Saturday, May 30—three days before the decisive California primary. Mrs. Rockefeller gave birth to a son, and the all-but-forgotten aspects of the New York Governor's private life were again front-page news. It would have been considered dirty politics for a political opponent to have made even an indirect reference to the old issue, but the divorces and remarriages were again before the voters, with the expected speculation on how it might influence the California primary.

The California primary results on June 2 were close, as expected, but the winner was Senator Goldwater with 51 percent of the votes. Governor Rockefeller had a healthy 49 percent, but close didn't count, and it was apparent that the results had destroyed his last chance for the Republican presidential nomination in 1964.

The dust had hardly settled on the California primary before Pennsylvania Governor Scranton and a few of his close associates started to push him as the logical man to head a "stop Goldwater" movement. For six months, the wealthy young Pennsylvania Republican had been receiving a major public-relations buildup, and syndicated columnists and magazine writers were finding qualities that made them characterize him as a "Repubican Kennedy" or a "Republican Stevenson."

For months, President Eisenhower had avoided any public endorsement of Scranton or anyone else, but Scranton saw the Rockefeller defeat as an opportunity to win the Eisenhower nod he felt was essential for a successful launching. Only four days after the California primary, Scranton went to Gettysburg for a private meeting with the former President. When he emerged, Scranton said that President Eisenhower had said he should make himself "more available" for the Republican nomination.

The simple statement that Eisenhower had asked him to be more available was certainly nothing definite, but even the vagueness of it added a mystery that is often much better than plain talk in national politics. Was it the forerunner of an Eisenhower effort to block Senator Goldwater? The fewer facts Scranton presented,

the more speculation he was able to create over the likelihood of
some dramatic move. When he had finished his talk with Eisenhower, Governor Scranton left immediately for Cleveland, Ohio,
and the Governors' Conference starting the next day, Sunday,
June 7.

Governor Romney was also acting in a strange manner in the
aftermath of Rockefeller's defeat in California. The Michigan Governor arranged a press conference, and made a point of
the fact that in doing so he was breaking a rule against engaging
in politics on Sunday. Suddenly, Governor Romney was gravely
concerned over the possibility that Senator Goldwater might win
the Republican presidential nomination. He wanted the Republican Governors to summon Goldwater to a conference in which
he would explain his position on national issues and submit to
questioning by the various Republican Governors.

"If his views deviate as indicated from the heritage of our party,
I will do everything within my power to keep him from becoming
the party's presidential candidate," Romney said.

Scranton also favored a decision by the Republican Governors
to summon Goldwater for a grilling on his political views, but it
was headed off by others. Arizona Governor Paul Fannin, later
elected to the Senate, bluntly asked what right Governor Romney,
who had run as an independent in 1962, had to summon Senator
Goldwater and cross-examine him, and make judgments as to
whether Senator Goldwater was deviating from "the heritage of
our party."

Governor Mark Hatfield, a long-time supporter of Governor
Rockefeller, declared the approach suggested by Governor Romney was pointless at this stage. He said that if Governor Romney
and Governor Scranton were so interested they should have
exhibited more concern months earlier.

"George, you're six months too late," Governor Hatfield said.
"If you can't add, I'll add it for you. Goldwater's got it. I'm not
happy about it. I'm going to vote for Nelson at the convention because I'm bound. But these are the facts, and neither you nor
anyone else is going to change them."

Hatfield's comments to Scranton were equally direct as he stated that both Romney and Scranton had been "gloriously silent" while Rockefeller tried to stop Goldwater.

The comments of Governors Hatfield and Fannin blocked Romney's suggestion to summon Goldwater. But they did not stop the dramatic last-minute efforts to stop Goldwater that wrenched the Republican Party apart and destroyed any hope there had been for unity against President Johnson.

Senator Hatfield's calculations on Goldwater's strength were accurate. F. Clifton White, a key strategist in the Goldwater campaign, estimated that immediately following the California primary they had sewed up 665 delegates—ten more than needed to assure nomination on the first ballot. Within two weeks after the California primary, the Goldwater total had increased to 679, according to White. It was only necessary to hold tight and avoid incidents which might cause those delegates to bolt.

Governor Scranton paid no attention to the solid indications that Goldwater would win the nomination, but bounced about the country meeting with Republicans who had supported Rockefeller, Nixon, and Lodge. Optimistic reports continued to roll out of his press conferences of "new gains." These reported gains were apparently only shifts from Rockefeller, Lodge, or other so-called liberal Republican candidates to Scranton.

When the Republican convention opened at the Cow Palace in San Francisco on July 13, 1964, Senator Goldwater's strength remained firm. Governor Romney continued as a favorite-son candidate, and he was still unwilling to accept the Goldwater nomination as inevitable. To some of those close to the Michigan delegation, Romney seemed ready to swing to Scranton if it seemed opportune, or even to make the supreme sacrifice and accept the Republican presidential nomination himself.

For the first three days of the convention, Governor Scranton went through an amazing series of political acrobatics in a desperate effort to gain attention and to become the focal point of an anti-Goldwater drive. The Pennsylvania Governor received plenty of attention by his vicious attacks on the man he had often called his "good friend." His earlier announced "overriding interest in unity within the Republican Party" was pitched overboard in his effort to keep his presidential ambitions afloat. He became more a subject of ridicule for irresponsibility than a symbol of a courageous man fighting for a principle.

Whatever his personal ambitions were at that time, Governor Romney wisely kept his own counsel, stayed clear of the Scranton assault, and limited his public position to the submission of planks for the Republican platform that in many respects seemed to be designed to provide a middle ground upon which the Rockefeller-Scranton and the Goldwater factions could agree.

One amendment suggested by Romney was to denounce extremism without naming the John Birch Society or any other specific organization. It was recommended by Romney as a substitute for a Scranton-sponsored amendment that specifically named the John Birch Society. Goldwater advisers said they could have accepted the Romney amendment, but feared it would be interpreted as a sign of weakness. Romney, of course, interpreted it as a sign of unreasonableness and a support of extremism.

Ineptitude on the part of Scranton destroyed his effort, and solidified and increased Goldwater support. Goldwater's tally on the first ballot was 883 votes. Scranton had 214 votes; Governor Rockefeller, 114; Governor Romney, the 41 votes of the Michigan delegation; Senator Margaret Chase Smith, 27 votes; former Representative Walter H. Judd, of Minnesota, 22 votes; Senator Hiram L. Fong, of Hawaii, 5 votes; and Ambassador Lodge, 2 votes.

It was on Governor Scranton's motion that the Goldwater nomination was made unanimous by acclamation, but that belated gesture for Republican unity was not enough to heal wounds caused by the bitter activity of several weeks. Nor were other Scranton gestures for "unity" able to repair damage done during the convention and the weeks that preceded it.

On August 12, 1964, a "Republican unity" conference was held at Hershey, Pennsylvania, for the purpose of permitting Goldwater to talk with other leading Republicans, and as Karl Hess explained, "to calm the fears of the Rockefellers and the Romneys." It was also an opportunity for Senator Goldwater to introduce his campaign staff, including Dean Burch, the young Tucson,

Arizona, lawyer who was to serve as Republican national chairman.

The major issues were civil rights and law enforcement, and all the top Republican political figures, including former President Eisenhower and former Vice President Nixon, were present to try to bring a spirit of harmony.

Scranton, as Governor of Pennsylvania, was host, and he started the meeting by saying that he was "thrilled when Barry Goldwater called me and suggested this meeting be held here." It seemed a sharp reversal of form from a few weeks earlier.

The Republican Party platform on civil rights had pledged "full implementation and faithful execution of the Civil Rights Act of 1964 and all other such statutes to assure equal rights and opportunities guaranteed by the Constitution." Senator Goldwater assured the liberal Republicans he would carry out that pledge, and that he would not run a racist campaign.

Civil rights was one of the problems bothering Romney, but one after another the Republican figures applauded Goldwater as a man of integrity and as one who had been personally involved in fighting segregation in Arizona. His record was contrasted favorably with the record of President Lyndon Johnson when he was in the House and the Senate.

Eisenhower commented on a *Wall Street Journal* article on President Johnson and his pals. "If you haven't read it, you should," he said. "Then you would begin to see what we are talking about here in . . . return to trustworthy government, government that is thinking of the nation and just not of the pocketbooks of some favorite people."

Senator Goldwater reinforced assurance on the civil-rights plank, and said that when he pledged faithful execution of the laws, he meant just that. He said that he and William E. Miller, the Republican vice-presidential candidate, "repudiate the character assassins, vigilantes, Communists, and any other group such as the Ku-Klux Klan, which seeks to impose its views through terror or threat or violence."

Governor Romney did not inject himself into discussions until late in the conference. Then he expressed concern about the implications of a comment by Charles Percy, the young Chicago business executive who was the Republican candidate for Governor of Illinois.

In an assessment of issues in Illinois, Percy had commented: "The backlash group certainly is there, there is no question about it. And we will campaign, but on the right issues—and on the areas of fear of movement in the neighborhood, and so on. We will try to do it on a sound, sensible basis."

Governor Romney said he did not understand what Percy was saying: "I'm not sure whether Chuck said what I thought he said with respect to this racial situation. Did I understand your problem was how to suddenly encourage the backlash?"

"No, no," Percy replied. "We will not give any consideration to that, George, in Illinois, other than that we will campaign intensively among the nationality groups, for the Polish vote, the Lithuanian vote; we'll only appeal to them. . . . We have been told we should not campaign for the Negro vote because that would antagonize the so-called backlash. We are paying no attention to that whatsoever."

Turning to Senator Goldwater, Romney said that he had asked the question "because we have a very difficult situation in Michigan.

"I have been over it with you and I don't want to take up time here," Romney continued, "but a good deal of it relates to this question of the race situation. For years we have been pointing out in Michigan that the Democratic Party has been divided, in that you have the Southern Democrats who are taking one position on civil rights, and the Northern Democrats [who] have taken another position, whereas the Republican position has been a consistent position."

Romney said that the new support Goldwater was receiving from the South created some bad impressions in Michigan, and raised the question "of whether the campaign is a racist campaign."

The Michigan Governor said that he had heard Goldwater's statement and was satisfied with his personal viewpoint, but added, "On the other hand, I would have to say that in Michigan there is not an understanding of your private viewpoint, but rather an understanding of the public's position as they understand it, which is quite different. And that constitutes quite a problem because I have always found, in any field of activity, what people think is more important than the facts themselves."

"You are talking about image and not reality," Eisenhower commented.

"That's correct," Romney responded. "And I don't know how you pick up this other vote [in the South] and at the same time retain the Negro in our area. We had eight to nine percent of the Negro vote in 1962 in Michigan. The last polls show we had thirty percent interested. . . ."

Representative Miller declared that as Republican national chairman he had "tried to build a two-party system in the South, and I think that we have done this." He declared that the hard-core segregationists in the South were largely Democrats, and that "all the leaders of the Ku-Klux Klan for years and years and years have been Democrats."

Romney said that all he was trying to do was to indicate that "people [in Michigan] are concerned about whether this is a racist campaign, and that this point had to be dealt with effectively."

While accepting Miller's explanation, Romney declared that an impression had been created "that needs to be reckoned with."

"And I have got to reckon with it in Michigan," Romney said. "I have people ready to move out of the party, just as Chuck (Percy) has indicated he has, because they are determined on this point and on a few others."

Romney said a chain of events touching on civil rights caused the concern. He mentioned first that while the Republican Party talked of the need for local and state responsibility on civil rights, many Republicans did not have a record of actual involvement in trying to solve civil-rights problems at the local level. "We are doing it in Michigan," Romney said proudly.

The fact that Governor George Wallace had dropped out of the presidential race immediately following the Republican convention was another dramatic development, since Wallace was satisfied with the Republican nominee, Romney said.

To cap it all, Romney said that with all the resistance to civil rights across the South indicating that a majority of the people does not favor applying human rights and civil rights "we [the Republicans] suddenly emerge with the majority" of the voters.

Romney declared that he believed that some of the support swinging to the Republicans following the convention was based on the race issue.

"All I can ask you to do is to believe that I am an honest man and I will put my record on civil rights against any man in the United States," Goldwater replied. "I have never gone to the South . . . . I haven't explained my position as being totally against segregation."

Goldwater told Romney that "racism down there [in the South] is not the big screaming thing that it is in the North."

"In the cities in the South they are making real progress in the suburban areas," Goldwater said. "In the country is where you find the diehard segregationists who are Democrats."

The Republican presidential nominee related that even in that week, a columnist in *Newsweek* magazine had tried to point out "that I am no good for them because I have a better civil-rights record than Hubert Humphrey in the Congress. So I am . . . sort of damned if I do and damned if I don't. It gets hard to know which horse to ride."

Goldwater repeated his record as a former member of the NAACP, as a founder of the Urban League of Arizona, and added, "I have done as much as any man in that state to bring about what I consider to be probably the highest degree of integration ever achieved in the United States."

He declared that he had cast only one vote against a civil-rights bill because of the manner in which it would have injected the Federal Government into it.

Romney replied that in Michigan they were trying to do their best to win national and state victories for the Republican Party, and he declared that on civil rights Goldwater had "an enviable personal record—and it is an enviable personal record at the local and state levels."

Romney urged that Goldwater speak out "with firmness and

emotion" to show that he meant business across the nation and that individuals should become involved.

"That is what is missing," Romney said. "And when you don't do that, you leave this impression that you are trying to finesse this. . . ."

"George, I don't know how I can say it any stronger or any oftener than I have said it," Goldwater responded. "I have been talking on this subject for twelve solid years across this nation. . . . The speech I made when I opposed the civil-rights bill was mostly based on this, on that personal responsibility. I will just have to do more of it, that's all."

Nixon did a summary on the meeting, stressing Goldwater's integrity. "This is a man of character and idealism and principle," Nixon said. "We can say a lot of things about Lyndon Johnson in the White House, but we can't say any of those." He recalled that Johnson had been the conservative candidate for the Democratic presidential nomination in 1960, but that the Democrats found no problem in accommodating themselves to a Kennedy-Johnson ticket and going on to win.

He declared that it would be necessary for all the Republicans to go out and work to overcome "this image thing" that had become a major drawback. It was a valiant effort to achieve unity behind the Goldwater-Miller ticket, but it never was accomplished.

Late in the 1964 campaign, Senator Goldwater's entourage invaded Michigan for one day of intensive campaigning, which included several platform appearances with Romney and concluded with a huge rally at Cobo Hall in Detroit. The big question with the press was the relationship between the two men, and reporters watched every word and every exchange of glances for indications of whether Romney might endorse Goldwater. Or perhaps they were interested in seeing just how he would handle the problem if he failed to endorse the Arizona Republican.

Senator Goldwater and his supporters were realistic about the practical political problem. Senator Goldwater was willing to praise Romney for his leadership in Michigan and his administration of Michigan government, and he was willing to ask the voters of Michigan to reelect him. But he understood that there had been some success in making "Goldwater" a bad word by painting him as an opponent of civil rights. Senator Goldwater wanted Romney's endorsement and felt that Romney and other Republicans in Michigan could have done a better job of straightening the record relative to his extensive personal activity on behalf of integration in the Arizona National Guard and the Phoenix schools at a time when Lyndon B. Johnson represented a major opponent of civil-rights legislation in the Congress.

Prior to the evening rally at Cobo Hall, Governor Romney and Goldwater met privately for more than half an hour to discuss issues which had developed since the so-called Republican "unity conference" at Hershey, Pennsylvania, on August 12. According to those who attended, both men were genial as they went over everything from law enforcement to the sticky issue of civil rights. Governor Romney appeared to be in agreement with the manner in which Senator Goldwater was conducting the campaign, and there seemed to be special rapport on the need for stressing the lack of integrity in the Johnson Administration, the need for dramatizing the irresponsible fiscal policies of President Johnson, and the need for firm action in enforcing laws.

Even the civil-rights issue, one of the most difficult for Romney in Michigan, was discussed in what seemed to be the same agreeable manner. Governor Romney emphasized one of his constant themes—the need for personal involvement and the need for more action on the local level. Senator Goldwater couldn't have agreed more, for local responsibility and local action had been one of his pet themes, and he felt that his own record of personal involvement should have satisfied Romney. He reminded Romney of his actions to change the policies of the family department store in Phoenix to make it the first major business in the community to hire Negroes. His role in integrating the Phoenix schools and the Arizona National Guard were also mentioned.

Senator Goldwater explained that he had rejected a Romney platform suggestion putting additional stress on local action only because it seemed too much like a Goldwater plank, because he had been speaking on the subject for years. The Arizona Senator said that the terminology would have added nothing to the Republican platform, but that the words might have been twisted into an expression of some hidden racism by his opponents.

Romney and Goldwater agreed they were both interested in elimination of segregation, and in full civil rights for all citizens. It seemed to observers in the Goldwater camp that there had been a meeting of the minds on all the difficult issues, removing some of the friction that had existed between the most ardent Goldwater and Romney supporters in Michigan. No endorsement was expected.

It was no surprise to Goldwater that Romney did not endorse him in the speech at Cobo Hall, but it was irritating to read news accounts of interviews Romney held after their meeting in which he indicated that he had strong differences with Goldwater on civil rights. What angered Goldwater more was to learn that the Romney organization was distributing instructions to voters on how to split the ticket and vote for President Johnson as President and for Romney as Governor of Michigan.

Senator Goldwater felt that Romney had not been quite fair in dealing with him, and the sting of that incident was to color his whole later relationship with Romney. The Arizona Republican was totally sophisticated about practical politics, and understood that Governor Romney was concerned about going down to defeat in what already had taken on the appearances of a Johnson landslide. Deep bitterness enveloped Goldwater's closest advisers, for they regarded Romney's actions as "dishonest politics."

"He didn't have to go as far as he did," said Karl Hess, who was the chief Goldwater speech writer on the campaign. "If he felt he had to do it, he could have told the Senator what he was going to do."

Could Governor Romney have survived in Michigan if he had endorsed Barry Goldwater in 1964? That question can never be answered, but the election returns indicated massive ticket splitting by Michigan voters. In piling up the biggest popular vote in history, President Lyndon B. Johnson carried Michigan by a record-breaking margin of 1,076,463, while Governor Romney posted a 382,913-vote margin over Representative Neil Staebler, a one-term Democratic Congressman.

Again it was a personal victory for Governor Romney, whose appeal to Michigan voters was demonstrated to be far above the appeal of the Republican political party.

Although the bitterness among Goldwater supporters was to create a persistent problem for Governor Romney, the fact that he polled 55.9 percent of the vote in the face of the Johnson landslide put him in the running immediately as a potential candidate for the Republican presidential nomination in 1968. All he had to do was patch the political problems with Goldwater and continue to show a winning form in Michigan.

FIFTEEN

"Dear George" and "Dear Barry"

As a Republican survivor of the 1964 Johnson landslide, George Romney was an oddity. The 57-year-old former automobile company executive had stamped himself as a figure worthy of national attention. While he was eager to get on with the job of putting the Michigan government in order, no one doubted any longer that the energetic Mormon crusader had his eye on the Republican nomination and the White House.

The unusually confident Governor Romney lost no time in asserting a leadership role within the Republican Party. At the Republican Governors' Association meeting in Denver, Romney took the initiative in telling the Governors and the public what had been wrong with the 1964 campaign waged by Senator Barry Goldwater. Romney now believed he possessed the credentials of a political professional, and no one could quarrel with him in view of his 380,000-vote victory.

In Romney's estimation, the 46,670,000 votes that went to President Johnson and Senator Hubert Humphrey, the Democratic candidate for Vice President, were vivid proof of his contention that the Goldwater appeal had been too exclusive and failed to be inclusive. Johnson had received the largest number of votes ever received by a presidential candidate—more than 15,800,000 over the Goldwater total. The 61.3 percent of the total vote Johnson received had topped the 60.8 percent that went to President Franklin D. Roosevelt when he defeated Kansas Governor Alfred Landon in 1936.

On the CBS program, "Face the Nation," Governor Romney told reporters what was wrong with the Goldwater campaign, and of the need for a candidate with broad appeal to win liberal as well as moderate Democrats and Republicans to the GOP side in the 1968 presidential election. Senator Barry Goldwater, still smoldering from the humiliating defeat, watched Romney's television performance and burned with resentment at what he considered unfair implications of some of the Governor's comments.

On the next Tuesday, December 8, 1964, Senator Goldwater wrote to Romney to correct the record and to challenge the Michigan Governor's facts relative to the 1964 campaign. If George Romney hadn't realized the extent of the political problem he had caused by his refusal to endorse the Goldwater-Miller ticket, he did when he received the sharply worded letter accusing him and New York Governor Nelson Rockefeller of running out on the Republican Party "when the chips were down and the going was hard."

That December 8, 1964, "Dear George" letter follows:

At no time during the Governors' meeting in Denver did I have any intention of injecting myself into your very proper discussions, but after watching you and listening to you on "Face the Nation" Sunday afternoon, I cannot allow the things you said to go uncorrected.

You constantly referred to a discussion in Jamaica as if there had been some top-level meeting down there. What happened was that Dean Burch, Bill Knowland, Denny Kitchel, and myself took ourselves a holiday for the purpose of playing golf, which we did. At no time while we were there, either seriously or half-seriously, did we talk about labeling the Republican Party "conservative" and the Democratic Party "liberal." What happened was that during a television interview I was asked a question to the effect of, did I think that the election would tend to realign the parties into conservative and liberal groups, and I replied something like this: that I felt ultimately something like that might happen, and it might be a happy thing, but I did not think that it was going to happen now or in the near future.

You referred frequently to the statement of principle which you drew up in Denver—a statement, by the way, with which I can find no quarrel—but I am confused about your language: "We need to become inclusive rather than exclusive." Who was it, in 1960, that pleaded with all Republicans, regardless of their philosophic bent, to work under the tent of the Republican Party to elect Dick Nixon? If you don't remember, it was me.

Now let's get to 1964, and ask ourselves who it was in the party who said, in effect: "If I can't have my way, I'm not going to play"? One of these men happens to be you.

So this brings up the question of who is exclusive and who is inclusive.

You further state, "We need to win elections and serve America as a broad-based political party." How does that statement possibly square with the actions of leaders like you and Nelson Rockefeller? Where was this broad-based feeling on your part when you repeatedly refused to back the national ticket?

You stated during your television interview that you would never compromise your principles, but you made it rather clear that you expected me and others to compromise theirs. Now, George, I happen to be just as proud of my principles as you are of yours, and I don't intend to compromise any basic feelings of mine any more than you do.

Frankly, I don't understand what principles of mine you disagree with. And in that respect you said on the show that I was never willing to meet with you. George, that statement was just not true. You and I met in my office at considerable length one day. Later I came to Michigan to appear before the delegates and give them ample time to question me and you ample time to do the same. If my memory serves me correctly, you and I had at least one other opportunity to bury what differences we had. But I am still in the dark as to just where we differ.

Now to get back to Dean Burch. Perhaps I should say, "Now to get back to me," because I am convinced that it was Barry Goldwater at whom the efforts of some at the Governors' Conference were directed. I am convinced that I am the one your group would like to see out of the party, not Dean Burch.

I should like to defend Dean Burch on one important point you raised. The statement on liberal and conservative labels made at Jamaica was made by me. It was not made by Dean Burch, and I happen to know that he disagrees with me on this matter.

About the Governors' Conference policy statement: I can find only one difference between your statement and the language contained in the Senate-House Statement of Principles of 1962 and the Republican Platform of 1964, and that is your long-overdue explanation of what you mean by "extremism." Had you offered this definition to me at any time, I would have been in complete agreement with it. But when you stood on the floor of the Convention and tried to get through an amendment against extremism after refusing to offer it to the Platform Committee, you left us all confused. Frankly, George, this is the first language with which you and Nelson have had a hand that makes some sense to me out of your opposition to so-called "extremist groups." I might say in this respect that Dean Burch feels just as strongly about this as you do. And you will see, if you read the interview with me which will shortly appear in *U. S. News & World Report*, that I have touched on this same subject.

Your talk about supporting all necessary action, public or private, to eliminate discrimination merely echoes what I have said time and time and time again. Let me quote from one of my own statements: "The key to racial and religious tolerance lies not in laws alone, but ultimately in the hearts of men. Individual actions by every American— this and this alone will one day eliminate the stigma of discrimination from our society." I further promised, as an individual candidate, to uphold the law of the land, and this included the civil-rights law, which I voted against because I questioned the constitutionality of two sections.

So, I repeat, I find nothing in your statement with exception of the expression on extremism that has not been said time and time again by Republican candidates, by our leaders, by the National Committee, by the various state committees, and in the Republican Party Platform.

At the end of your interview, you spoke of your great fear of the centralization of governmental power in Washington. And I must remind you that I have been warning of this for many years. But where were you, George, when the chips were down and the going was hard? I don't claim for one moment that had you, Governor [Robert E.] Smylie [of Idaho], Governor Rockefeller, Senator [Kenneth B.] Keating [of New York], Senator [Jacob K.] Javits [of New York], etc., supported me, I would have won. But I can tell you that many rank-and-file Republicans got a bad taste in their mouths when they saw leaders of their own party failing to support a national ticket.

You state that you have been waiting for the National Committee to make some overtures to you in furtherance of a policy of inclusion. Might I suggest that the time is long past due for you to make some overtures of inclusion toward the National Committee, and perhaps toward the candidate who suffered from your lack of support. I doubt if you will ever see a united party when one element of that party refused to cooperate 100 percent with the top of the ticket.

I would like—as one who has always looked upon you as a friend —to have an explanation from you on the points raised in this letter. I've given you many opportunities to do this in the past, but you have never taken advantage of them. Now here is a chance to get this done before the language you used before the American people on Sunday and the inference left from the Governors' Conference are taken to heart and we see blood on the ground again.

The letter was signed "Sincerely, Barry Goldwater." In addition to the sharp challenge presented in the private letter, there was also the hint that a public interview by Goldwater scheduled for the December 21, 1964, issue of *U. S. News & World Report* might bring the fuss into the open.

Governor Romney did not reply to the letter until after he had read the Goldwater interview in *U. S. News & World Report,* and then it was a long twelve-page missive aimed at placing the blame for disagreement on Goldwater or members of his campaign staff. It had to be written with the awareness that someday both letters might become public, and that the political embarrassment had to be kept to a minimum.

Governor Romney had to be aware that his relationship with Senator Goldwater could be the difference between success and failure at the 1968 Republican convention. It was unlikely that he could expect to make Goldwater an enthusiastic supporter, but it was essential that he do everything possible to avoid an active Goldwater campaign against his nomination. The December 21, 1964, Romney letter to "Dear Barry" follows:

Thank you for your letter of December 8. My apologies for not having answered it sooner.

You have requested "an explanation" from me with respect to certain matters raised in your letter. I will try to cover them as frankly and fully as I can.

First, as to your remarks in Jamaica concerning the possible realignment of the Republican and Democratic parties into "conservative" and "liberal" parties: Whatever the circumstances of the statement, you have indicated that you believe this might be "a happy thing." I disagree.

We need only look at the experience of some ideologically oriented parties in Europe to realize that chaos can result. Dogmatic ideological parties tend to splinter the political and social fabric of a nation, lead to governmental crises and deadlocks, and stymie the compromises so often necessary to preserve freedom and achieve progress. A broadbased, two-party structure produces a degree of political stability and viability not otherwise attainable.

I believe, therefore, that we should exert every effort to broaden and strengthen our Republican Party, as a means of presenting a strong two-party system, which is an essential element in a free country.

Next you state that you are "confused" about the language of the Denver statement that "we need to become inclusive rather than exclusive." It seems to me that the arithmetic of the election should make this unmistakably clear.

A political party which drops from 35 million votes in 1960 to 27 million votes in 1964 has certainly narrowed its orientation and support. The party's need to become more broadly inclusive and attractive should be obvious to anyone.

Then, and I suppose this is the point which really prompted your letter, you repeatedly indicate that I was at fault for not "backing," "supporting" and "co-operating 100 percent with" the top national ticket. I suppose I could give you a short and summary answer to this, but, to try to resolve misunderstanding, I will cover the point in some detail.

First, let me point out that, based upon careful analyses, I'm satisfied that, without changes in your campaign, an endorsement from me would not have made any significant difference in the results of your election.

In Michigan, it would have shifted the state campaign from our Republican record of state progress to the national issues and candidates. Your 33 percent of the total Michigan vote included about 70 percent of the Republicans, 30 percent of the independents, and 5 percent of the Democrats. Reliable polls show that these percentages remained relatively constant from well before the San Francisco convention all the way through to the election.

The figures appear to have become fixed without regard to any comments or positions of mine. The presidential campaign dominated Michigan's political consciousness, as I'm sure it did elsewhere. People made up their minds based upon your public positions and your campaign.

I don't make this point to duck responsibility. It's just a fact that should be recognized, and you appear to recognize it when you say that "I don't claim for one moment that had you (and others) supported me I would have won."

Second, I believe I made every reasonable effort to bring about circumstances under which I could have "backed" and supported the national ticket. Long before San Francisco—going back to the fall of 1963—I expressed concern about my lack of understanding of your views on several matters which I regarded as vitally important.

In September of 1963 I requested, through your representatives, an opportunity to meet with you to discuss these matters privately and in depth.

You refer in your letter to the meeting we had at my request much earlier in 1963 in your office in Washington. That discussion was largely limited to three points: (1) the fact that I had a commitment to the people of Michigan that I would not be a candidate for national office in 1964; (2) my invitation to you, as to other candidates, to appear in Michigan; and (3) my concern that your campaign in Michigan avoid, if possible, the involvement of individuals who might make it difficult to preserve party unity and harmony.

(At that time I was inclined to support your possible candidacy because the issues that subsequently became of grave concern to me were not then particularly apparent. As a result, I didn't even mention them, and discussed a few other matters only incidentally in that meeting.)

At any rate, the meeting I requested in September of 1963 did not occur.

During the winter of this year, after my earlier requests had been repeatedly renewed, your Mr. Clifton White did tell me he had talked with you and that you would meet with me after the California primary. However, the meeting did not materialize.

Instead, at the Cleveland Governors' Conference, shortly after the California primary, where I had hoped to be able to meet with you, Paul Fannin handed me a copy of a statement of your positions on some issues, printed for use in the California primary.

In the newspaper I read that when you were questioned about our getting together for what by this time was my well-publicized desire for a discussion in depth, you said you had sent me a printed statement of your positions, and if I didn't understand it, I could get in touch with you.

Let me interject that by that time the need for such a meeting had become all the more important. You were just about to take a position on the 1964 Civil Rights Act contrary to that of most elected Republicans in and out of Congress, and there were disturbing indications that your strategists proposed to make an all-out push for the Southern white segregationist vote and to attempt to exploit the so-called "white backlash" in the North.

The delegates' mail was beginning to contain much of what I'm sure you would regard as "extremist," "hate" literature, backing you. A clear understanding of your position was needed, and I persisted.

I invited you to Lansing to meet with the Michigan delegates. You accepted. I then telephoned, inviting you, through Mrs. [Edna] Coerver, because you were attending a meeting, to come early enough for dinner at my home and a thorough private discussion.

This was first accepted by telephone and then canceled because, I was told, "the boys said" you could not leave Chicago in time. I then indicated, in writing, my willingness to come to Chicago and fly back with you, so that we could visit on the plane. This was rejected and several days later reproposed by you, but, unfortunately, only after I had made other unbreakable commitments.

You will then recall our chance meeting at the Washington Butler Airport on June 29. You indicated you could come to Lansing earlier than expected on the following day, and that you would call me when you left Chicago.

The next day I not only received no call, but you arrived half an hour late for your meeting with our delegation. We talked pleasantries with others present riding in from the airport and briefly in your suite before the meeting of the delegation. I conducted the meeting on the basis of written questions previously prepared by the delegation and used in a similar meeting with Governor Scranton. In my personal view, some of your comments in response to delegates' inquiries, particularly on civil rights and extremists, raised more questions than they resolved. However, I did not regard that relatively open meeting as an appropriate place for me to express to you my concerns. The meeting ended, and without saying anything about your failure to arrive on time or of our long-sought "discussion in depth," you left.

Following this all-out effort at such a discussion, I decided it was futile to try further before San Francisco.

However, my efforts to bring about circumstances under which I could support the ticket continued. In my public statements and actions, I placed heavy emphasis on the vital importance of a sound platform.

In a memorandum submitted to Congressman Laird [chairman of the Resolutions Committee] at his request a week before the convention, I spelled out some recommendations of my own, and some offered on behalf of the Republican Governors. This memorandum dealt importantly with positive steps to avoid centralization in government, emphasizing state, local, and individual responsibilities. It also included the points on civil rights and extremism which were later to be the basis for my proposed amendments to the platform.

I presented this memorandum in person and in writing to the entire Platform Committee on July 8 in San Francisco. My testimony specifically urged, among other rights, that the platform pledge federal, state, local, and individual action to promote the civil rights of all Americans. I also urged the repudiation of extremists who might attach themselves to the party or its candidates. My proposals were subsequently presented in written form to the Platform Committee in debate and were rejected.

Contrary to your statement, my amendment on extremists was offered to the Platform Committee by Richard Van Dusen, the delegate from Michigan, and was rejected. Both amendments were next presented, and before the convention consideration of the platform, to your Platform Committee representative, Congressman Rhodes, and he rejected them. I personally discussed the importance of such amendments, briefly and separately, before their being offered on the floor with Congressman Rhodes, Paul Fannin, and Richard Kliendienst.

These were not amendments which called for any compromise of your principles, if in fact you find no quarrel with the Denver statements on civil rights and extremism. But they were essential if the party was to be soundly positioned for the campaign on the basis of principles I am convinced are essential to the future of freedom in America and around the world.

Further, a platform whose basic emphasis was in state, local, and individual rights and responsibilities but which failed to pledge state, local, and individual action in the civil-rights field was clearly vulnerable to charges of inconsistency, and, more important, of bowing to the segregationists in the South.

With respect to the extremist amendment, as I said at the time: "Experience shouts, the differences between success and failure are small. I do not believe our country will survive present perils unless the Republican Party provides the program and the leadership that will recapture the interest, respect, and support of a majority of voting Americans.

"With extremists of the right and left preaching and practicing hate, and bearing false witness on the basis of guilt by association and circumstantial rationalization, and with such extremists rising to official positions of leadership in the Republican Party, we cannot recapture the respect of the nation and lead it to its necessary spiritual, moral, and political rebirth if we hide our heads in the sand and decline to even recognize in our platform that the nation is again beset by modern 'know-nothings.' "

The failure of your representatives to accept these concepts left the party in an exposed and vulnerable position. A leading Southern delegate in a private discussion with me, opposing my civil-rights amendment after it was introduced but before it was offered, made it clear that there had been a platform deal that was a surrender to the Southern segregationists, contrary to the entire tradition of the party. And it appeared that there was a willingness to accept, perhaps even welcome, the support of irresponsible extremists such as those you clearly reject in the December 21, 1964, *U. S. News & World Report* interview.

Serious as this weakness was, you could still have corrected it by speaking out clearly and unequivocally. Unfortunately, your acceptance speech moved in precisely the opposite direction, seeming to approve the platform as adopted and to throw down the gauntlet to those who had dared to suggest it could be improved. Then the replacements made on the National Committee executive committee by your appointee, Dean Burch, added to the evident intention to restrict direction of the campaign and the party to those who had supported you before the convention. The very ones needed to give the campaign broad and inclusive direction were replaced.

Despite these developments, I still kept the door open for an endorsement of you. On July 15, 1964, as the convention ended, I said,

"As the national campaign progresses in a . . . responsible manner, free of hate-peddling and fear-spreading, and devoted to the issues of the day, I will be happy to support it."

Just ahead of the Hershey conference, you invited me to Washington for the type of "discussion in depth" I had persistently sought for most of the nine months before San Francisco. At that meeting I reviewed the reasons behind the proposed platform amendments on civil rights and extremism, only to be told by you that you had only read a few sections of the platform and didn't know what amendments were being offered.

On that occasion I told you of a leading Southern delegate's revelation that a deal had been made on the platform's civil-rights language which our Michigan amendments violated. I also urged you to recognize the need to overcome the effect of Governor Wallace's withdrawal and some Ku-Klux Klan endorsement.

You cited your personal dedication and action to eliminate discrimination and human injustice, as you did many times before and during the campaign—a personal attitude I do not question now and did not question then or at any time. However, I did my best to point out the inconsistency between your personal record and public record, including the arbitrary rejection of my San Francisco amendment which was offered separately from the Rockefeller-Scranton amendment because it dealt only with the principle and was not related to the candidacy fight.

While this made no apparent impression on you, at the end of our conference, which also included a shorter discussion of the extremism issue, you asked me to let you have any suggestions before the Hershey conference. This I did in writing, urging a public statement at Hershey that would include this key language:

"The enduring solution must be a personal solution in the hearts and minds of individuals. That is why we must encourage civil-rights actions by individuals, in families, in neighborhoods, and at the community and state levels of government.

"The rights of some must not be enjoyed by denying the rights of others. Neither can we permit states' rights at the expense of human rights. The basic principles of individual rights and states' rights are indivisible from individual responsibilities and states' responsibilities."

My extremism suggestion recommended this statement on your part:

"Extremism in defense of liberty is not a vice, but I denounce political extremism, of the left or the right, based on duplicity, falsehood, fear, violence, and threats when they endanger liberty.

"A political extremist in my view is one who advocates overthrow of our Government through either peaceful or violent means; one who uses threats of violence or unlawful or immoral means to achieve political ends; or one who believes that the political end justifies the use of any means, regardless of the effect on others.

"Such political extremism destroys liberty, and is a vice.

"With one or two exceptions, I cannot condemn groups as groups. Guilt by association is contrary to American principles of justice."

In the subsequent inadequate opportunity for discussion at Hershey, it was apparent you were not planning to make such strong clarifying statements. As a result, three times in the group meeting I tried to point out your need to recognize and correct the conflict between your personal and public record. My final plea was voiced in essentially these words:

"Barry, in essence what I'm urging is that you urge others to do in the field of civil rights what you say you have done at the private, local, and state levels—to advocate it with such conviction that everyone will know you mean exactly that."

In one response, you said that I was questioning your honesty.

As far as the campaign itself was concerned, I ran as a Republican on a record of state progress built with the assistance of Republican candidates and appeared with hundreds of them. I instructed the GOP State Central Committee to extend full support based on Republican accomplishments. I ran as a Republican and I won as a Republican.

Despite our landslide losses in local and state offices, we have stopped the progressive membership shrinkage of the Republican Party in Michigan and have started to broaden its base. We are now in the process of taking steps in Michigan similar to those recommended in the Denver Governors' statement designed to broaden and strengthen the party nationally. To the extent I can, I want to help in this effort.

I cannot accept the blame for the divisiveness in the party when you, your representatives, and your campaign strategy refused to encompass those of us who had reservations based on basic American and Republican principles. My reservations I voiced privately to your representatives and publicly on many occasions for some months before the San Francisco convention. Dick Nixon, since you draw the analogy, was astute enough to reach understandings with you and Governor Rockefeller in 1960.

At no time before or during or immediately following the convention did you move effectively to restore the unity of the party. You certainly knew the Hershey conference had failed to do so. Points of principle raised in discussion were not resolved, nor did the conference have any apparent influence on the campaign.

Many in the party detected intransigence in your attitudes before, during and after the 1964 convention, culminating in your acceptance speech, which, among other things, said:

"Any who join us in all sincerity, we welcome. Those who do not care for our cause we do not expect to enter our ranks in any case."

Indeed, the conduct of the campaign and the November 3 election results demonstrated that your campaign never effectively deviated from the Southern-rural-white orientation. Preconvention discussion and post-election discussions with some who were active in your campaign brought to my attention distressing evidence that this was part of the strategy.

Now, Barry, I do not assert you were aware of this strategy or the author of it. I frankly can't believe you shaped it. You didn't read the platform adopted in San Francisco and you didn't know what amendments were being offered on the floor, so you were obviously leaving many vital things almost entirely up to others, vital things about which you were not personally informed. This may account for your inability to see the inconsistencies I tried so hard to help you recognize.

However, for these philosophical, moral, and strategic reasons, I was never able to endorse you during the campaign. Of course, millions did because they believed your leadership would inspire a rebirth of Americanism and a strengthening of constitutional government.

I, too, am one dedicated to these objectives, but I know they cannot be realized if foundation principles of American freedom are compromised. The chief cornerstone of our freedom is divinely endowed citizenship for all equally, regardless of pigmentation, creed, or race.

It is true I said on the "Face the Nation" television interview that I did not endorse you because I was not willing to compromise one iota the principles I fought for in San Francisco. But this did not make it "rather clear that you expected me and others to compromise theirs," as you assert. I have never suggested that to you or anyone else.

One reason I was so anxious to talk with you in depth before the convention was because I felt sure we would be in agreement in principle on the above issues and others, providing there was adequate opportunity to discuss them, but I was denied this opportunity until it was too late.

Now, I realize that our busy schedules contributed to the problem, but I sincerely tried over a nine-month period to arrange a discussion. Our relatively public meetings were hardly appropriate "to bury our differences," as you put it. So, if our positions were really closer than it appeared, all I can say is that I made my position known on many occasions and did my best to discuss them with you personally and in depth.

As to the governmental centralization, we do share a common apprehension and concern. But then you ask me, "Where were you, George, when the chips were down and the going was hard?" Well, Barry, for a long time I've been right on the firing line.

All Republicans (and, I believe, most Americans) are increasingly concerned about constant centralization, but many of us believe we must have a positive rather than negative approach to this increased federal control.

At San Francisco, I offered a detailed program for stronger state and local government cooperation and activity, plus recommendations that could result in a recovery of certain functions from federal control. On behalf of the Republican Governors' Association, I urged the Resolutions Committee to adopt these proposals. For the most part, the recommendations were ignored by the committee and in your campaign.

In Michigan, I entered public life to help modernize Michigan state and local government as an essential step in slowing and reversing the constant flow of responsibility to Washington. It is futile to talk about stopping centralization and the eventual nullification of our Constitution without removing the antiquated obstacles at the state and local level that prevent meeting the needs of the people effectively in the right place.

I do not believe we can prevent unsound solutions to current problems by sheer opposition. My experience convinces me we must present sound solutions based on applying our proven principles to current problems in the development of specific, positive programs.

Only in this way can we stop the adoption of unsound national programs to fill personal, private, local, state, and national vacuums. For instance, talk about states' rights will not be an adequate substitute for state responsibility. We are beginning to prove in Michigan, and in some other states, what it takes to deal with centralism.

In light of your recent public statements joining me with Nelson Rockefeller, may I point out that at no time did I publicly or privately say or do anything to create "the bomb scare" or "Social Security scare." I never discussed them. Nor was I part of any stop-Goldwater effort before or at the convention.

Finally, this has been a difficult letter to write. It is all too apparent that we have differing interpretations of the events of this hectic year. What I have tried to do is to answer your questions about the past. Having done so, I—as I believe you are—am much more concerned with the party's future than its past.

Just as I believed in full and frank discussion of intraparty differences (and agreements) before the election, I believe in it now. The sooner we can get together and discuss the recovery of the GOP, the better. The sooner we can get together with others, as well, the better.

Your agreement with the statement of principles and unifying recommendations adopted by the Republican Governors' Association bodes well for productive, future conversations. I urge your early, direct public endorsement of it.

I also urge you to take the initiative in calling the leadership-planning-group meeting that is recommended instead of fighting the implementation of that hopeful agreement. This would be constructive and a big step in the right direction.

The real challenge for us lies in the expansion of voter support for the Republican Party in all parts of the country, urban or rural, North or South, colored or white. Without common dedication to this fundamental, our rehash of 1964 positions may become of interest only to the historians of defunct political institutions.

I believe an intraparty leadership conference representing all elements of the party is essential to unifying and strengthening it. Based on our experience at the Denver Governors' Conference, I know it will take a schedule that provides adequate time for the frank, sincere, searching discussion that is essential in resolving misunderstanding and hammering out agreement on principles and programs.

The Denver conference is the only one in which I have participated involving representative party leadership from any party segment where such a procedure was used and such a result achieved.

It was a significant accomplishment to arrive at unanimous agreement in a group representing the diversity in viewpoint of a Paul Fannin and Nelson Rockefeller. It was also significant that a preponderant majority exercised restraint and did not force their position into the approved statement contrary to the views of a significant minority.

I hope you will actively support the Denver recommendations designed to achieve needed national leadership agreement and understanding. I regret such a leadership conference could not be convened ahead of the Chicago meeting of the National Committee. This I advocated but reluctantly abandoned as being impossible considering the time problem.

You may be sure I am prepared at any time to meet with you or other party leaders to increase our effectiveness in strengthening our party for the essential task it faces of arousing the nation to the developing national crisis and providing the programs that will get us back on the road to realizing America's divine destiny.

Barry, from a personal standpoint as well as a party standpoint, I wish the past year had turned out differently so I could have followed my personal attitude toward you as a friend and endorsed you.

Lenore joins me in wishing the new year will be one of health and happiness for you and Peggy and your loved ones.

Sincerely,

George Romney

Senator Goldwater did not reply to the letter, and the matter appeared to be settled. Governor Romney busied himself with running Michigan, preparing for the 1966 gubernatorial race, and trying to acquire familiarity with such increasingly important international issues as the Vietnam War.

SIXTEEN

Winning with Coattails—1966

On August 2, 1964, the Johnson Administration announced that three North Vietnamese torpedo boats had attacked the U. S. destroyer *Maddox,* which was on patrol in international waters about thirty miles off the coast in the Gulf of Tonkin. The next day, President Johnson ordered the Navy to send another destroyer to patrol with the *Maddox* and ordered the Navy to tell the commanders of the destroyers and combat aircraft "to attack any force which attacks them in international waters, and to attack with the object not only of driving off the force but of destroying it."

That incident set the stage for approval of the Gulf of Tonkin resolution in the Senate, but President Johnson's campaign was based upon the claim that we had "proved that we could stand firm in the defense of freedom" while "we patiently labored to open new avenues of peace." He said he would not send American boys into a land war in Vietnam, and he left the clear impression that Barry Goldwater was a "trigger-happy" irresponsible figure who would put the United States into a full-scale war in Southeast Asia.

Despite his assertions that his Administration patiently labored to open new avenues of peace, President Johnson felt it necessary in 1965 to take essentially the same steps he had warned that a Barry Goldwater might take. In early February, the United States combat role in the Vietnam War was widened as President Johnson ordered carrier-based fighter planes to bomb and strafe the Dong Hoi military base in North Vietnam in retaliation for a Viet Cong guerrilla attack on a United States installation at Pleiku, in South Vietnam.

More than 3,500 Marines landed in South Vietnam in the second week in March to guard the strategic U. S. Air Force base at Danang. Although President Johnson told a press conference on March 13 that "our policy is still the same" as established by President Eisenhower and President Kennedy, there was no doubt that there had been a significant escalation of the United States' role.

The President's April 7 offers for "unconditional discussions" to end the war in Vietnam were rejected by North Vietnam, the Soviet Union, and Communist China. The air war intensified in late April, and by May 9 the Defense Department said that the United States had a total of 42,200 men in Vietnam. By mid-June, the Defense Department announced that more Army and Marine troops had been sent into South Vietnam and the total was estimated at more than 70,000 men.

By the time the Fifty-seventh Annual National Governors' Conference convened in Minneapolis, Minnesota, in late June, the American commitment in Vietnam had become an issue of some significance. President Johnson wanted the bipartisan support of the nation's Governors to buttress his own political position.

On the morning of June 28, 1965, the Governors interrupted their proceedings to watch a press conference in which President Johnson explained his position on Vietnam. Governor Carl E. Sanders, a Georgia Democrat, immediately offered a resolution to put the Governors' Conference "on record in support of the

President of the United States and the policy he has just announced."

Oregon Governor Mark Hatfield, who had been critical of the President's policies in Vietnam, wanted a clarification of just what the Sanders resolution meant. "If it [the resolution] says we want a strong America, standing up to Communist aggression, I can be in full support. But if we are talking about techniques and manner in which the war is being waged in Vietnam, I am not in favor."

Sanders declared that his resolution was "not about techniques, but about one nation in support of one President in the effort to protect the Free World in Vietnam. I am not trying to say anything about escalation or nuclear weapons."

Governor Hatfield was not satisfied that the resolution was specific. He did not want to sign a "blank check" on Vietnam, and Governor Romney had the same reservations.

"For some time now, the information we have been receiving on Vietnam has obviously not been accurate," Governor Romney said during the debate on the resolution. "We've had optimistic predictions that have not been borne out."

The Michigan Governor noted that President Johnson had invited the Governors to come to the White House for a briefing on the Vietnam War, and he expressed the opinion that it would be best for the Governors to wait until after the briefing before voting endorsement of the Johnson Administration's policies.

"I have no way of knowing if the course of action the President has taken is right or wrong," Romney said. "I hope it is right, but the lack of information is disturbing. He told us nothing new that would indicate why he had taken the course he has."

Romney argued that any actions by the Governors would be much more significant after they had been briefed at the White House. He submitted an amendment to the Sanders resolution to try to postpone any action until after the White House briefing. Although most of the Republicans voted for the Romney amendment, it was defeated in a voice vote.

Only Romney and Hatfield dissented on the vote on the resolution pledging support of President Johnson's actions in Vietnam. Following the briefing at the White House the next day, Governor Romney indicated that he now felt he could voice general sup- port for the Johnson Administration's action in Vietnam.

In October, Governor Romney, accompanied by other Gover- nors, traveled to Japan and then to Vietnam for a firsthand look at the war. Romney and the other Governors had conferred with Gen. William C. Westmoreland and other United States and South Viet- namese officials. Romney's State Department escort officer on the trip was Dr. Jonathan Moore, a protégé of Assistant Secretary of State William Bundy and the son of Charles O. Moore, a retired vice-president of the Ford Motor Company and a former consult- ant to New York Governor Rockefeller. When the trip was over, Governor Romney reiterated his general support for President Johnson's policies in Vietnam.

There were approximately 150,000 American servicemen in Vietnam at the time of Governor Romney's visit in the fall of 1965, and the number was to increase steadily as one Administra- tion prediction after another went astray. By mid-January 1966, Governor Romney had serious doubts about where the Johnson Administration policies were taking the nation. On January 15, 1966, he declared that President Johnson's State of the Union Mes- sage had "failed to deal with the tough problems" on either the international or the domestic front.

With regard to Vietnam, Romney said some difficult decisions had to be made relative to further commitment in Vietnam: "If we should face the alternative of further military commitment in South Vietnam to the point where it ceases to be a support of South Vietnam's defensive efforts to resist and drive the aggressors out, and it's going to become an American war, we should follow con- stitutional procedures." He explained that he meant that there should be debate in Congress and formal consideration of a declar- ation of war if the United States were to change its role as he understood it.

By mid-February, Governor Romney was critical of the proce- dures followed by the Johnson Administration. On February 12, he declared: "We have taken major steps in escalating our position in Vietnam without adequate confrontation with the Congress and the people." He insisted that the Vietnam policy "does not have the degree of public understanding it should have," and added that we have failed in our foreign policy ventures because "we have largely tried to buy the favor of the world with material handouts and military strength."

On June 13, 1966, Romney appeared on the CBS program "Face the Nation" and emerged sounding like a hawk. He commented that it was ridiculous for the United States to be bombing trucks carrying gasoline from North Vietnam while placing restrictions on bombing the oil-storage facilities near Haiphong. The Michigan Governor questioned whether the United States should ever have permitted itself to be pulled into a land war in Southeast Asia in the first place. However, having raised his doubts about the initial involvement, Romney went on to declare that after making the decision to commit American men, there should be an adequate policy in terms of military results. As Romney saw it, there was neither "an adequate policy in terms of military results nor an adequate policy in terms of negotiated settlement."

"I don't think that you can bring the North Vietnamese to the bargaining table by simply saying that you are going to demonstrate to them that they can't win," Romney said. "Now, I think they have to be confronted with the fact that they are going to lose."

The Romney position was not unlike that of Senator Richard Russell, the Georgia Democrat who headed the Senate Armed Services Committee, or Senator John Stennis, the Mississippi Democrat who headed the Senate Preparedness Subcommittee. Both Senators had seriously questioned whether the United States should have become involved in the Vietnam War. However, after the Johnson Administration made the decision that it was "in the national interest," both Senator Russell and Senator Stennis gave total support to the Vietnam War, and their major criticisms involved the restrictive bombing policies and limited response that they felt hampered the United States war machine and gave away the advantage to the North Vietnamese.

When the 1966 Fifty-eighth Annual National Governors' Conference convened in July in Los Angeles, Governor Romney said, "There is ample reason to wonder if the people of South Vietnam really want us" (in their country). He did not suggest United States withdrawal, but declared that the recent escalation, including the bombing of oil-storage depots, had increased the possibility of a major war with Communist China and the Soviet Union.

Another Democratic effort to obtain broad endorsement for President Johnson's policies in Vietnam was put aside after it appeared that a bitter partisan battle might develop. Vice President Hubert H. Humphrey appeared before the Governors as the leading spokesman for the Johnson Administration. He declared that the United States was "gaining on all major fronts." In a news conference he said the "North Vietnamese and the Viet Cong will be defeated."

"I do think there are flickering bits of evidence that are not solid or concrete that Hanoi spokesmen are wandering around wondering if there is some way out," Humphrey said.

Romney charged the Administration with "fundamental mistakes" and said he was more and more concerned over the trend in the war. He said he was flatly opposed to a "blank-check" resolution for Vietnam or any other place.

Texas Governor John B. Connally, Jr., a friend of President Johnson, was a key figure in presenting the initial resolution that would have endorsed "containment of Communist aggression in Southeast Asia" and said it was "initiated under the Eisenhower Administration and honored and implemented by the Kennedy and Johnson Administrations."

Republicans insisted that this entire paragraph be eliminated, and in its place there be a simple statement in support of a "bipartisan American foreign policy continuing through four Presidents' Administrations."

The other major change demanded by the Republicans was in the final paragraph. The original draft by the Democrats had stated: "This conference affirms to the President and the American public, the servicemen and women of the military forces of the United States and our allies, our absolute support of our global commitments and the policy presently being followed to honor them."

As revised, the word "absolute" was changed to "resolute," and the sentence was ended after "commitments," leaving it only an affirmation of support of "our servicemen in Vietnam" and "our global commitments."

In the course of less than a year, Governor Romney had swung away from the cautious general support he had voiced after his trip to Vietnam to one of sharp criticism of the manner in which the war was being fought.

Even before Romney's campaign for reelection as Governor was well under way, he was pushed into the national political arena by New York Governor Rockefeller. Governor Rockefeller announced in early June that he was out of the presidential race "forever." He suggested a 1968 ticket headed by Governor Romney and Senator Jacob Javits of New York.

Governor Romney shrugged off the talk of a Romney-Javits ticket as "pure speculation" and declared that "the first thing Republicans have to do is make a comeback in 1966." It could have been that he also remembered the disasters that seemed to plague those who had been front runners for the Republican nomination, including Governor Rockefeller.

Among the professional politicians, former Vice President Richard Nixon had considerable popularity as a result of friendships built up over the years in national politics and particularly for his work for the national ticket in 1964. In April 1966, the Gallup Poll gave Nixon 27 percent of the Republican vote—double the 14 percent registered for Governor Romney. Although Romney showed some gains over the summer, without doubt Nixon was the most popular among Republicans and particularly among Republican organization people.

A Gallup Poll taken in August showed increasing public interest in Romney as a result of his activity on the national political scene. While Nixon still led Romney by a margin of 55 to 40 among Republican voters, with 5 percent undecided, Nixon had only a narrow 44 to 43 margin among independent voters, with 13 percent undecided. Among Democrats, Romney was favored over Nixon by a margin of 50 to 36, with 14 percent undecided.

Romney's demonstrated political strength in Michigan did not impress many of the Republican regulars any more than it impressed the loyal Goldwater men, who resented the attention the Michigan Governor was receiving. Romney was unorthodox. He was not a team player, complained Republicans who noted that he had run virtually without a party label in 1962 and had failed to endorse the Goldwater-Miller ticket in 1964. Romney's victory margin in 1964 was discounted because he had not pulled other Republicans into office with him.

Representative Melvin Laird, of Wisconsin, a devoted Nixon supporter, declared that Romney would have to be given serious consideration only if he was able to elect Senator Robert Griffin, who was running in Michigan against the well-known and popular former Governor G. Mennen Williams.

Governor Romney and his supporters bristled at such comments, and there were many, because they seemed to handicap Romney unfairly in the race for the Republican nomination. Duplication of the 380,000-vote victory of 1964 was all that should have been expected, in Romney's view. Although he and his supporters felt it unfair for political figures and columnists to burden him with a handicap, he went to work with his Romney Action Team to try to do what some Republicans considered impossible in the face of the organizational strength of the AFL-CIO and the UAW in Michigan.

In the summer and fall of 1966, Governor Romney traveled all about the country making new political contacts, ran the State of Michigan, and conducted as vigorous a campaign as had ever been waged. It was a team action to prove that he was not "Lonesome George." Romney appeared on the platform with all the other Republicans, praising them, endorsing them, and cooperating with them in joint political advertising. As usual, he was a tireless campaigner, and he ended the wearing weeks on the stump with a last-minute blitz that left his younger colleagues and his opponent, Zolton A. Ferency, swinging futilely.

Both the *Detroit News* and the *Detroit Free Press* endorsed Romney for his third term as Governor of Michigan. The *Free Press* declared: "By any objective standard, George Romney is the clear choice. He has been an excellent Governor for two terms now, and if he is willing to take on a third term, the people should be eager to ink his contract."

The October 24, 1966, *Free Press* editorial paid tribute to the "good job of campaigning" done by Zolton Ferency, the young lawyer drafted by the Democratic Party for the unenviable job of opposing Romney. Although Ferency was praised as an articulate speaker and witty debater, the *Free Press* concluded that he "had three strikes against him" in a race against Romney.

Ferency had been unable to generate any debate over issues "simply because there aren't any genuine issues in the gubernatorial campaign."

"He [Ferency] has tried to deny that George Romney, in his almost four years as Governor, has changed Michigan from Michigan on the rocks to Michigan on the march. But the facts counter him," the *Free Press* said. "He has tried to argue that any Governor could have taken a state from a deficit to a $167-million surplus, given the booming national economy. But the Democratic Administration in Washington hasn't done it, and neither has any other Governor in the nation produced such a showing."

The *Free Press* said Ferency had attempted to portray Romney as an enemy of the little guy who has built up the surplus at the expense of the needy.

"But the facts are that our workmen's compensation program, among the last in the nation four years ago, is now the leader," the *Free Press* noted. "We have for the first time a minimum-wage law and a construction-safety law. And these are only a few of many."

The *Free Press* questioned the judgment of Ferency in fiscal matters. "In a boom year, he said, in which tax collections are high, he would spend it all and save nothing for a rainy day. When the rainy day came, he would propose deficit financing. The workmen's compensation law, he says, is only half of what he wanted. He blames Romney for its not being better. Yet it is the most generous in the nation. Ferency, apparently, would give the whole state away."

In concluding as laudatory an editorial as could be written about any candidate, the *Free Press* said Romney had been "an excellent

Governor, one of the best. He has balanced human needs with financial possibilities. He has increased almost every aspect of Michigan's duty to its people, while at the same time strengthening the state economically. He has made Michigan a better place in which to live, work, and do business."

The *Free Press* was willing to accept the fact that Romney might have presidential aspirations for 1968 that could cut his term in half. "It would hardly be realistic to hold that against him, especially since he has more than fulfilled his commitments to the state," the *Free Press* said. "And if he succeeds, Lt. Gov. William Milliken would be a worthy successor."

It was significant that the *Free Press* and the *Detroit News* were equally laudatory in speaking of Romney's accomplishments as Governor, for these were large newspapers with a real stake in the stability of Michigan and with the insight into Michigan government that can only come by living with the problems from day to day.

Disillusionment with the Johnson Administration permeating the nation as the 1966 election approached gave added impetus to the campaign Governor Romney was directing on behalf of all the Republican candidates. In the final *Detroit News* poll published on November 6, 1966, Governor Romney had what poll expert Richard W. Oudersluys called "a margin of landslide proportions."

The *Detroit News* poll indicated that there had been some swing to Ferency after the mid-October poll had indicated that Romney would receive a whopping 64 percent of the votes. The October poll gave Ferency only 33 percent of the votes. The poll taken the week before the election and published the Sunday before the election gave Romney 61 percent of the votes and Ferency 36 percent.

The polls indicated that Romney's tremendous popularity would probably elect a Republican United States Senator and several new Republican congressmen. Under the new Michigan constitution, Romney and the Republican candidate for Lieutenant Governor were linked together on the ballot, and a Romney win was to mean an automatic win for William G. Milliken.

While Romney was demonstrating the much-needed coattail

strength in many races, he was failing in two races for state office in which the Democratic candidates were well known and had some personal appeal of their own. Lawrence B. (Larry) Lindemer, former Republican state chairman and a Romney intimate, was trailing behind Democratic Attorney General Frank J. Kelley by 39 to 54 percent in the final poll. Likewise, George Washington, the Negro nominated by the Republicans for Secretary of State, was trailing the Democratic incumbent, James M. Hare, by a margin of 35 to 59 percent of the vote.

The poll showed that Washington, the first Negro ever nominated by the Republicans for state office, and Lindemer led the incumbent Democrats "only among predominantly white rural voters." Both trailed by large margins among Negro voters and among trade-union members.

Romney was outpolling Ferency in every category except Negroes and union members, and even among the Negroes he had boosted his percentage from 37 to 43 percent. He held steady with about 46 percent of the union members, which was astounding in the light of all the AFL-CIO and UAW money and effort that had been put behind the Democratic ticket.

When the votes were counted on November 8, 1966, Governor George Romney had done better than anyone had expected of him. The evangelistic Republican polled 1,524,583 votes, compared with 956,135 for the Democratic candidate, Ferency. In piling up that 568,000-vote margin he was able to win approximately 50 percent of the labor vote, and more than 34 percent of the Negro vote. Senator Griffin owed his election over former Governor Williams to the coattail strength of Governor Romney, and so did five new Republican House members.

George Romney had accomplished what he had set out to do as well as any man could do it, and on the basis of the statistics alone he merited the most serious consideration as the Republican presidential candidate in 1968. In an election which had pushed many new Republican names to the front, Governor Romney seemed to be the most credible as a presidential candidate. He did not have former Vice President Richard Nixon's two election losses to overcome. He had more in the way of age and experience than Senator-elect Charles Percy, 47, of Illinois, or Senator-elect Mark Hatfield, 44, who had served two terms as Governor of Oregon. He did not have the race handicap that was a practical barrier for Senator-elect Edward Brooke, of Massachusetts. He did not carry the handicap of a career as an actor that made it difficult for many to visualize California Governor-elect Ronald Reagan as a presidential candidate.

Governor Romney did have a handicap almost as great as any carried by the other 1966 victors, for he had stepped on the sensitive toes of many conservative Republicans. And in his file the exchange of correspondence with Senator Goldwater was a constant reminder of an old bitterness which could flare into the open at any moment and seriously damage his presidential aspirations.

SEVENTEEN

Front Runner—
A Precarious Role

On the strength of the landslide victory in 1966, George Romney was hailed as the Golden Boy of Republican politics. His standing in the polls soared, and major magazine articles dealt with him as the front runner. It was expected in Michigan, where Romney boosters were chanting, "Romney's Great—in Sixty-eight" long before the votes were counted. Even Republican Party officials, with a personal preference for former Vice President Nixon, found Romney's winning image appealing. It was difficult to argue with the Michigan win and the manner in which Romney had climbed in the polls.

Even before the election, the last Gallup Poll had indicated that Romney had the best chance to defeat President Johnson. That poll showed Romney lagging by only two points, at 49 percent to 51 percent. In another Gallup Poll Romney had forged ahead of Nixon among Republican voters by a 39-to-31-percent margin.

The Louis Harris Poll taken just after the election rated Romney as a 54-to-46-percent favorite over President Johnson, considerably the best showing by any Republican when matched against the President.

Governor Romney had become the man to beat, and in that respect he became the target of not only the conservatives but also the supporters of all of the other aspirants.

Within weeks after election, it was announced that a Romney-for-President headquarters would be opened in Washington, D. C., in early 1967. The question was being asked: Is it possible to stop the Romney drive and the "bandwagon" psychology which seemed to be developing?

Possibly the leaders of the conservative wing of the Republican Party could band together to try to wreck Romney, and they would almost certainly have a helping hand from the more liberal Republicans, who wanted to keep the 1968 Republican Convention an open fight in the hopes of landing the nomination.

But as Governor Romney was emerging with popular appeal, questions were raised about his ability to handle foreign-affairs issues, and particularly the sticky political problem of the Vietnam War. Those questions were to be raised with increasing frequency as the months moved by, but the major question in December 1966 became Romney's relations with Senator Goldwater.

Romney's popularity seemed to be at a peak less than a month after the election when the old fuss with Goldwater suddenly emerged again. Romney's twelve-page letter to Goldwater, written on December 21, 1964, was leaked to the *New York Times*, and all the old wounds plus some new ones were opened.

The questions arose immediately: Had Goldwater or his supporters leaked the letter to put a crimp in Romney's bandwagon, or had the Romney forces leaked it to air the problem as early as possible and get it out of the way? Both Governor Romney's office and Goldwater's political aides made flat denials of any knowledge of how the Romney letter got to the *New York Times*.

The Romney letter was printed in the *New York Times* on November 29, 1966, and subsequently the Goldwater letter to Romney and the hitherto unavailable transcript of the August 12, 1964, "unity conference" at Hershey, Pennsylvania, were published.

An almost immediate decline in Romney's popularity resulted in the *Baltimore Sun*'s story on December 4 that "George W. Romney's glittering triumph . . . has lost some of its luster."

In addition to the expected bitterness from Goldwater supporters, a new problem was created by Romney's allegation that the Republican Platform Committee had been involved in some "deal" with "southern segregationists" with regard to the civil-rights plank in the 1964 platform.

"The charge is amazing to me," said Representative Melvin Laird of Wisconsin, who served as chairman of the Resolutions Committee that drafted the platform. Laird pointed out that the civil-rights plank had been drafted under the direction of Representative William M. McCulloch, the Ohio Republican who had been a sponsor of the 1964 civil-rights law.

"I am certain there was no deal," Laird said. "Bill McCulloch is the leading authority in our party on civil rights. He does not make 'deals.' "

Representative McCulloch, the ranking Republican on the House Judiciary Committee, declared "there was no 'deal' with anyone." He said he was never approached by Senator Goldwater or any southern delegates, and that neither Senator Goldwater nor any southern delegates had anything to do with the wording of the civil-rights plank.

"The language of the civil-rights plank is broad and comprehensive, and carries on even now as adequate to the needs of our times," the Ohio Republican said.

Governor Romney declined to identify the individuals involved in the alleged deal, and the matter was dropped, but it left a sour taste with a number of members of the Republican convention committees involved in the writing and approval of the civil-rights plank. Some of them were moderate Republicans who would have had little problem in accommodating to Governor Romney's brand of Republicanism.

Although the problems created by the Goldwater fuss were to persist, Governor Romney paid little attention to them and went about the business of creating a nationwide political organization while engaging in a hectic schedule of speeches. He used the same blunt approach in North Carolina, New York, or Colorado that had served him so well in Michigan. In Charlotte, North Carolina, he told a Chamber of Commerce dinner group that "as far as I am concerned, states have no rights. Only people have rights."

"I know that some of those who shout the loudest about states' rights are laggards in state responsibility," Romney told the Southern audience. "Obstructionism masquerading as states' rights is the height of folly."

In New York to address the National Association of Manufacturers in December, Governor Romney declared that he found that organization had improved over the years and was now "less obstructionist" than a few years earlier when, under his leadership, American Motors had resigned from the organization.

In spite of some drop in the polls, George Romney was riding high as 1967 opened, and there seemed to be plenty of time to do the work on problems confronting the Michigan Governor. The problems as they existed in January and February were difficult, but they did not seem unsurmountable for a man of Romney's energy and eighteen months before the 1968 Republican Convention. To assure winning the Republican nomination, Romney had to do these little chores:

1. Create a national political organization among moderate and liberal Republicans to break through the large network of Nixon supporters within the Republican organizational structure. While Romney was most popular with voters as a whole, Nixon still held a margin of about two to one among Republican functionaries.

2. Woo Barry Goldwater and the conservative wing to move them to a position of neutrality rather than one of armed aggressive resistance. This required personal contact with Goldwater and the type of in-depth informal discussions Romney and Goldwater did not have in 1964.

3. Establish a reputation for competence in discussing foreign-affairs issues, particularly Vietnam. Some fumbling with the Vietnam issue at the Governors' Conference in Los Angeles in June 1966 had resulted in a rash of news stories and columns comment-

ing on his "confusion" and questioning his ability to handle the issue in a tough campaign.

4. Achieve the long-sought tax reform in Michigan, including a 2.5 percent individual income tax, a 5 percent income tax on business, and an 8 percent income tax on banks and financial institutions. The booming automobile sales and a rising economy in Michigan had shielded Romney from tax troubles, but new state services had boosted the budget for fiscal year 1968 to a record $1.153 billion, and an additional $331.4 million in taxes were needed. Although Michigan's budget projected a small surplus for the fiscal year ending June 30, 1967, estimates pointed to a $182 million deficit in fiscal 1968. The new Michigan constitution barred deficit spending, so new taxes were essential unless there was a sharp cutback in some state services. The issue was loaded with political hazards.

In January 1967, Romney started to put together the political team he hoped would deliver the Republican presidential nomination. The team included Leonard W. Hall, the former Republican national chairman, who was to head the Romney-for-President Committee in Washington. Robert J. McIntosh, a former Congressman from Port Huron, Michigan, was to be the number-two man on the Romney-for-President Committee. Richard C. Van Dusen, a wealthy Detroit lawyer and close personal friend, served as a legal adviser and as a personal confidant.

The leading financial supporters of the Romney drive were J. Willard Marriott, an old friend from Washington, D. C., who owned the Marriott Motor Hotels and Hot Shoppes restaurants; John Clifford Folger, of Washington, a Nixon fund-raiser in 1960; and Max M. Fisher, a wealthy Detroit industrialist.

His press entourage eventually included William G. Murphy, former secretary to Governor William Scranton in Pennsylvania; Travis O. Cross, a former assistant to Oregon Governor Mark Hatfield before Hatfield was elected to the Senate; Charles E. Harmon, formerly a reporter for the Booth Newspapers in Michigan; and Jack Vandenburg, a former Washington reporter for the United Press and a former state capitol correspondent at Lansing. Richard

L. Milliman, formerly Romney's press secretary, took leave of absence from his job as publisher of the Mt. Pleasant, Michigan, newspaper to work as a speech writer for the Lansing political organization known as Romney Associates.

Lawrence B. Lindemer, the former Michigan Republican chairman, was assigned the job of coordinating the midwestern states. Dr. Walter B. DeVries, an associate of Romney's since serving as a delegate to the Michigan constitutional convention, also had major chores as researcher and speech writer in Romney Associates.

Other key figures in Romney Associates included S. John Byington, a lawyer-pharmacist who was Romney's campaign manager in the 1962 gubernatorial campaign; L. William Seidman, a well-to-do operator of a Grand Rapids accounting firm; and Dr. Jonathan Moore, a foreign-policy expert who was a fellow at the Institute of Politics of the John F. Kennedy School of Government at Harvard. Dr. Moore, then a special assistant to the Secretary of State for Far Eastern Affairs, was Romney's escort officer when Governor Romney visited Vietnam in October 1965.

Dr. William B. Prendergast, formerly director of research at the Republican National Committee and for the House Republican Conference, was named in mid-1967 as research director of the Romney-for-President Committee.

Though George Romney tried to avoid labels throughout his political career, he found himself aligned most of the time with the so-called liberal wing of the Republican Party. In dodging labels, he was often heard to say, "I am as conservative as the Constitution, as liberal as Lincoln, and as progressive as Theodore Roosevelt before the Bull Moose Movement."

The Michigan Governor might have added that he was also as energetic as Teddy Roosevelt, one of his boyhood heroes. He plunged into national politics in early 1967 with a vigor that would have done justice to Roosevelt on his most unrestrained health binge. Although he was approaching the age of sixty, Romney set a schedule for himself in February 1967 that would have broken many a younger man.

In a week-long western tour, Romney whipped through six states on the same kind of tight schedule expected in a presidential campaign. According to his aides in Romney Associates, the swing through Washington, Alaska, Utah, Idaho, Albuquerque, and Phoenix had a threefold purpose. It was to give Romney and his staff some practical experience in the planning of a national campaign, to give Romney an opportunity to become better acquainted with national political writers, to test himself at a series of press conferences, and to give him an opportunity to make contact with political leaders far in advance of the heat of the 1968 political year and to see what kind of personal commitment and rapport might be forthcoming.

The 8,500-mile western tour included a chance to confer with Washington Governor Daniel J. Evans on Friday, February 17, and an opportunity to forge a close political link with Alaska Governor Walter J. Hickel. In the twenty-four-hour period in Anchorage, Romney won the highest praise from Governor Hickel, who told six hundred Republicans at a fund-raising dinner that "there is no question whether he [Romney] should decide to run for President. It is the duty of every American citizen to convince him that he should run."

It was interpreted by reporters as the most open endorsement Romney had received since New York Governor Rockefeller had spoken out in early January. Governor Hickel also pledged that he would line up help for Romney in the twelve-member delegation Alaska would send to the Republican Convention, despite the fact that he said former Vice President Nixon could probably win a state convention endorsement if it were put to a vote at that time. Governor Hickel described Romney as being "knowledgeable, competent, but not too political."

Reaching back into his years as the Rambler salesman, Romney on Saturday night told the Anchorage audience that "the Great Society is just the New Deal turned into a gas-guzzling dinosaur."

On Sunday, February 19, Romney did not engage in political campaigning, but he and Mrs. Romney spoke before the Alaska Stake of the Mormon Church.

Many of the thirty reporters who accompanied Romney on the western tour found it difficult to tell the difference between his evangelistic political speeches and his religious discussions before the more than 850 members of the Mormon Church, dealing with the problems of social justice for the slums and the need for "respect for law" while attacking the slum problem.

"We must accelerate our progress in conformity with the law," Governor Romney told the Mormon audience comprising one fifth of the total Mormon church membership in Alaska. Mrs. Lenore Romney also spoke, and her theme was the usual one dealing with the need for higher moral standards and religious training as well as more personal involvement in cleaning up the slums.

Governor and Mrs. Romney and their press entourage arrived in Salt Lake City on Monday, February 20, and it was a warm homecoming for the local boy who had earned wealth and a national reputation.

Chauffeur for the occasion was his boyhood friend, Occie Evans, who had taken a fling at professional baseball before returning to the hometown of Salt Lake, where he was serving as a deputy sheriff. Romney and Occie Evans had played football and basketball together in high school, and it was Occie who had first introduced George to Lenore.

"George was just the same fellow he's always been," Evans said later. "Every time he comes out here, a few of us get together, and he and Lenore are just like they always were. There is none of this big-shot stuff with him."

In Salt Lake, Romney attended a family dinner in the home of Mrs. Amy Pratt Romney, his aunt and stepmother. He also made a social call on the 94-year-old David O. McKay, president of the Mormon Church, and spoke before a group of Protestant and Catholic clergymen at a Catholic mission hall.

Governor Romney assured the clergymen that there was nothing in the Mormon religion to prevent him from a full effort to combat racial discrimination and prejudice. "If there were, I would not belong to it," Romney said, "but that is not the case."

The Michigan Governor was questioned about the doctrine of the Mormon Church which permits Negroes to become members, but bars them from the priesthood that is required for lay leadership and for admission to the Mormon Temple.

He declined to discuss the doctrine of his church, but said, "My faith has influenced me to believe . . . that every human being is a child of God as I am . . . and that they should have every opportunity I have. I have fought for twenty-five years in Michigan to eliminate discrimination. I believe I'm entitled to be judged on the basis of my actions, not someone's ideas of what may be the precepts of my church."

When a Negro minister, the Reverend Dr. Palmer S. Ross, asked that Romney "disown" the Mormon position on Negroes, Romney declared that he would resign from the church "if my church prevented me from working to eliminate social injustice and racial discrimination, as I have worked for twenty-five years."

Governor Romney challenged the Reverend Ross or anyone else to "name me one other man in the Republican Party in 1964 who went as far as I did to fight for a complete expression of civil rights in the platform."

Romney addressed the Utah legislature, and two Republican fund-raising dinners, then took a midnight flight to Idaho Falls for a nostalgic visit to his boyhood home in Rexburg. At political meetings in Idaho Falls and Pocatello he tried to win a share of the fourteen delegates that Idaho would send to the Republican Convention.

His religion was an asset in Idaho, where Mormons make up about one fifth of the state population, but he received only a cool reception from Governor Don Samuelson, a conservative with a strong inclination toward former Vice President Nixon or California Governor Ronald Reagan.

While making his tour of Rexburg with reporters and local politicians, he visited the gray stone Washington Grade School where he was eighth-grade valedictorian, and stopped at the Rexall Drugstore. One of the biggest thrills of his youth was going to the drugstore for a banana split, Romney said, and then in a comment totally out of character he added, "While you were there, you probably swiped fifty cents' worth of candy and other stuff." Reporters gasped at the exposure of this questionable activity in his youth.

After Idaho, the Romney party left for Albuquerque, where the Michigan Governor touched base with the new Governor, David J. Cargo, and received as enthusiastic a reception there as he had

in Alaska and Utah. The next day, February 23, Romney invaded
Barry Goldwater's hometown of Phoenix, and considering the
problem of 1964, it was a reasonably warm reception from Republican Governor Jack Williams and Harry Rosenzweig, the Arizona
Republican chairman and a close personal friend and supporter
of Barry Goldwater. Goldwater was out of the city on some long-
standing engagements in Ohio and Washington, but he extended a
hearty welcome to Romney and an invitation to speak at a Republican fund-raising dinner on October 21, 1967.

Romney's speeches in Arizona dealt with the need for national
fiscal reform, and Barry Goldwater could have endorsed everything he said. Rosenzweig told reporters that he did not believe
there was much bitterness left from the 1964 race, and added,
"This is a new ball game." Romney hoped it was as he flew back
to Detroit.

Although Romney tried to patch things up in Arizona by declaring he would work to reelect Goldwater to the United States Senate,
Senator Goldwater told reporters that he had not been able to forget the 1964 campaign and said his traveling around the country
indicated that there were many other Republicans who felt the
same way. Goldwater indicated he would not try to block Romney
from the Republican nomination, but declared himself for Dick
Nixon.

Romney hopped back to Detroit in preparation for meetings
with Senator Charles Percy, the Illinois Republican who was considered one of the best possibilities to pick up the presidential ball
for the moderates if Romney stumbled. In what Romney had believed was an off-the-record talk with reporters, the Michigan Governor used the term "opportunist" in speaking of Senator Percy.

A Detroit newspaper printed the story, and it called for a lot of
explaining by Romney as he prepared for a meeting with the influential young Republican he had hoped to win to his side. Romney
said he did not use the term in the bad meaning of the word, but
meant it as "one who recognizes the right time to act . . . a constructive and useful quality."

As Paul Hope of the *Washington Star* pointed out at the time, the
Romney definition was not in line with Webster's dictionary, which

described an opportunist as one who practices "the art, policy, or practice of taking advantage of opportunities or circumstances, especially with little regard for principles or ultimate consequences."

Despite Romney's problem with word definitions, Senator Percy said he thought Romney's political swing was a success, although he had doubts about the wisdom of such a swing so early in the campaign. While he said it was too early to endorse any candidate, Percy said he admired Romney as a man with "progressive attitudes" who knew how to solve problems.

The western trip was viewed by reporters as having been of mixed value to Romney. It had been generally successful as a method of meeting political leaders and developing pleasant relations. It had served the Romney Associates staff as a shakedown cruise on travel plans, and had given Romney broad exposure to about thirty national political writers.

However, Romney's dealings with the newspapermen and women was hardly an unqualified success, for there had been considerable friction and a lot of news copy over what reporters considered to be inconsistencies in the Michigan Governor's stand on the Vietnam War.

The picture in Vietnam was a changing picture, and Governor Romney had been in enough controversy on the subject in 1965 and 1966 to last him the whole campaign. Prior to the western tour, Dr. Jonathan Moore, his foreign-policy adviser, had suggested that Romney say no more about Vietnam because of the complicated issues that made oversimplification and misunderstanding so easy.

Dr. Moore suggested that Romney say only that it was wrong to get bogged down in a large land war in Asia, that some mistakes had been made by President Johnson, but that the United States had to remain firm until there was an honorable conclusion. It was recommended that Romney suggest only that Republicans had the advantage of being able to take a "fresh look" at the Vietnam problem without the impediment of having been involved in earlier mistakes.

As the trip started, Romney appeared to have followed Dr.

Moore's advice reasonably well, but as time went on, Paul Hope reported in the *Washington Star* that the Michigan Governor "seems almost to have a compulsion to comment on a question even if not to answer it."

In commenting on Vietnam, Romney on one occasion stated critically that Johnson's policies were "ambivalent and completely flexible" and explained that he meant that the President was flitting constantly between emphasis on military drives and peace moves.

Later, Romney declared that the President was locked in a rigid position and had lost his options for the kind of flexibility needed.

Upon completion of the trip, friction had developed with a number of reporters because Romney declined to specify the mistakes he felt had been made by President Johnson, or because he had failed to clarify his position on Vietnam.

The *Detroit Free Press* commented that the Michigan Governor had returned from the tour "with his lean heel exposed." The *Detroit News* declared in an editorial that "even the benefit of hindsight hasn't improved the Governor's logic or his grasp of elementary facts about the Vietnam situation."

Although the Romney ramblings on Vietnam were to create more problems for him in a short time, the Michigan Governor continued as a front runner in many of the polls as the Republican who would be most likely to defeat President Lyndon B. Johnson. However, among Republican voters, Vice President Nixon held a consistent lead.

According to a Gallup Poll published on March 18, 1967, Nixon held a 39-to-30-percent edge over Romney when Republican voters were asked which of seven Republicans they "would like to see nominated" as the candidate in 1968. Nixon held a smaller margin, 39 to 34 percent, when Republican voters were asked which of the seven Republicans "would make the best Presidential candidate" in 1968.

With the choice at the convention narrowed to Nixon and Romney, the Republicans gave Nixon a 53-to-41-percent margin over Romney in March 1967, with 6 percent undecided. This was a sharp contrast to November 1966, when Romney had held a

51-to-42-percent margin over Nixon, with 7 percent undecided.

The Louis Harris Poll of April 24, 1967, indicated Governor Romney would defeat President Johnson, but that the President would defeat Nixon by a margin of 54 to 46 percent. Likewise, a Gallup Poll of the same week showed that although Nixon was stronger with the Republican organization, Romney would rate a much better chance of defeating President Johnson. The Gallup Poll indicated that Nixon and Johnson would run neck and neck, with each receiving 48 percent of the vote, but that Romney would overwhelm Johnson by a margin of 52 to 43 percent of the vote.

Indications were that Romney had lost ground from his peak in November and early December 1966 as a result of the fuss over the exchange of letters with Goldwater, and as a result of news stories and editorials that had painted him as "confused on Vietnam."

Democrats, fully aware that Romney might be the strongest Republican foe, tried to whittle him down to size by placing emphasis on what Senator John Sparkman, the second-ranking Democrat on the Senate Foreign Relations Committee, called Romney's "confusion, frustration, and inconsistency" on foreign affairs. His was only one of many speeches attacking the Michigan Governor, and charging that Romney's criticism of President Johnson was for "purely political purposes."

Although Romney continued to cling to a lead with voters generally, the increased strength registered by former Vice President Nixon served as an ominous warning. Within the Democratic Party an interest increased in getting Romney to move deeper into the treacherous waters of Vietnam policy, for he would either have to back the Johnson Administration or risk the political scorn which had been heaped upon so-called doves.

The month of March 1967 was not a very good period for George Romney. It started with Governor Romney sharing the platform with California Governor Reagan, former Vice President Nixon, Senator Percy, and former Senator Goldwater at a Republican Party fund-raising dinner in Washington, D.C.

Although the Republican gala party pulled a million dollars into the party treasury, it was a flop as far as George Romney was con-

cerned. The sincere Mormon was just out of his element. In the
first place, it was a Republican crowd oriented toward regular
organization people, and the applause for Nixon and Goldwater
was deafening, although they were only introduced. Even more
applause followed the smooth and witty speech by Governor Reagan.

Sincere George should have stuck with his serious lines, for his
ability to tell a joke is limited at best. Even an anti-Johnson audience didn't find it funny when Romney quipped: "LBJ is down at
the ranch riding horseback so he can improve Gallup." The applause was barely polite.

Polls published in March were the first strong indicators that
Romney's comments on Vietnam on his western tour had dam-
aged his image. The dip in Governor Romney's strength came in
the face of a continued upward surge for Nixon, whose supporters
insisted he was better qualified to handle foreign affairs.

By late March, it was apparent things were going wrong for Governor Romney in Michigan. His tax-reform measure was in serious trouble after the state Senate rejected his income-tax proposals
by a vote of 23 to 14. The Republicans had a majority in the
Michigan Senate, but six of the Republicans joined with the
17 Democrats to defeat Romney.

Romney had given the tax measure top priority on his legislative list, and had urged that it be passed by April 1 so it could become effective on July 1, 1967. To emphasize the importance of
early passage, Romney had declared that he would sign no appropriations bills for the next year until he knew where the money
was coming from.

Although hopes for passage of the tax-reform measure looked
bleak, indications were that chances might improve if the Republican Governor could squeeze some additional time out of campaigning for the presidential nomination to tend to Michigan business. Absence from the state and the lack of time to explain the
financial predicament to the voters and whip the Republican conservatives into line were credited as part of the reason for the
March 30, 1967, defeat of his tax-reform measure.

As the polls dropped and the tax-reform crisis grew, Romney

was under increasing pressure to prepare a definitive statement on Vietnam to establish his ability to deal with foreign affairs. Some of the pressure was from friends with genuine belief that a comprehensive statement would make it easier to sell him as presidential timber. Pressure was also applied by Democrats and anti-Romney Republicans who saw the opportunity to get the Michigan Governor hopelessly ensnared in the morass of an insoluble Vietnam mess.

Governor Romney and his top policy advisers ignored warnings of the dangerous area they were invading, as dramatized by the futility and inconsistency of President Johnson, and the long record of misjudgments by Defense Secretary Robert S. McNamara. The President and the Defense Secretary had access to all the information available on Vietnam, and had access to the fact-gathering machinery of the entire Federal Government plus the propaganda machinery of the whole bureaucracy, but they were still in political trouble because they had been unable to devise a salable policy on Vietnam. Much of the problem of the so-called credibility gap arose out of the inconsistencies of the President and the Defense Secretary on this issue.

Yet, Romney, with his meager staff, felt compelled to make a definitive statement on an issue that was shifting month by month and which could swing 180 degrees before the Republican Convention. Romney, with the help of Dr. Moore and others, prepared his statement on Vietnam for delivery on April 7 in Hartford, Connecticut, before a crowd celebrating the 150th year of the *Hartford Times*.

The Romney foreign-policy declaration was long, touched on nearly every aspect of the Vietnam issue, and mingled criticism of the past conduct of the Vietnam War. Romney declared he would "neither give encouragement to Hanoi's aggressive course, nor undermine our President in sincere efforts to bring peace to Vietnam." He declared that it was unthinkable that the United States should withdraw from Vietnam. He also declared that the United States "must use military force as necessary to reduce or cut off the flow of men and supplies from North Vietnam, to knock out enemy main force units, and to provide a military shield for the South.

(See Appendix A for the entire Romney speech at Hartford, Connecticut, on April 7, 1967.)

President Johnson expressed gratitude and appreciation for what he called Romney's "strong endorsement of the Administration's position on Vietnam."

There was considerable editorial applause for the Romney position, and the *Washington Post* said the Michigan Republican should be credited with having skillfully mingled legitimate criticism of past conduct with forthright endorsement of American objectives.

"His [Romney's] most important foreign-policy utterance passes the first test of statesmanship—it offers no quick, easy, painless, or inexpensive solutions for a difficult, complicated, and costly situation," the *Post* said. "It will reassure his friends and give no comfort to his country's enemies."

The *Washington Star*, on April 10, 1967, declared, "The charge of 'fuzziness' in his thinking on the war in Vietnam can no longer fairly be brought against George Romney."

However, some of the news stories flowing from President Johnson's "gratitude" made it appear that Governor Romney was a near total supporter of the Johnson Administration's policies. This was not what Romney wanted. On April 19, the Michigan Governor declared that his statement should not be taken as "blank-check approval" of the Administration's policies.

"I do not consider my Vietnam speech to be a blanket endorsement of the President's program," Romney said. "If the speech is read carefully, it will be seen that I was not indicating blank-check approval of all the methods we've been using."

At least for the moment, it appeared that Romney had been successful in neutralizing the Vietnam issue, and he was ready to deal with the equally knotty problem of tax reform, which was reaching crisis proportions.

"Tax action must be the number-one job of this legislative session," Governor Romney had told the Michigan legislature on January 12. "The inequities and weaknesses of Michigan's tax structure have been documented time and again. . . . The time has come for action. The stark fact is that the cost of state services demanded by the public is outrunning the revenues produced by present taxes."

Complaints that Romney's administration was costly could not be denied because each year had resulted in substantial increases in the budget. His first budget was a $20 million increase over Democratic Governor John Swainson's last budget. From his $550 million start, the Romney budgets had jumped to $684 million, to $820 million, and then to $1,007 million in fiscal 1966, to $1,101 million, and then to a record $1,153 million for fiscal 1968.

"It is not because of state governmental waste, costly frills, duplication, or inefficiency," Romney defended. "Tax-supported services, particularly education, are serving a sky-rocketing population. Michigan has over 200,000 more school-children than just four years ago, and over 100,000 more college students. In addition, the public demands that government do more to deal with crime, mental illness, water and air pollution, hospital and medical care, recreational needs, juvenile delinquency and rehabilitation, poor housing, racial tension, and traffic safety. All of these cost money."

Governor Romney had spelled out other rising costs for wages and equipment and buildings, and he declared that the choice was "whether these new revenues should come from increased rates on present taxes, coupled with a variety of new nuisance taxes, or from an overhaul of the present tax structure."

The Michigan surplus crested at $167 million in July 1966, but it was falling rapidly and was certain to drop below $50 million by July 1, in Romney's estimation. He had insisted that there be action by April 1, but a balky coalition of Democrats and anti-Romney conservative Republicans had rejected his plea. Many of the Democrats wanted to load more taxes on the already heavily taxed corporations doing business in Michigan. Conservative Republicans from wealthy areas were opposed to new individual income taxes, corporate income taxes, and taxes on financial institutions proposed by Romney.

Having failed to get his tax-reform measure through in 1963 and in 1965, he had been saved from crisis by the booming economy and business growth that brought in more taxes, but action was needed.

He had said it before, but Romney declared with more determination in 1967, "I do not intend to sign any appropriation bills for next year until I can see where the money is coming from— until I can see sufficient revenue to meet the costs of government."

The Michigan Republican rejected those who wanted an additional sales tax rather than an income tax, because the sales tax would put a greater burden on low-income groups. He admitted frankly that "low-income families will pay less in state taxes" under his proposal, but he argued that he would also eliminate a business activities tax on gross receipts that had nothing to do with the actual income of large business, and replace it with a corporate income tax related to net income.

In addition to a 2.5-percent personal income tax, a 5-percent business income tax, and an 8-percent income tax on banks and other financial institutions, Romney proposed an increase from three cents a package on cigarettes to ten cents a package.

Romney explained the purpose was a more equitable distribution of the tax load. He said his formula would bring in more than $300 million a year in taxes and provide a more stable base than the one which had caused the crisis of the "payless paydays" for state employees only a few years earlier.

By mid-May, Governor Romney had another reason for pushing hard on the tax reform. The polls indicated his political fortunes were lagging, and he could not afford the luxury of a loss before the Michigan legislature. He needed to show he had not lost his winning touch with the Republican legislature.

Ironically, it was Romney's political popularity in 1966 that had made it possible for the Republicans to win control of the House and Senate in Michigan. This Republican control was more of a drawback than an asset, for whatever happened would then be a Republican problem.

Governor Romney had planned a trip to South America in May, one of three foreign trips in 1967 to project an image-building program to overcome what critics called his "weakness on foreign affairs," and to give his comments a ring of authority.

The financial crisis in Michigan could not be turned over to others, and after elaborate planning Romney canceled his South American trip. Nothing less than an all-out effort by Romney himself could overcome the opposition—an opposition which did not hesitate to point out that the Michigan Republican had spent a lot of time out of the state pursuing his presidential political ambitions.

Weeks of persuasive efforts were futile, and on June 21 Romney initiated steps to cut spending for schools and mental health, to lay off state employees, and to eliminate all the new state programs. This was no bluff, he told the press and the members of the legislature. It might hurt Michigan, but it was essential in the face of the attitude of the balky legislature, he said. He insisted it would not hurt his national image.

"If I were only thinking of my personal situation, I would have gone after an austerity budget in the beginning," he said. "Across this country people are fed up with taxes."

By June 23, an air of crisis prevailed in the Michigan capitol where a shirt-sleeved Romney started working night and day to persuade reluctant Democrats and Republican legislators to see their "public responsibility" and to prepare for spending cuts, if required. It was not easy, and the tough bargaining extended over five days and kept Romney from attending the Republican Governors' Association meeting at Jackson Lake Lodge, near Jackson, Wyoming. Mrs. Romney, Press Secretary Travis Cross, and Walter DeVries, his long-time confidant of Romney Associates, attended the Governors' meeting to try to do a little fence-mending with liberals and moderates.

New York Governor Nelson A. Rockefeller and Rhode Island Governor John H. Chafee worked futilely among the Republican Governors to obtain firm commitments for Romney delegates for 1968, while Romney was in Lansing putting the last pressure on the Michigan legislators.

A tentative compromise was reached on Thursday afternoon, June 28, but it wasn't until 1:30 A.M. the next morning that the 62-to-44 vote was taken in the House that gave Governor Romney the assurance that he would get his tax reform. The Senate had acted earlier. Republicans only had control of the House by a margin of 56 to 54, but forty-two Republicans and twenty Democrats reluctantly joined forces to put through the slightly compromised program to raise an estimated $270 million a year in new revenue. The main features were a 2.5 percent personal income tax and a 5.6 percent tax on business profits.

The House action was in doubt up to the end, for Romney wanted assurance that twenty Democrats would vote for the measure to kill the partisan flavor, while Democrats demanded that key Republicans, including William P. Hampton, Republican floor leader from Bloomfield Hills, go on record for the bill.

Hampton, from Romney's Oakland County, was reluctant until he was called into the Governor's office for what was later reported to be a "tough" talk from Romney. When he emerged, Hampton said he would vote for the bill. "I never said I would vote against it," he commented. "I only had some hesitation about it."

Minor compromises solved slight differences between the Senate and House versions, and George Romney gained what the *Detroit News* called "another dramatic home-front political victory in his drive for the Republican presidential nomination." Romney needed it, for his presidential drive was lagging with increasing discussion of California Governor Reagan and former Vice President Nixon.

EIGHTEEN

Detroit Riots

Black Power advocates threatened a "long hot summer" in 1967, and officials in the nation's largest cities braced for trouble. Governors and mayors still had a vivid recollection of the six days of rioting that swept the Watts section of Los Angeles in August 1965, leaving thirty-five dead and more than $200 million in property damage. Aspiring political figures remembered the smaller Watts riot in March 1966, in which two were killed, twenty injured, and forty arrested.

Governor Edmund G. "Pat" Brown, a Democrat, had gone down to a crushing defeat at the hands of Republican Ronald Reagan in November 1966 in the aftermath of the problems at Watts, campus riots at Berkeley, and a dozen smaller incidents. By promoting liberal social programs, Governor Brown had tried to avoid incidents which gave rise to riots. When they took place anyway, he was the political victim. Reagan, a movie actor and a novice in politics, campaigned on a platform stressing strict law enforcement, and won a lopsided victory with a margin of 965, 898 votes.

In an atmosphere of emotion and growing racial tension, no political career was completely safe. National, state, and local figures were treading a fine line trying to promote those programs which demonstrated humanitarian instincts without abdicating the responsibility to retain law and order in the community.

When California Governor Pat Brown failed the political test, every realistic political figure recognized the slim line between success and failure. Some trouble spots had been obvious, while others seemed most unlikely.

The summer of 1967 saw rioting at Nashville, Houston, Cincinnati, Newark, and finally Detroit. Although Detroit had been pinpointed as one of dozens of possible trouble spots, many reasoned the Motor City would be spared. In addition to the State Civil Rights Commission created by the new Michigan constitution, Governor George Romney had been as outspoken an advocate of civil rights as any Governor in the nation.

Romney and Mayor Jerome P. Cavanagh of Detroit, a young liberal Democrat, had marched in civil-rights parades with representatives of the National Association for the Advancement of Colored People. They were credited as among the most progressive public officials in the nation, taking all possible steps to create good relations between Negroes and whites and eliminating irritating practices of police and other government officials that so often caused resentment.

Jobs in the automobile industry put Detroit's large Negro population among the best-paid workmen in the nation. Constant pressure of the liberal United Automobile Workers union and Walter Reuther were believed to have reduced the racial tensions to a practical minimum. The horror of one bloody race riot in Detroit in 1943 lingered with hopes that lessons had been learned from the experience.

"Nobody has to throw a brick at City Hall to get our attention," Mayor Cavanagh declared. A liberal police commissioner, Ray Girardin, named by Cavanagh, was one of the most active and successful lobbyists for antipoverty-program funds. Detroit, under Cavanagh's leadership, obtained more than $200 million from a wide variety of education, job-training, and recreational programs.

Neither Mayor Cavanagh nor Governor Romney were complacent, but they were stunned by the racial insurrection that tore Detroit apart in the last week of July 1967.

An insignificant police problem in a West Side ghetto area on Twelfth Street mushroomed. On July 23, police made a 4 A.M. raid on a "blind pig"—an illegal after-hours club. As the police started to load the more than eighty prisoners into police wagons, there were shouts and imprecations. Black-Power advocates and Black Nationalists jeered and cursed. The unruly crowd pelted the officers with rocks and later resorted to bricks.

Windows were broken in stores in the neighborhood of the blind pig, one brick smashed the window of a police car, and the trouble intensified.

Initially, regarded as only a local police problem, responsibility lodged firmly on the shoulders of Mayor Cavanagh and Police Commissioner Girardin. Fearful of having police involved in an incident resulting in charges of "police brutality," Mayor Cavanagh and Girardin cautiously flooded the area with police patrol cars while avoiding a direct confrontation with the crowds of angry Negroes.

Regarded as a sign of weakness, that formula did not work. It only opened the way for the mobs to bomb, burn, and loot as they pleased.

Serious though it was in the first hours, it appeared the rioting could be contained by the Detroit police. Michigan state police and Robert Danhof, legal aide to Governor Romney, kept in touch with developments. By 8 A.M. Danhof called Governor Romney at his home in Bloomfield Hills to express grave concern. He explained briefly how the rioting started, reported that Michigan state police thought it extemely serious, and noted that Detroit police were operating under restrictions from Mayor Cavanagh. Danhof recommended that Governor Romney urge Detroit officials to "do everything possible to curb the situation."

Romney instructed Danhof to get in touch with Mayor Cavanagh, express his concern, and notify him of the immediate availability of Michigan state police and about 1,200 National Guard troops conducting Sunday morning drill at the Detroit Armory.

Normally the National Guard troops drilled and went home, but Romney ordered them to remain on duty throughout the day to be readily available if needed in the streets.

Optimistic reports in the middle of the morning indicated the rioting was being brought under control, and that Detroit police could handle it with help.

It was about noon when Mayor Cavanagh made his first call to Romney to explain that he believed Detroit police could contain the rioting. Their conversation was devoid of political hostility when the Republican Governor told the Democratic Mayor to contact him if he needed help from either state troopers or the National Guard.

Conditions deteriorated in the early afternoon, and at about 2 P.M. Mayor Cavanagh requested assistance from the Michigan state police. At 4 P.M. he called again, indicating he might need the National Guard. Arrangements had already been made to alert 350 Guardsmen at Flint and about the same number at Grand Rapids, and Brig. Gen. Noble O. Moore, at a Guard encampment at Grayling, had been notified to report to Detroit to take charge in the event the Guard moved into the streets.

Rioting continued unabated, and at 6 P.M. Danhof alerted the National Guard encampment at Grayling that Romney wanted the entire Guard moved the two hundred miles to Detroit ready for emergency duty.

Romney remained at his Bloomfield Hills home throughout the afternoon, worked on a foreign-policy speech with Jonathan Moore, and kept in touch with developments by telephone. At 8 P.M. he was driven to Detroit Police Headquarters, where he talked with Cavanagh and Police Commissioner Girardin prior to making a helicopter flight over the city for a firsthand examination of the riot area.

Rioters surged from the western part of the city to the eastern part, burning, looting and sniping. By 2 A.M., fires extended throughout a two-by-four-mile area, and the Detroit Fire Department was being hampered by the snipers. Officials seriously questioned whether 1,500 Detroit police, 350 to 400 Michigan state police, and 4,000 National Guardsmen could restore order.

A conference of Detroit and Michigan police officials and National Guard officers determined that about 3,000 additional men would be needed, and Governor Romney arbitrarily increased it to 5,000 with the declaration, "We've got to be on the safe side; we've got to make sure that we get enough men so we can contain this thing, so we can keep this thing from getting further out of hand." Mayor Cavanagh and Colonel Fredrick E. Davids, the Michigan Commissioner of State Police, agreed that 5,000 federal troops should be requested.

Without telling Romney, Mayor Cavanagh and Detroit Police Commissioner Girardin left the room and telephoned Vice President Hubert H. Humphrey, who was in Minneapolis, to inform him of what had taken place and to ask him about the procedures for getting federal troops. Governor Romney walked into the room where Mayor Cavanagh was on the telephone, and the Mayor asked him if he wished to talk to Humphrey. Romney and Cavanagh were instructed to call Attorney General Ramsey Clark.

It was 2:40 A.M. when Romney made his first call to the Attorney General, briefed him on the riot conditions, and said that he and Mayor Cavanagh wanted 5,000 troops as soon as they could get them. Romney later recalled that Clark said he should give careful consideration to the precedent that such a request would set, and to be sure they knew what they were doing.

Romney assured the Attorney General that the request had been given the most serious consideration and asked if anything was needed other than an oral request. Attorney General Clark assured him that only an oral request was needed.

On the basis of that call, Romney and Mayor Cavanagh informed reporters shortly after 3 A.M. that they had requested federal troops. As the press conference was concluding half an hour later, Governor Romney was handed a note stating that Attorney General Clark was on the telephone and wanted to talk with him.

The Michigan Governor was informed by Clark that an oral request for troops would not be enough, that the request had to be in writing. He also questioned the need of the troops, relating that the Commanding General of the Fifth Army had talked with Maj.

Gen. Cecil Simmons, the commanding general of the National Guard, who said that the Detroit rioting could be handled without federal troops.

"I did not withdraw my oral request," Romney related later. "I told him I'd get into the matter further and I'd call him back."

Romney returned to the press conference, and told reporters some unexpected developments made it necessary to reevaluate the request for federal troops. Then Romney assembled all those who had been in on the initial decision, summoned General Simmons, and in this meeting General Simmons agreed with the judgment that 5,000 federal troops were needed.

At 5:15 A.M., Romney again called Attorney General Clark to inform him that General Simmons now agreed the troops were needed. Attorney General Clark then related that not only would Governor Romney be required to make the request in writing, but that he would have to state that an insurrection existed which was out of control.

"I told him that I was in no position to indicate with complete certainty that with the arrival of the National Guard we couldn't control the situation, but that none of us believed we could, and the reason we had requested federal troops was because we wanted to be sure we had enough forces to prevent this thing from getting out of control," Romney recounted his version of the conversation later.

Romney said that he argued that "if we had to wait until this thing was out of control to get federal troops, we'd have a much worse situation to deal with than if we could have adequate personnel to deal with it at that stage."

Attorney General Clark refused to change his position, and Governor Romney concluded that the Attorney General "was making more of a political request than a legal request." Despite this, he said that he told Clark he would consider his request and get in touch with him later.

Governor Romney, Mayor Cavanagh, and their advisers discussed the matter further, instructed Robert Danhof and Charles Harmon, Romney's press secretary, to draw up a telegram requesting federal troops, and made another tour of the riot area.

It was approximately 7 A.M. when Romney called Attorney General Clark to read the telegram recommending that federal troops be sent and spelling out in detail the circumstances that made it necessary to request the troops. The Attorney General, who was in close touch with the White House, told Romney the telegram was not adequate. He insisted that the word "recommend" be changed to "request," and there was a heated and lengthy discussion over whether the Johnson Administration was going to wait until the riot was out of control before sending troops.

Romney declared he could not certify that the Detroit riot was out of control, and Clark finally agreed that he would act if Romney only certified that there was a reasonable doubt of the ability to control the riot.

It was after 9 A.M. when the second telegram was completed, and Romney again called, read the telegram to the Attorney General, and was told that it should be addressed to President Johnson. It was not until sometime after 10 A.M. that the message signed by Romney and Mayor Cavanagh was given to Western Union for transmittal to the White House.

Governor Romney, angry at the delay of more than seven hours caused by what he considered "political red tape," went home for lunch, where he received a call from Attorney General Clark notifying him that President Johnson had sent a reply, sending troops, and appointing Cyrus Vance, a former Deputy Defense Secretary, to go to Detroit to represent him. Vance was put on the telephone, and he informed Romney he was leaving Washington immediately and would be at Selfridge Field near Detroit in an hour and a half. Romney calculated that this would be about 2 P.M. or 2:15 and made arrangements to have key city and state personnel there to meet him.

Romney was at the airport at 2 P.M., but when Vance did not show up at the appointed time, he went back to the Detroit police headquarters to complete planning. Vance did not arrive until 3:07 P.M., and it was approximately 4:30 by the time he arrived at police headquarters.

An airlift of 137 aircraft carried two brigades of paratroopers—one from the 82nd Airborne Division at Fort Bragg, North Car-

olina, and another from Fort Campbell, Kentucky—to Selfridge
Air Force Base, which was about forty miles from the trouble area.

Governor Romney wanted the 4,700 federal troops brought into
Detroit immediately, but Vance declared that he thought the rioting could be handled without federal troops.

Romney and Mayor Cavanagh united in a forceful demand for
using the troops to end the possibility of major disorder. Vance repeatedly refused to change his position, and Romney asked him
if there was any further action on his part that was needed. Vance
assured the Governor that he could do no more than he had already done to bring the federal troops in.

Governor Romney, Mayor Cavanagh, Vance, and Gen. John
Throckmorton, who was in charge of the federal troops, then
made another inspection of the city. As they rode about the city,
Vance urged Romney and Cavanagh to make public statements
assuring the community that more men were on hand and that
they were better organized to handle any problems on Monday
night.

At an 8 P.M. press conference, Romney led off with a statement that the Detroit police, Michigan police, and National Guard
were much better organized to handle the situation than they had
been on Sunday night. It was no modification of the request for
federal troops.

Vance followed with a comment that he believed that the local
officials could handle the rioting without federal troops, and Mayor
Cavanagh conceded local forces were better organized but stated
specifically that he wanted federal troops used immediately and
did not necessarily agree with those who did not feel federal troops
were needed.

The sequence of events gave some reporters the impression
that Romney was one of those who did not feel federal troops were
needed, and he later insisted that this was not true because he had
been consistently demanding federal troops since 2:40 A.M.

Governor Romney, Mayor Cavanagh, and Vance met with
about twenty Detroit Negro leaders, most of whom were demanding that federal troops be brought into the downtown Detroit area
immediately. Only two of the Negro leaders did not want immedi-

ate action to stem the looting and terrorism which had rocked the Negro areas on Sunday night. Still, Vance declined to move, contending that there was "a division" in the Negro community on the issue.

Repeated demands for the troops continued to be rejected by Vance, and when Governor Romney received the 9:30 P.M. police reports he showed them to General Throckmorton and said with some agitation, "General, those figures are higher than they were last night. We've got to have those troops."

Since General Throckmorton had no authority to act, Romney took the figures to Vance and said he realized that the fact that he was making the request for troops "might be a factor in the reluctance to commit them."

Romney declared that he was the one running the major political risk in asking for troops, but that he wanted them "regardless of the consequences to me personally."

Vance motioned him over to a corner, Romney related later, and then confronted him with the same question Attorney General Clark had asked that morning: "Are you ready to certify that you have an insurrection that is out of control?"

Romney replied that he could not certify that there was an insurrection that was out of control, but that he believed it would get out of control, and that he had stated frequently that they needed the federal troops and needed them urgently. Romney added that he had spelled out all the facts in a telegram to the President that morning, and, irritated at what he considered "playing politics" with tragedy and riots, he wheeled and walked out.

It was about 9:45 P.M. when Romney left Vance, but there were other political forces at work. Representative Charles C. Diggs, Jr., Democrat, one of the two Negro Congressmen from Michigan, and United Automobile Workers Union president Walter Reuther called the White House to demand troops.

At 10 P.M., Vance announced that the troops were being moved from Selfridge Air Force Base into the fairground in Detroit. At 10:30 P.M., Vance indicated that the federal troops would be used in the streets because of mounting rioting and terrorism.

It was not until 11:25 P.M. that President Johnson issued an executive order to use federal troops to "restore law and order." The troops were not actually on the streets until nearly 2 A.M.

By the time the order was issued, the Detroit riot problem had become deeply involved in politics. Even before Vance had left for Detroit, there were Democratic lawmakers publicly deploring the fact that Governor Romney could not maintain order in Michigan without making a request for federal troops.

The Republican Coordinating Committee, meeting in Washington on Monday, July 24, issued a stinging report blaming President Johnson for racial riots. "Widespread rioting and violent civil disorder have grown to a national crisis since the present Administration took office," stated the Republican report authored by former Republican presidential candidate Thomas E. Dewey. ". . . This Administration has failed even to make a proposal to protect our people on the streets and in their homes from riots and violence."

Governor Romney, a member of the Republican Coordinating Committee, was unable to attend the meeting because of the riot and had no role in the attack. In addition to Dewey, those on hand to approve it were Senator Bourke B. Hickenlooper, of Iowa; Senator Thomas H. Kuchel, of California; Representative Leslie C. Arends, of Illinois; Representative Bob Wilson, of California; Governor John A. Love, of Colorado; and Governor Raymond P. Shafer, of Pennsylvania.

Whether sparked by the attack by the Republican Coordinating Committee on Monday afternoon, or whether merely following out a plan made earlier, President Johnson's announcement of the use of federal troops ended up as an effort to undercut Governor Romney. In his television message, President Johnson mentioned Romney more than a dozen times in an effort to leave the implication that Romney's lack of ability to handle such serious matters was the only reason federal action was needed.

"Law and order have broken down in Detroit," President Johnson told the television audience. He said he was authorizing use of federal troops "only because of the clear, unmistakable, and undisputed evidence that Governor Romney of Michigan and the local officials . . . have been unable to bring the situation under control."

Governor Romney was furious, for as he reviewed the entire day, it seemed to him that it had been one effort after another by Attorney General Clark and by Vance to lay political traps for him rather than to take reasonable and sound steps to restore order in Detroit.

Riot conditions still persisted on Wednesday, and for the remainder of that week Governor Romney withheld his views on President Johnson's action. Other Republicans were not so hesitant, and the newsletter of the Republican Congressional Committee characterized Johnson's statement authorizing use of federal troops as a "reluctant and apologetic announcement, tinged with politics."

When the rioting was over and the curfew lifted, Governor Romney reported to the people of Michigan that more than 40 persons were killed, at least 300 injured, and more than 4,000 arrested in Detroit and the nine other cities where violence had broken out in Michigan's week of horror. Detroit, with more than 1,600 fires and damage estimated at more than $500 million, overshadowed smaller riots in Grand Rapids, Flint, Saginaw, Muskegon, Benton Harbor, Kalamazoo, Albion, and Pontiac.

In an address before the National Association of County Officials on July 31, Governor Romney pointed out that Detroit has been regarded as a leader in race relations and yet had been devastated by a tragic holocaust. The Michigan Governor was furious over a story that appeared in *The New York Times* quoting unidentified White House sources commenting on "Governor Romney's indecision for nearly twenty hours about the need for troops."

Governor Romney avoided any attack on President Johnson during the address before the nonpartisan county officers group at Cobo Hall, but he held a private press conference to rip into the implications of the *Times* article and the White House unnamed officials who had given this version to reporter Max Frankel.

Romney reviewed in detail his many requests for federal troops, and vehemently denied any indecision on his part when he had periodically requested troops since 2 A.M. on Monday, July 24.

"I think the President of the United States played politics in a period of tragedy and riot," Romney declared bluntly, as he blamed the Johnson Administration for the twenty-two-hour delay in the arrival of troops.

He repeated the details of his dealings with Ramsey Clark and Cy Vance, and commented that both were in close contact with the White House and President Johnson, leaving no doubt in his mind as to who was calling the shots.

Romney told reporters he first became aware of a political factor in his second telephone conversation with Clark "when the Attorney General began to insist on this certification that we had an insurrection that was out of control and didn't seem to be particularly impressed with the fact that we needed the troops to keep the situation from getting out of control."

The Michigan Governor declared that "it would have made a difference" in the amount of damage and violence if the federal troops had been moved in earlier on Monday. Riot experience in Los Angeles, Newark, and other cities demonstrated that such violence was rarely limited to one day and night and that it was "the unanimous judgment of state and local officials and Michigan military establishment" that the rioting would continue at least through Monday night unless a large force was on hand to stop it.

Governor Romney told reporters that the reluctance of the White House to put troops on the streets in Detroit "stands in marked contrast" to the Federal Government's offer of federal troops to the Democratic Governor of New Jersey, Richard J. Hughes, at the time of the Newark and Plainfield riots.

The *Washington Star* was only one of many newspapers to take notice of "the low blows" thrown at Governor Romney by President Johnson. The *Star,* on July 26, was no less critical of the Republican Coordinating Committee for issuing a statement "which reeked of partisanship" in trying to blame the Johnson Administration for the rioting and violent civil disorder.

"The injection of partisan politics into the problem of handling the riots that are wrecking so many of our cities is utterly deplorable," the *Star* commented. "The violence affecting our cities these days is not an issue out of which either party can make political hay. The situation is too serious for this kind of nonsense—and the voters, if not the politicians, surely know it."

The *Washington Post* declared:

". . . The Detroit riot is the greatest tragedy of all the long succession of Negro ghetto outbursts. In other cities it has been possible to seek causes in the ineptitude of governments, the hostility of employers and unions, the destitution of the slum's people.

Detroit's poverty program has been repeatedly cited as the most effective in the United States. Its police force is considered a model of temperate restraint. Its inner-city schools are one of the country's leading examples of forceful reform in education. The United Automobile Workers have done more for racial equality than any other union in the history of American labor, and they have been met with the steady cooperation of the automobile manufacturers. . . . The source of these riots lies beyond any easy explanations in the social and economic statistics.

The *Wall Street Journal* on July 31 commented that though it may be deplored, "this summer's riots are a legitimate political issue," but added, "President Johnson scored no points by delaying dispatch of federal troops to Detroit while he made it clear that the order was inspired by Michigan's Governor Romney, who may oppose him for the presidency in 1968."

Governor Romney said the riots demonstrated that "the greatest threats to our nation are not from without." He said the riot conditions are fed by "a decline in religious conviction . . . a decline in moral character and a decline in family life."

Standards are lacking, he said, when young people in a slum area see that "a pimp and a prostitute and the owner of the property" that is not kept up to habitable standards are the wealthiest people in the neighborhood. The moralistic Michigan Governor said dissatisfaction is often created by the lack of economic equity when "a schoolteacher gets less than a janitor," and when a veteran policeman gets less pay than a carpenter's helper, and when farmers are receiving only $1 or $2 an hour for their labors.

The Michigan Governor placed a large part of the blame on the "private power blocs" in organized labor that he said are "distorting our whole concept" of equity. He also blamed those in politics who have "created expectations and hopes that could not possibly be realized."

While supporting government social programs to achieve an equity among citizens, Governor Romney warned that these matters cannot be left to government but must involve personal commitment. Periodically he warned that for any groups to achieve progress there must be a stable society, adding, "Maintaining law and order is the only solid basis for a stable society. We must enforce the law firmly, fairly, and in proper time. We must make it plain that the public policy is respect for law and order. . . . There can be no such things permitted as a little looting, a little rioting, a little sniping, a little arson. We must be firm in this resolve."

In speeches immediately following the riots, Romney stressed the need for more strict law enforcement and he declared that the Federal Government should treat such Black Power activists as Stokely Carmichael as traitors.

"I am not making a racial statement," Romney told an audience of about ten thousand at the Chautauqua Institution in Chautauqua, New York. "I have just gone through civil guerrilla warfare in Detroit, and those Americans who preach revolution and preach the use of guns should be charged with treason. There is a criminal element in all races, and we must enforce the law without fear or favor among the races."

Romney's theme was popular in the aftermath of a summer of the worst rioting in history. At the same time, considerable editorial comment criticized President Johnson for stooping to "politics" in the manner in which Romney's request for troops was handled. It even looked as though the "Romney luck" had turned the misfortune of the Detroit riots into a political bonus.

As a result of President Johnson's heavy-handed political efforts, Governor Romney emerged from the Detroit riots in a stronger political position. Nothing in his performance could be considered spectacularly successful, but he had avoided errors and gained some sympathy.

George Romney needed to gain ground, for his political fortunes had been falling for several months. In early February, Romney had started his campaign with a substantial edge over President Johnson in both the Harris and Gallup polls as well as a half dozen regional polls. He had started to slip in March following his western trip, lost momentum while bound up with Michigan tax matters, and in May dropped below President Johnson.

The Detroit riots had moved Romney back on page one of the newspapers, and the polls began to climb again.

Gallup Poll figures in mid-August showed Romney had moved ahead of President Johnson by a 49-to-41-percent margin.

But, as Romney was reviewing his first optimistic polls in weeks, touchy new problems were brewing with regard to Negro demands for open-occupancy ordinances in various Michigan cities. While Romney urged passage of local ordinances as an expression of local support for equality in housing opportunities, he declined to push for state open-occupancy legislation. It was his contention that the Michigan Civil Rights Commission, established under the new Michigan constitution, provided all of the authority needed in this field. A test case was pending in the Michigan Supreme Court, Romney explained to reporters and to Negro demonstrators.

If the Supreme Court upheld the full authority of the Michigan Civil Rights Commission, there would be no need for new civil-rights laws, for the ultimate in civil-rights protection would be established in the Michigan constitution. His legal advisers believed the Supreme Court would uphold the authority of the Michigan Civil Rights Commission. If the authority of the Civil Rights Commission was not sustained, then Romney promised to make state open-housing legislation the first order of business.

Complaints in Michigan about Romney's refusal to push for state open-housing legislation at that time were of little consequence as a national political issue. But even before he had settled all his riot troubles, Governor Romney was drawn into more discussions on the sticky subject of the Vietnam War. Comments on the Vietnam War had given him serious problems on several earlier occasions, and friends and advisers warned him to steer clear of it.

President Johnson, Secretary of State Dean Rusk, and Secretary of Defense Robert S. McNamara had been unable to outline a sound and consistent policy on Vietnam even with access to all the information and personnel in the vast federal establishment. But George Romney seemed obsessed with the need for talking about Vietnam and winning national recognition as a man with depth understanding of international affairs. The obsession was leading toward more political trouble than he had yet experienced.

NINETEEN

"Brainwashing"

"Gas-guzzling" became identified with George Romney when he used it in his campaign to ridicule the ever larger cars produced by the Big Three.

"Brainwashing" became equally identified with him in his campaign to extricate himself from the ambivalent position in which he found himself regarding the Vietnam War.

Historians and practical politicians will be certain to classify it with "rum, Romanism, and rebellion" for its disconcerting impact on a political campaign. Regardless of the outcome of Romney's try for the nomination, brainwashing became the subject of cartoons, editorials, and jokes which assured it a place in the American political dictionary.

Political professionals have a horror of the candidate or one of his associates uttering that one word or phrase which will destroy months of image-building. Governor George Romney had been in trouble as a result of seemingly contradictory positions on the Vietnam War, but none of the slips would permit his critics to characterize him as either heartless, cruel, or ridiculous.

In fact, in late August 1967, surveys indicated that the Michigan Governor had managed a miraculous political recovery in the wake of the Detroit riots and his tough talk about treating the instigators of riots as traitors. The Gallup Poll published on August 20, 1967, showed Romney had again overtaken President Johnson and was leading by a margin of 49 to 41 percent, with 10 percent of those polled undecided.

Overwhelming public support for stronger actions against rioters and stronger criminal penalties for those taking part in riots was indicated. The Minnesota Poll, published by The Minneapolis Star and Tribune Company, reported that 79 percent of those polled in August 1967 agreed that "what is needed are strong penalties for those taking part in riots."

The Minnesota Poll on September 3 reported that Governor Romney was favored over President Johnson by a margin of 47 to 28 percent. The same poll showed President Johnson with a 44-to-38-percent margin over former Vice President Richard Nixon. Both polls had assumed that Dr. Martin Luther King was in the presidential race as a "peace" candidate, and former Alabama Governor George C. Wallace was in the race as a states' rights candidate.

The Iowa Poll, published by the Des Moines Register and Tribune Company, taken just prior to Labor Day weekend (published September 17, 1967), showed Governor Romney leading President Johnson by a 54-to-26-percent margin in a two-way race, with 20 percent undecided. That poll also revealed that Governor Rockefeller, Richard Nixon, or California Governor Ronald Reagan would receive 49 percent of the vote, against 31 or 32 percent that would go to President Johnson.

Although the nationwide Harris Poll of September 4, 1967, gave President Johnson a narrow edge over Romney, the 45-to-41 percent margin was not discouraging to Romney, and it could hardly offer comfort to the President when 14 percent of the voters were listed as "not sure."

After a long slump, things seemed to be breaking right for George Romney, and it was not surprising that the hard-driving Michigan Governor was relaxed on August 31 as he and press secretary Travis Cross entered the studios of WKBD-TV in Detroit to tape a question-and-answer show. The program was "Hot Seat," and the questioner was Lou Gordon, a pleasant and amicable Detroit radio and television commentator.

Although it was the premiere of Gordon's show as a national program, neither Governor Romney nor Cross had felt a need for special preparation. After all, as in other shows of recent weeks, questions could be anticipated on everything from race riots through Republican politics and the Vietnam War.

Reporters and columnists had taken some delight in the controversy over Romney's comments on the Vietnam War, and pressed him for more and more statements on just what he felt would be the proper way to handle the diplomatic and military problems. Romney had changed his position on the Vietnam War since giving it rather solid support in November 1965, shortly after he and nine other Governors had visited the area for briefings and personal examination of the problems that existed.

In the intervening two years since his Vietnam visit, Romney had become more and more disillusioned with the conduct of the war by the Johnson Administration and with what he considered misleading and inaccurate information that the President and Cabinet officers were feeding the American people. For a period of time, Governor Romney was considered a hawk because he backed the Johnson Administration regarding Vietnam, although he had reservations about the kind of war we were fighting, with unrealistic restrictions on bombing. As 1967 wore on, Romney had been categorized by many as a dove, although he constantly insisted that he had not strayed from the framework of the major foreign-policy speech he had delivered at Hartford, Connecticut, on April 7, 1967.

Governor Romney, garrulous and rambling on the subject of Vietnam, left both friend and foe confused from time to time with positions seemingly contradictory. Always, Romney insisted his remarks were simply an elaboration of statements in his much-praised Hartford speech, and a close examination usually disclosed this to be true, for the Hartford speech itself was broad as the whole outdoors. In that discussion of the history of the Vietnam conflict, he had taken up almost all the alternatives and options ever suggested. He did not endorse them, but he touched them with just enough emphasis to say he had discussed the issue at Hartford.

The interview with Gordon started on subjects totally unrelated to Vietnam. Romney explained why he had canceled a scheduled European trip to tour the slums of American cities and "look at the innovating things that are being done around the country."

The Michigan Governor was neither cheered nor dismayed when Gordon brought up the subject of the polls and President Johnson's obsession with polls. Gordon wanted to know if Romney carried polls around in his pocket as President Johnson did, and the Governor replied: "No, polls are interesting and certainly they're one aspect of the total national picture, but they are not the primary consideration."

"If I'd been running around with polls in my pocket of what people thought about a compact car, we'd never have tried to sell a compact car," Romney quipped.

"You probably wouldn't be here where you are today," Gordon injected, and Romney commented, "That's right."

From a review of the Detroit riots, and another pass at the Mormon Church doctrine barring Negroes from the ministry, Gordon shifted to the Vietnam War. Gordon quoted Romney as saying in November 1965 that the Vietnam War was "morally right" and "necessary" to cause a "shift in the balance of power greater than if Hitler had conquered Europe."

"In recent weeks, you said you didn't think we should have been involved in it at all . . . if President Johnson's decision to expand the bombing wasn't going to resolve the problem," Gordon prefaced his question. "Isn't your position a bit inconsistent with what it was, and what do you propose to do now?" he prodded.

"When I came back from Vietnam, I just had the greatest brainwashing that anybody can get . . ." Romney replied. "Not only by the generals, but also by the diplomatic corps over there, and they did a very thorough job. . . . Since returning from Vietnam I've gone into the history . . . , all the way back into World War II and before that, and as a result I have changed my mind in that. . . . I no longer believe that it was necessary for us to get involved in South Vietnam to stop Communist aggression and to prevent Chinese domination of Southeast Asia."

Already having given too long an answer, the loquacious Michigan Governor continued,

"I've indicated that I think it was tragic that we became involved in the conflict, and that if Eisenhower had remained President of the United States, I don't think we would have become involved in the Vietnam War in Southeast Asia. But . . . we're there, we are involved, we have created this conflict that now exists between Communism and freedom there, and this is the complexity and difficulty of the situation. And . . . we have involved other nations in Southeast Asia, and we have to deal with it on the basis of the current circumstances rather than what might have been if there hadn't been an overreaction . . . in dealing with the Vietnamese problem."

When questioner Lou Gordon finally managed to squeeze into the act again, he apparently did not find the brainwashing topic worth further probing, or he had lost it in the extensive answer. He called Governor Romney's attention to a speech by House Republican Leader Gerald R. Ford, also a Michigan man, at the American Legion Convention in Boston, Massachusetts. Ford had said that he believed the United States should step up the bombing of the Haiphong harbor area, and Lou Gordon offered the opinion to Romney, "I detect your position is more dovish."

"I don't know that there is any real basic difference of opinion," Romney responded. "It might be that he feels that bombing is somewhat more effective than I feel it is. The one thing I've been saying about the bombing is that we can't win the war by bombing the North; this can't be a decisive aspect."

Later, Gordon turned the questioning to politics, and Romney said he was sure Governor Nelson Rockefeller was backing him, and did not intend to seek the Republican nomination. "He [Rockefeller] indicated publicly many times—and privately—[that he is not going to become a candidate] and I think Nelson Rockefeller is an honest man, and I think that he is doing it in line with what he is indicating publicly," Romney said.

In connection with his relations with Nixon, Romney said he

first met him in 1954 at an Automobile-Show dinner in New York.

"We've been good friends since, and he encouraged me in 1960 to run for the United States Senate for Michigan," Romney said. "I didn't do that because I was concerned about state problems. . . . Richard Nixon was the first man of any significance who ever indicated [in 1962] that the party ought to take a look at me as a possible presidential candidate."

Romney said he had had contact with Governor Reagan on two or three occasions, and he restricted his comment to saying he is "performing in a more creditable manner than many people thought he would."

"Would you take a vice presidential spot with either Nixon or Reagan?" Gordon asked, and Romney snapped out a quick, "No."

"Would you take a vice presidential spot, period?" Gordon followed up, and Romney answered: "No . . . I'm not interested in that."

The press release prepared for the program was headed: MICHIGAN GOVERNOR SAYS NO TO VICE PRESIDENTIAL POST. It only mentioned that he "discussed Vietnam, recent riots in the Midwest, the Mormon Church, and his background and experience." There was not a word about brainwashing.

Travis Cross was unconcerned over the term "brainwashing" when Romney answered the question on Vietnam. Many of the nation's Governors used it in connection with White House briefings on Vietnam. Cross, who had been press secretary to former Oregon Governor Mark Hatfield, explained later that it had developed into a standard joke by Governors invited to the White House to be "brainwashed" by Lyndon Johnson. "It was used interchangeably with the current comments on the 'LBJ arm-twisting,' " Cross said.

When the filming was completed, Lou Gordon shook hands with Governor Romney and Cross, commenting that it was a "great show" and that he believed Romney had handled himself well. Though trite, Cross felt it was genuine and relaxed.

Basking in the contentment of a job they felt well done, Romney and Cross left the studio with no premonition of trouble. The transcript would be distributed to the press on Saturday, September 2, and scheduled to be run at 11 P.M. on Labor Day, Monday, September 4.

Dr. William B. Prendergast, in charge of research for the Romney for President Committee, did not see the transcript, but the first news stories on September 5 hit him with cold shock. Reporters had pulled the one word "brainwashing" out of the transcript for a colorful lead from coast to coast.

Bill Prendergast, an old pro and formerly director of research for the House Republican Conference, immediately understood the dangers inherent in that one colorful term. It was made to order for devastating barbs by political critics, cartoonists, and pundits.

Cross and Prendergast hoped the whole problem would simply fade away in the wake of other issues. But within twenty-four hours it became the theme of critics and columnists searching for something to give a little life to politics while Congress was away for a Labor Day recess.

Democratic national chairman John Bailey helpfully added fuel to the flames by stating: "Governor Romney's statements this week have proved that anybody who tries to brainwash the Governor has very little to work with." Senator Gale W. McGee, a Wyoming Democrat, quipped: "Governor Romney must have an awfully clean brain because he changes it so often."

Democratic chairman Bailey followed up with a comment that anyone who would admit that he had been brainwashed on a visit to Vietnam certainly was no fellow to put in charge of dealings with the Soviet Union. He enthusiastically poured out press releases to ridicule the man who up to that time loomed as the toughest foe the Democrats could face in the 1968 presidential race.

These were cruel thrusts, but George Romney had volunteered to play in the big leagues. In addition to the Democratic broadsides, Republican critics sniped at Romney, hoping to give their favorites a chance. Romney, once hailed as the articulate business genius of American Motors, was called "stupid" and "naïve." Washington cocktail parties now had a new conversational target in the Man from Michigan. Romney's sensational political victory for the Republican Party in Michigan a few months earlier was forgotten, and the man portrayed as having real know-how in Republican politics now was depicted as "inept" and lacking stability needed in a presidential candidate by his unwise choice of words.

Governor Romney and his associates realized an immediate response was needed to turn the issue. Earlier they had planned to make the "credibility gap" a strong talking point, for the polls had consistently disclosed general public distrust for President Johnson. The comments of Democrats and Republicans in Congress and unanimous reports by a number of committees of Congress challenged the accuracy of the testimony of Defense Secretary Robert S. McNamara on a wide range of important issues.

Leonard W. Hall, who headed the Romney for President Committee, suggested that the credibility gap should be used to dramatize the difference between Governor Romney, the nonsmoking and nondrinking boy scout of politics, and the man in the White House, who had gained the reputation of being a crafty political animal of the most questionable credibility.

Weeks before the appearance on "Hot Seat" and the brainwashing comment, Hall, Cross, and Prendergast had agreed that Romney should attack President Johnson's credibility and make it his issue. Romney himself decided his first significant speech on the credibility gap would be at a Republican fund-raising dinner in Portland, Oregon, on September 7. (See Appendix B for the text of Governor Romney's "credibility gap" speech of September 7, 1967, at Portland, Oregon.)

There would have been no way to forecast just how much he needed that speech as he met the tide of the brainwashing ridicule. Combining his defense with offense, he stressed that the Johnson Administration had been brainwashing the American people on Vietnam in the same manner that an effort was made to brainwash him on the 1965 trip to Vietnam with nine other Governors.

In a quick swing through Washington, D. C., on September 6, to meet with Republican National Committee members, Romney was questioned extensively about his brainwashing statement. He replied, "If you want to get into a discussion of who's been brainwashing whom, I suggest you look at what this Administration has been telling the American people . . . about Vietnam. The information has not been accurate." A dozen or more unanimous reports by committees of Congress would have made his point for him, but Governor Romney ignored the work of the Senate and House Armed Services Committees, the Joint Committee on Atomic Energy, the Senate Preparedness Subcommittee, or the Senate's Permanent Investigating Subcommittee. Instead, he rummaged through his pockets and pulled out a copy of a news service story on a meeting between President Johnson and Defense Secretary McNamara at the LBJ Ranch in Texas only three days before the 1966 election. There was a sarcastic ring in his voice as Romney read the news account predicting that draft calls could be cut in 1967, the man-power buildup in Vietnam reduced, increases in bombing attacks avoided, purchases of rockets, bombs, and bullets reduced and a tax increase avoided.

Romney declared generally that the information has not been accurate. "We've been told repeatedly that just one more step will handle the situation successfully, or that we'd be able to bring the boys home by the first of the year. . . . This hasn't happened." McNamara's inaccurate and misleading statements on Vietnam and Pentagon finances were so well documented by Congress that it was reasonable to believe that there would be no reply to Romney's statement. However, one prediction by McNamara was accurate, and the Defense Department seized the opportunity to fire back at the potential 1968 Republican standard-bearer.

Within a few hours, the Pentagon press office was declaring that McNamara's prediction on reduced draft calls had been accurate. "The fact is that draft calls for the first ten months of 1966 totaled 314,980, whereas for the first ten months of 1967 they have totaled 178,500," the Pentagon press office reported in a clever denial of something that was not charged. "It is the Governor who is giving inaccurate information to the American people."

Everywhere, public-relations officials, political appointees, and political officeholders rallied to try to shoot holes in Governor Romney. United States Embassy officials in Saigon reported that Governor Romney was given the same standard briefing that was given to the other nine Governors. Iowa Governor Harold E. Hughes, a Democrat, was one of the first to get into the act with a declaration that he had seen no evidence of any attempts to influence the Governors' thinking. Other Governors on the 1965 trip were John H. Chafee, of Rhode Island; Carl E. Sanders, of Georgia; Tim M. Babcock, of Montana; John H. Reed, of Maine; Philip H. Hoff, of Vermont; Clifford P. Hansen, then Governor of Wyoming and later elected to the Senate; John A. Burns, of Hawaii; and Henry Bellmon, then Governor of Oklahoma.

Governor Hoff, one of the most ardent Johnson backers, denounced Romney for using what he called "McCarthy tactics of guilt by innuendo" in charging he had received a brainwashing. Hoff declared that during the Vietnam visit, Romney made himself "conspicuous" by the number of questions he asked officials who briefed the Governors.

"It was my experience that Ambassador Lodge and General Westmoreland were extremely forthright and candid," Hoff said. Governor Sanders declared that he had seen no indication that the Johnson Administration had presented anything but a realistic picture in Vietnam.

Even the Republican Governors and former Governors, Chafee, Babcock, Reed, Hansen and Bellmon, did not want to make an admission that they might have been brainwashed. Governor Chafee, a warm supporter of Romney for the 1968 Republican presidential nomination, told reporters that he had no feeling that he was being brainwashed in Saigon. But he hurried to add that this was a personal feeling and that "I don't want to disagree with what someone else felt."

Most Republicans avoided a direct criticism of Romney, but there were some exceptions. One was former Governor Bellmon, who had just taken over as director of the Nixon for President Headquarters in Washington. He could not ignore the opportunity to harpoon the man Nixon had to beat. Bellmon told reporters that Romney's use of the term "brainwashing" demonstrated "weaknesses [that might be] damaging in a presidential campaign."

Democratic Chairman Bailey followed Hoff's charges and suggested Romney should make a public apology to Ambassador

Lodge and General Westmoreland. Romney said he was not contending that Ambassador Lodge or General Westmoreland had misled him, but declined to name those who had performed the brainwashing.

Defense Secretary McNamara was the next big Administration figure to engage in the effort to discredit his old Detroit friend, Romney. "I think he is blind to the truth," McNamara declared with intensity. "I am confident that Ambassador Lodge and General Westmoreland spoke to him as factually in Saigon at a time he says he was brainwashed as I did last November in Texas at the time he claims I brainwashed the public."

McNamara again focused attention on the draft-call figures, which did decrease, as he had predicted, but he ignored the other areas in which he had been demonstrably inaccurate and misleading in his comments and predictions. He declared that Romney was a man who cannot "recognize the truth when he sees it or hears it."

Romney was in Portland at the time he received the report on McNamara's attack and declared he had "difficulty in believing that Bob McNamara said that." However, assured that McNamara had indeed said just that, Romney declared that he would be "delighted to compare my record on Vietnam with McNamara's." He said he would have more to say on the subject when he returned to Washington, where a meeting of the Republican National Committee was to wind up its sessions on Saturday.

The sudden controversy over brainwashing had become a major topic of conversation among delegates trying to pick a winner for 1968. Iowa Republican state chairman Robert Ray said it was "an unwise choice of words" on Romney's part, and would do some damage to Romney's campaign. He felt Romney was highly popular, and that it would take some time to determine if the comment would have any long-range impact.

The Iowa Republican chairman was typical of delegates who felt that Romney had been wise to turn attention to the credibility gap, which they believed could be one of the most important issues in 1968. Ray commented that the public no longer trusted President Johnson or Secretary McNamara, and with regard to Mc-

Namara's attack on Romney, he said, "If I had to pick my enemies and Mr. McNamara were one of them, it wouldn't make me mad."

In a most serious vein, Ray added: "It didn't sound particularly good that a person of his [Romney's] caliber could be brainwashed."

Romney arrived in Washington the evening of Friday, September 8, with no outward signs of concern over the storm being created. He said he didn't believe the comment on brainwashing would hurt his try for the Republican nomination, and told reporters he would have more to say on the whole issue at a press conference on Saturday morning.

Concern was apparent among Romney's staff members, but Len Hall tried to make the best of it with a hearty laugh and a quip: "If it gets down to a question of whether the American people are going to believe Goerge Romney or Bob McNamara, I don't have any doubt about whom they will believe."

"I believe the credibility gap is a good issue, and the Republicans here think it's a good issue," Hall said. "George Romney has grabbed it for his issue. There was probably a better way to approach it, but it is now his issue."

Devastating news from Detroit followed Romney and his party to the Washington Hilton Hotel. Martin Hayden, editor of the *Detroit News* and a long-time Romney backer, had written a blunt editorial stating that Romney's use of the term "brainwashing" was only illustrative of "Romney's incapacity to achieve stability and consistency in presidential politics, his inability in answering substantive national questions with something other than nervous bombast."

Though planned for Sunday use, a copy was available at the Republican meeting, and news stories had been written dealing with it. It stated clearly: "The *Detroit News* believes that the time has come for Governor George Romney to get out of the presidential race—and for Governor Nelson Rockefeller to get in." The men around Romney were crushed by the blast from a formerly friendly editor.

Romney jammed the editorial in his pocket and continued to greet members of the Republican National Committee with a friendly exuberance that gave no hint of the black cloud that had arisen on his political horizon.

The fact that the *Detroit News* had stated it was acting "with regret" did not soften the blow. "Consistently and with pride we have supported all previous political aspirations of George Romney," the editorial said. "We watched with interested expectation Romney's inevitable projection as a 1968 Republican presidential candidate running on his reputation as a winner and doer in Michigan.

"But for months we have chronicled and puzzled over his inexplicable blurt-and-retreat habits in the unfamiliar realms of national and foreign affairs. Patiently we have awaited the day when he finally would organize and coordinate a purposeful campaign and articulate specific goals.

"We now conclude that he never will become so organized. The accumulated evidence leading to this conclusion was climaxed last week (Monday) when Romney said in a television interview that he came home from Vietnam in 1965 calling for support of the war effort there only because he had been 'brainwashed' by American diplomats and generals. . . .

"The plain truth is that on July 29, 1965, Governor Romney emerged from a presidential briefing in the White House and endorsed the Administration's conduct of the war in Vietnam. That was months before the alleged Saigon brainwashing."

The *Detroit News* also raised the question of just how long the brainwashing had lingered: "Eight months after his Vietnam trip —on July 13, 1966—Romney said on a Washington TV panel that the United States should have bombed installations around the port of Haiphong and that there was no danger of Red China becoming involved in the war."

The *News* recalled Romney's Hartford speech in which he had said that "we must have victory," and had seemed to give full backing to President Johnson.

"But now we must believe that these were but the views of a man not yet recovered from the brainwashing," the editorial said. "Some may accept the explanation. Others may take the view that the Governor is either incapable of maintaining a stand on so vital an issue, or, less charitably, that he trims his Vietnam position to accompany prevailing political winds."

The *Detroit News* noted its agreement with Romney's Hartford speech, in which he said that there could be no retreat from Vietnam without betraying those who have died there in the belief that America's pledge will be redeemed.

"We do not demand that every presidential candidate agree with us on our Vietnam stand," the *News* said. "But there is a requirement that every candidate have firm policy on so critical an issue and a capacity to state it. Governor Romney fails that requirement."

In questioning Romney's requirements for the presidential race, Hayden recalled that the *News* had urged him to run for Governor and "supported him in three successful campaigns and hails him today as the ablest Michigan Governor in the last four decades." They were sweet words on his performance in Michigan, but George Romney was not interested in praise about past performance. He had his eye on the future.

The *Detroit Free Press*, which questioned United States involvement in Vietnam, was kinder in its September 7 editorial. "As readers of these columns know so well, we thought the Governor must have been brainwashed during his visit to Vietnam back in 1965," the *Free Press* said. "He returned to Michigan convinced that this nation's role was both necessary and proper and that we ought to pour out our treasure and sacrifice our sons to prop up a palpably weak military regime in that land."

The *Free Press* found it commendable that "the Governor is willing to admit his earlier mistake."

"Far from censure, he deserves high praise. When he becomes susceptible to error, he becomes a bit more human, and when he digs into a difficult subject and changes his mind about it, he demonstrates fine qualities too rare in public officials today."

The *Free Press* concluded: "In our view, the nation would be better off if the President would follow Governor Romney's lead. Let Lyndon Johnson admit that he's also been brainwashed. Let him confess error. Let him end this horribly wrong war."

At Romney's press conference on Saturday, September 9, Travis

Cross had copies of the *Detroit Free Press* editorial. It did not compensate for the shattering blow of the *Detroit News* editorial, but it was a ray of sunshine on a rather bleak day.

Romney strode vigorously into the room where the press was waiting, with no sign of the despondency that plagued some members of the staff. When he was asked if he would support Governor Rockefeller for the 1968 Republican nomination, as suggested by the *Detroit News*, Romney noted that he had a high regard for Rockefeller and shared the judgment of the *News* on this. He said that Rockefeller had stated he would not be a candidate, and that the New York Governor had reiterated recently that he was backing Romney.

When he was asked if he believed his problems with the term "brainwashing" was comparable to the incidents in 1964, when Senator Goldwater had spent much time explaining inept statements, Romney replied with a short, "Nope."

Governor Romney read a prepared statement to deal with the brainwashing charge, and in doing so tried to broaden the area of dispute, "While what I said about my experience in Vietnam started a controversy, that is not the important aspect of matters now under discussion. The real question is whether the American people have been told the truth about the war in Vietnam. Has there been a systematic continuation of inaccurate reports, predictions, and withholding of information?"

From that start he accused President Johnson of trying to do "a snow job" on the American people on Vietnam. He declared that in his brainwashing statement he "wasn't talking about Russian-type brainwashing." He was "talking about LBJ brainwashing." Romney declared that a Johnson brainwashing involves the "credibility gap, a snow job, manipulation of the news, hogwash."

"It is not easy to say this," Romney said, "but I believe the American people are as shocked as I am that we can no longer rely on the statements made by our Government and our leaders."

The Michigan Governor spelled out a bill of particulars relative to erroneous statements by Secretary McNamara. He quoted McNamara as saying, "The major part of the U. S. military task can be completed by the end of 1965, although . . . there may be a continuing requirement for a limited number of U. S. training personnel."

Romney recalled that on October 21, 1964, in the presidential campaign, President Johnson had pledged: "We are not about to send American boys nine or ten thousand miles from home to do what Asian boys ought to be doing for themselves." He also quoted Johnson as stating on August 29, 1964, that "there are those that say you ought to go north and drop bombs, to try to wipe out the supply lines, and they think that would not escalate the war. We don't want our American boys to do the fighting for Asian boys. We don't want to get involved in a nation with seven hundred million people and get tied in a land war in Asia."

Governor Romney said he considered that a pledge on President Johnson's part, and he declared that the Johnson Administration had been just as deceptive and misleading in dealing with domestic affairs.

Johnson Administration officials had suggested to reporters that it might be embarrassing to Romney to be asked if he had been brainwashed by the State Department escort officer who had accompanied him on the 1965 visit to Vietnam. It was pointed out that Dr. Jonathan Moore had been Romney's escort officer, and since that time Dr. Moore had been hired as Romney's foreign-policy adviser. Some of the reporters were aware of the two roles that Dr. Moore had played, and had commented on the difficulty the young foreign-policy expert must face as a former member of the Johnson Administration, as a warm admirer of Assistant Secretary of State William Bundy, and as an adviser to one who criticized the foreign policy as severely as Governor Romney.

Dr. Moore stood fidgeting uneasily in the background while Romney described his young aide as only "a technician" while serving as his escort officer, and said he had no policy role. It was not particularly helpful to Dr. Moore's stature to describe him to the press as only a technician, but it absolved him of any role in the brainwashing.

When Romney had completed his press conference, there was rather general agreement that the Michigan Governor had handled himself with assurance, and had avoided the long, rambling answers that had created some of his problems in the past. He had pulled a packed house for the Saturday-morning press conference, and some staff members commented that the brainwashing problem had made him the focal point of attention during the meeting of the Republican National Committee. It might also be said that a man standing on the gallows is the focal point of the crowd's attention, but to those who had tied their wagon to the Romney star that was a weekend for scratching around for any optimistic signs.

As Romney left the Washington Hilton with his friend Bill Marriott, he said he would have more to say about the credibility gap later. However, he was slated to leave on a month-long tour of slum areas on the following Monday, and he said he did not expect to say much about either Vietnam or the credibility gap until that tour was completed. "It would take attention away from this other problem," he said. "There will be plenty of time to discuss other things when this is over."

There was no opportunity at that time to question Romney about his relationship with Defense Secretary McNamara, who was certain to be one of the major targets of any assault on the credibility gap of the Johnson Administration.

Understandably, Romney had avoided earlier criticism of McNamara, for they had been friends in Detroit, and the Defense Secretary was not involved directly with Romney in what he considered "playing politics" with the safety of Detroit. Now the situation had changed. McNamara, whether on his own volition or as a result of White House insistence, had struck out at Romney in a manner that seemed totally inconsistent with any continuing personal friendship even among tough-hided politicians.

On the record, McNamara had treated Romney with contempt in saying he wouldn't know the truth if he saw it or heard it. Several newspapers carried reports that the Defense Secretary had been more disparaging in private comments, and had dismissed Romney as an inconsequential "idiot."

When Romney was questioned about his relationship with McNamara, his comments were amazingly devoid of any anger or hostility. "We've been very good friends," Romney explained in matter-of-fact tones that contrasted sharply to the intense anger he often displayed. "In Detroit, we got together a couple of times a week when we were organizing Citizens for Michigan, and then it was always once or twice a month for years. We saw the McNamaras socially, and liked both of them very much."

When questioned about his contacts with McNamara since he had moved to Washington, Romney replied that he had "seen him several times a year."

"When I've been down for Gridiron Club dinners or Governors' conferences at the White House, I've always seen Bob," Romney said. "It has always been as genial and friendly a relationship as when he was back at Ford."

"Wasn't it a little unusual for him to have such caustic things to say about you at that press conference?" Romney was asked. "Was there some change in your relationship before that, or has that changed your personal relationship with him?"

"No one could have been more surprised than I was when I was told what he said," Romney replied. "When I said at the time that I could hardly believe that Bob McNamara would say those things, I said exactly what I thought. You become accustomed to some surprises like that in politics, but I just didn't think Bob McNamara would do it."

Have there been any conversations with McNamara since that press conference? Romney was asked in a September 13, 1967, interview.

"We have had no conversations," Romney replied, "but there was an exchange of correspondence—an exchange of notes. Bob wrote me a warm friendly letter about the whole thing, and I replied in the same tone, accepting his letter in good faith."

"How did the Defense Secretary explain such highly critical and even personal comment?" Romney was asked. "Do you still consider him a good friend?"

"I accepted what he wrote as having been written in good faith," Romney said. "I hope it was."

Romney went on to say that "it may have been the way the reporters asked the questions that made Bob respond the way he did." The Michigan Governor seemed willing to accept whatever private explanations he had received from McNamara. "It may be that Bob was doing only what he was told to do. He assures me it was nothing personal that should interfere with our friendship. I accept him at his word."

Others in Washington had started developing doubts about some of the private assurances they received from the Defense Secretary, but Romney had concluded that he would at least say nothing that might add to the friction. It was pointed out to Romney that he and a number of other Republicans had declared that they believed the credibility gap would be an important issue in the 1968 political campaign. A large number of the critical Republican salvos had been directed at purportedly inaccurate and misleading statements made by McNamara.

"Do you believe your friendship with McNamara will interfere with your dealing with this issue aggressively?" Romney was asked.

"If you want to know if I can be objective about Bob McNamara, I can," Romney said with a sudden firmness. "I will deal with cases as they come up, and under the circumstances as they exist at the time. My friendship with McNamara will not interfere with doing what is necessary with this issue or any other issue."

Governor Romney did not want to disclose the letter from McNamara or the details of the special soothing syrup that McNamara had volunteered to minimize any lingering bitterness following his public attack on Romney.

Was Romney naïve to accept this private note from McNamara to smooth over a public dispute in which his political future was being hurt? One might judge him to be too trusting, and yet there was a hard glint in Romney's eye as he said he could deal objectively with McNamara and the credibility-gap issue.

It is difficult for close associates of Romney to assess his manner of dealing with McNamara in a campaign in the light of his tendency to go the extra mile before believing an adversary might not be dealing in good faith. Certainly, Romney might be considered naïve when compared with so many public officials who cannot be trusted and who are instinctively suspicious of everyone.

Yet, Romney's long-time admirers in the business and political worlds will tell you that he can be a pragmatic politician when a crucial juncture is reached. Gus Scholle, Romney's archenemy who heads the Michigan AFL-CIO, does not intend to be complimentary when he declares that Romney is "totally pragmatic" and "wears that sanctimonious mask to fool the voters and the politicians."

"Romney can find ways to do just about anything that suits Romney's purpose at the time," Scholle charges. "I told our people [in the AFL-CIO and the UAW] not to have anything to do with his Citizens for Michigan because he was going to use that nonpartisan deal to build himself up to run for Governor. A lot of them got sucked in, and they have lived to regret it."

From his friends and supporters, Romney is characterized as having a cautious capacity for self-preservation. "He may seem naïve, but he is plenty tough underneath," comments Ed Cushman, who lived with him through difficult labor problems and the crucial financial period at American Motors. Cushman and others will point out that Romney's shrewd capacity for self-preservation stood him well as a young lobbyist among the wolves of Washington, in the automobile business when faced with some of the greatest predators, and in the vicious political war in Michigan, which took place in the Republican Party as well as between the Democratic and Republican parties.

Romney survived, and Romney's political fortunes flourished. Friends say it is because of the ability, integrity, and courage of the sincere Mormon. From Gus Scholle, Walter Reuther, and other anti-Romney factions comes the claim that Romney was saved by a friendly Michigan press. "His political mistakes were buried by the big Michigan newspapers," claims Scholle in explaining the trouncings Romney gave the labor unions and the Democratic Party in 1962, 1964, and 1966. Scholle's Michigan AFL-CIO has published a thirty-page booklet entitled, *Who Is the Real George Romney?* to expose the "duplicity" of his foe from the time he worked on the Detroit committee to improve the schools.

Whatever complaints Scholle had about the Michigan press's protecting Romney, it could not be said that he was protected in connection with the brainwashing fuss. It lingered on for weeks in news stories, editorials, cartoons, and in the public opinion polls.

Romney's rise as a political figure was dramatic, and his fall in the polls was just as dramatic in the weeks following the brainwashing statement. The *Los Angeles Times* Poll taken immediately after the incident indicated that only 16 percent of the Republican voters in California would vote for Romney for the Republican presidential nomination. This compared with 35 percent who had noted Romney as their first choice in March from a field that included former Vice President Nixon, California Governor Reagan, and Senator Charles Percy of Illinois. Between March and September, Nixon had jumped from 32 percent to 43 percent in the same poll.

Nixon had always been strong among Republican voters and had registered consistent gains in both local and national polls. The Gallup Poll published on September 23 showed that a nationwide survey of Republican voters gave Nixon a 35-to-24-percent edge over Romney just prior to the brainwashing statement. In the next two weeks, Romney dropped 10 percentage points to 14 percent, while Nixon climbed 5 percentage points to 40 percent—23 percent ahead of his closest rival, New York Governor Rockefeller.

The Louis Harris Poll published on September 25 showed that a Rockefeller-Reagan ticket would tie a Johnson-Humphrey ticket, but that a Johnson-Humphrey ticket would overwhelm a Romney-Reagan ticket by a 52-to-39-percent margin.

Polls taken two weeks later indicated a drop in popularity of the Johnson Administration when matched with either a Rockefeller-Reagan or a Romney-Reagan ticket. The Gallup Poll published on October 4 indicated that despite Rockefeller's noncandidate status, a Rockefeller-Reagan ticket would hold a commanding 57-to-43-percent margin over a Johnson-Humphrey ticket. In the same poll, a Romney-Reagan ticket had a slim 49-to-47-percent margin over a Johnson-Humphrey slate.

The Louis Harris Poll published a month later, on November 6, indicated that Governor Rockefeller would defeat President Johnson by a 52-to-35-percent margin, with 13 percent of the voters "not sure." In that same sampling, reflecting all the voters, Governor Romney held a 46-to-37-percent edge over President Johnson, with 17 percent of the voters not sure. The poll indicated that President Johnson would receive 41 percent of the vote if paired against Nixon, but that Nixon would have 48 percent. Only 11 percent were listed as not sure when faced with that choice. Six candidates, including Reagan, Lindsay, and Percy, all topped President Johnson in that poll.

Representative Wayne L. Hays, an Ohio Democrat, used his position as chairman of the House Foreign Affairs Subcommittee to try to keep the Romney brainwashing incident alive. He invited Governor Romney and Dr. Jonathan Moore to appear as witnesses before his subcommittee to explain how Romney had been misled by United States generals and diplomats. Not expecting the Michigan Governor would agree to appear, he was giving a "put-up-or-shut-up" challenge to Romney.

To the surprise of many, Governor Romney replied on October 3 willing to testify in an investigation "to determine the accuracy and nature" of the official briefings in Vietnam. "Such briefings are, of course, conducted by both diplomatic and military personnel and are consistent with the general policy declarations made to the American people by the President, Secretary of State, and Secretary of Defense," Romney wrote.

"Their accuracy and nature constitute part of the larger issue of the candor and honesty of the Government with the American people. . . . As you are aware, I have challenged the tendency of the President and his spokesmen to mislead the American people concerning the war in Vietnam."

Romney enclosed a copy of his September 9 press statement and added, "The accuracy and reliability of statements by the Administration has also been challenged on many recent occasions by members of Congress, leading commentators, and experts outside of Government, as well as members of the general public."

The Michigan Governor not only said he would "be pleased to have the opportunity to appear" before the subcommittee, but he suggested that "a full congressional review would be very appropriate."

Representative Hays feared the Romney letter was an effort to turn his subcommittee into a forum for a broad-scale attack on the credibility of the Johnson Administration. "While we respect your right as a partisan politician to attack the Administration on any basis you choose, this subcommittee is not sponsoring 'Meet the Press,' " Hays said, backing away.

Hays interpreted Romney's letter as having answered the important question by "clearing" the State Department and the Administration of having brainwashed him. This was the Hays interpretation of Romney's statements that the briefings were "consistent" with general policy declaration.

"Our only interest was specific as to whether any State Department personnel had given you false information on your trip to Vietnam with other Governors," Hays wrote. "I take it from your letter that you are not attacking the integrity of the State Department, of Ambassador Lodge, of your 1965 escort Mr. Moore, or of General Westmoreland."

Later, in a House speech, Representative Hays commented caustically: "In view of Governor Romney's changing positions, I can only conclude that Duz did it or that he took a ride with intensified Tide." Hays suggested that Dr. Moore may have been the one who brainwashed him, and he even threatened to subpoena Moore if he did not come voluntarily. No one took the threat seriously, for this was regarded as political jockeying.

In the Romney camp, the exchange was heralded as a Romney win, and it was claimed that Hays had backed down. Hays contended that he still had an invitation extended to Romney to testify, but that he was simply putting him on notice that he would be questioned on "a pertinent issue" and would not be permitted to use the subcommittee "for a partisan political speech."

Undaunted by the fuss over the brainwashing comment, Governor Romney continued to use the term to create a greater hubbub by applying it to the Johnson Administration's "misleading and dishonest budgets."

"He misled us on the budgets from the moment he took office," Romney told a Republican conference in Denver in late October. "What a phony." He said the term "phony" was intended to apply to the budgets, not to the President, but he did not retreat on his characterization of the fiscal policies of the Johnson Administration. On this point he had firm support from Republicans as far apart as Senator Mark Hatfield, of Oregon, and former Senator Barry Goldwater.

Lack of credibility of the Johnson Administration was generally recognized as a strong issue, but in grabbing it Romney had become the object of ridicule. Three of the six Republican songs at the November 11, 1967, Gridiron Club Dinner dealt with Romney in an unflattering manner.

The "Romney Song" to the tune of "Did You Ever See a Dream Walking" started:

> Did you ever get a brainwashing? Well, I did.
> With the plunger and the Duz sloshing? Well, I did.
> Did you ever get your foot caught in your mouth,
> Just like me,
> And, gulping hard, find you've choked on your knee?

It ended on an equally devastating thought:

> Did the White House light stop beckoning bright,
> Fading right out of your view?
> Well, the thoughts that have wandered
> And the brain that gets laundered,
> They can make it pretty tough on you.

There was no more solace for the Romney club in the Gridiron Club's parody on "The Last Time I Saw Paris" dealing with Governor Rockefeller. A Winthrop Rockefeller character sang:

> The last time I saw Nelson
> He said he wouldn't run.
> And he was strong for Romney—but,
> Old Georgie's race is done.

Michigan Governor Romney was unwilling to accept the judgment of the Gridiron Club, the pollsters, or even the fickle voters.

"I've always been an underdog in everything I've ever done," Romney declared. "They said we couldn't win at American Motors, that we couldn't whip that school problem in Detroit, that we couldn't get a new constitution in Michigan, and that a Republican couldn't be elected Governor of Michigan."

If George Romney, front runner in November 1966, wanted an underdog position, he had it a year later. He said he was in to the end, and George Romney couldn't be counted out until the last crucial primary battle was over.

TWENTY

Underdog

"I'm used to being an underdog. I've been an underdog in everything I've gone into of consequence throughout my life."—*George
W. Romney,* on "Meet the Press," October 15, 1967

George Romney at sixty had the incurable optimism of a teen-age
boy. He believed he would win the Republican presidential nomination at the convention scheduled for August 1968 in Miami
Beach, Florida. He believed he would go on to be elected President
of the United States. Also, the Michigan Governor believes firmly
that the success he has experienced in business and politics has
been possible because of his dedication to God, to his family, and
to the Church of Jesus Christ of the Latter-Day Saints.

Critics have called Romney "corny" because he expresses
himself in terms of a straitlaced middle-class morality. He has
said he believes in hard work, integrity, and high purpose in public office, and often has been chided as being just too sincere.

He has been called "Good George" or "Saint George" in a deri-
sive manner by self-styled sophisticates. Critics have called him
"shallow" because he usually speaks in direct moralistic words

that reduce major issues to simple terms easy for the average voter to grasp. Romney has been described as "naïve" because he looks for the best in other men and has said he expects other men to respond in good faith if he meets them in good faith.

On the speaking platform, Romney does not have the easy wit of former President John F. Kennedy or California Governor Ronald Reagan. As a public figure he does not have the stature that President Eisenhower commanded as a hero of World War II, not the reputation of President Johnson as a hardheaded political operator who commands the Senate and knows how to get things done in Washington. Romney does not have the advantage of either a Barry Goldwater or an Adlai Stevenson as the patron saint of a vast ideological cult.

George Romney has not been all things to all men, nor has he tried to be. He was willing to make certain compromises on tax legislation or other small concessions that he did not consider to be matters of principle. However, when the political fights conclude on any issue, it is the same hard-working and moralistic George Romney who keeps moving forward, smiling, arguing with rich and poor alike, disregarding the sensitivity of the leaders of Big Labor and Big Business, and occasionally showing flashes of a hot temper that accompanies his intense righteousness.

On a twenty-day tour of America's slums, Romney questioned the poor, talked to public officials, and even spoke before hundreds of hippies in San Francisco. With the same zeal of his Mormon missionary days in England, he preached abstinence from drugs and alcohol to the flower children and refused to take the easy way of unqualified criticism of the war in Vietnam as a totally evil undertaking. Although he disapproved of the loose-living hippies, he spoke with compassion and understanding and asked them to save themselves with the common sense of Mormon ideals of physical and mental fitness.

Barred from a private welfare organization in Chicago, Romney did not retreat in the face of a bitter attack by Luis Cuza. Cuza, director of the Puerto Rican welfare organization, prevented Romney from entering the Casa Central Outpost building, and accused the Michigan Republican of answering the poor with "tanks and machine guns." On the door of the building was a sign stating: "We do not welcome politicians that call out National Guard on poor people."

Many political figures would have ducked a confrontation, but Romney met the issue in typical Romney style. He accused Luis Cuza of a despicable political attack on him, and when Cuza tried to retreat, the Michigan Governor grabbed him by the arm and declared, "You stand here and take it. You can't walk away after making charges that are false."

Other Puerto Rican leaders were impressed by Governor Romneys' action, and Juan Diaz, director of the Spanish Action Committee of Chicago, apologized. He said the actions of Cuza were not representative of the views of the Puerto Rican community.

As the slum tour ended, Warren Weaver, Jr., of the *New York Times,* concluded: "Perhaps the strongest characteristic the Governor put on regular display was persistence, a stubborn refusal to withdraw when he was stopped by men and women who wanted to challenge his politics, his economics, or his Mormon religion."

The *New York Times* political writer quoted one observer as commenting: "He [Romney] really hangs in there. When he believes himself, which he generally always does, the angriest militant can't talk him down."

He made no apologies for his religion, for his handling of race problems in Michigan, or for Michigan welfare programs. "I'm concerned about America," he told crowd after crowd. "I'm concerned about race relations. . . . I've been poor. . . . I know about poverty. My father went broke five times."

As he reached into his past to identify with the poor, Romney sought rapport with college students by characterizing himself as a lifelong dissenter. While encouraging dissent among college students, the Michigan Governor tried to draw a distinction between responsible use of free speech and the unlawful violence and inciting to riot that is creating a chaos in our society. (See Appendix C for the text of the speech on "dissent" by Governor Romney at Dartmouth College, Hanover, New Hampshire, on October 30, 1967.

He used the same direct campaign style he had found so effective in Michigan, and did not try to hide disagreements with rich or poor, weak or strong. His reaction to editorial criticism in the *Detroit News* was the same direct and undiplomatic reaction he had to the critics among the poor, the hippies, or the Republican conservatives.

Despite an initial quip that he was "amused" at the *Detroit News* editorial taking him to task for his brainwashing comment, Governor Romney was angry with Editor Martin Hayden.

He had regarded Hayden as a friend, and that editorial from a newspaper which had supported him inflicted serious damage to his political campaign. Romney called Hayden the day after reading the *Detroit News* editorial, demanding to know why Hayden hadn't at least consulted with him before writing an editorial stating he should get out of the presidential race in favor of New York Governor Rockefeller.

Martin Hayden was just as firm in explaining that the *Detroit News* was not in the habit of consulting with political figures on editorial policy. He said he had not consulted with Romney before writing favorable editorials supporting him, and that Romney had no right to expect consultation before being criticized.

Hayden had liked Romney and admired his handling of Michigan State Government. He was disappointed and irritated at Romney's comments on Vietnam. In his opinion, a great Michigan Governor did not necessarily make a good President of the United States.

Gus Scholle, Romney's old enemy from the Michigan AFL-CIO, saw the Hayden editorial in a different light. He interpreted the *Detroit News* editorial as "an effort to keep Romney in Michigan so he can run against [Democratic] Senator Phil Hart."

Scholle viewed the *Detroit News* as the most influential of the Republican press in Michigan. He contended that "the Vietnam issue and this brainwashing just showed Romney up for what he was all along—a phony who's had a little luck and the protection of the Republican newspapers in Michigan.

"All this Romney fumbling on Vietnam is nothing new," Scholle said. "He's the same old fumbling, duplicitous Romney we had in every campaign in Michigan. I've been saying it for years, but we got fifty Republican newspapers in Michigan, and they have been covering up his political mistakes for years or he would never have made it."

Scholle said that Romney had "even fooled some of the labor boys" for several years. "He gave the labor people this business about no politics in that Citizens for Michigan Committee. I warned them what he was up to, but they didn't wise up until it was too late."

As far as Gus Scholle is concerned, there is nothing naïve about Romney. "That's all a big pose," Scholle declares. "He's fooled a lot of people with that act."

Walter Reuther is less bitter in his criticism of Romney although he has opposed him in each try for public office. "He's a guy who was made by sticking with one good idea—the compact car," Reuther said. "He was with the right idea at the right time. It wasn't his original idea, but he stuck with it and it made him."

"I think George is a well-meaning fellow," Reuther explains his view of the whole man. "He wants to do what he thinks is right, but he just isn't very deep. He was lucky at American Motors and he was lucky as Governor. He has some ability, but I've just never seen the qualities that would make him presidential timber."

Of course, neither Walter Reuther nor Gus Scholle saw the qualities in Romney that would make him a good Governor, but his performance as Governor has won him wide public approval in Michigan as the man who straightened out state government.

The outcome of Romney's quest for the Republican presidential nomination is going to be contingent upon his ability to win the same kind of broad public approval in the presidential primaries in 1968. Governor Romney has to look like a winner, for that is the only basis upon which he can be sold to a Republican organization peopled by men and women who fear his unorthodox approach to politics.

Republican leaders cannot doubt that George Romney will be an able and an energetic candidate if nominated, but they have to ask themselves if he will be the candidate most likely to win in a contest with President Johnson. As they answer that question for themselves, the Republican leaders will be measuring Romney against a wide variety of regional and ideological prejudices that will be certain to color the final conclusions.

They will generally accept the fact of his excellent record as Governor of Michigan, and that in campaigns pitched to a Michigan audience he was able to sell himself and his theme of hard work, integrity, and financial stability in government.

In his first campaigns, George Romney was a loner. He worked within the Republican Party, but he was his own policy maker and policy executer. Within the boundaries of Michigan he found it possible to be an effective spokesman for himself, with the amazingly able help of Mrs. Romney.

When Governor Romney moved into close political association with Senator Robert Griffin and other Republicans in 1966, it was the voice, the energy, and the image of George Romney that dominated the scene. By 1966, George Romney was a familiar salesman who knew the territory. He was selling himself to people who had listened before, and over a period of ten years had come to believe in him as an honest, able man who delivered on his promises.

A most important question was this: Could George Romney, who had been pretty much of a one-man band, adapt himself to the huge ensemble of a national Republican organization to meet the political power generated by an incumbent President?

The political power combining the AFL-CIO and the Democratic Party, though substantial in Michigan, is small beside the power plays launched by incumbent President Lyndon B. Johnson.

The President can inaugurate new programs or attack an adversary from the lofty pedestal of a presidential press conference. He can initiate prestige-building international conferences to take the spotlight away from any opposing candidate. He can obtain exposure to a national television audience in prime time by merely indicating that some subject of grave importance to the nation is to be discussed, and then merely discussing it with proper gravity to make it a subject of grave importance.

Equally formidable is the fact that any theme launched by the

President, whether valid or invalid, can be projected and ampli-
fied by Cabinet officers and men operating from leadership positions in the House and Senate. The "Amen chorus" of prestigious
Cabinet officials and congressional leaders is likely to drown out a
single Republican, regardless of the right or the righteousness of
his message.

Nothing less than the full power of a united Republican Party is
likely to be heard above the din expected in 1968 from President
Johnson, his Cabinet officers, and loyal congressional Democrats.

In December 1966, it had appeared that George Romney was
the man most likely to unite the Republican Party in 1968. At
that time it had also seemed that he was the Republican most
likely to win the large number of Democratic votes essential to
victory in a national election.

Although his fortunes dropped sharply in the year following
his 1966 election sweep, it is not safe to count Romney out until
the primaries are concluded.

Governor Romney made the announcement of his candidacy on
Saturday, November 18, 1967, admittedly an underdog. Former
Vice President Nixon had a greater following among Republicans
and particularly among the Republican organization workers with
whom he had labored over a period of many years. Governor Nelson Rockefeller, though continually pushing Romney's candidacy,
loomed as the most popular of the Republicans in polls of Democrats, independents, and Republicans.

Among Republican leaders there was near-unanimity of opinion
that George Romney would be beaten by either former Vice President Nixon or Governor Rockefeller. But, even as they started to
write Romney off, the Republican leaders and political writers
stated that a series of victories in the 1968 presidential primaries
could again project Romney as a leading contender.

His pledge for a "new America" at home and a "just peace" in
Vietnam were said with the same sincerity he had pledged to rid
Michigan of the AFL-CIO domination of political affairs and to
bring Michigan fiscal stability and tax reform.

The Romney statement officially announcing he would seek

the Republican nomination started with an unusual tribute to "my wife, Lenore," whom he characterized as his greatest earthly inspiration. "She excels in eloquence, the poetry of words, empathy, and graciousness," the Michigan Governor said.

Concern for family, community, and the moral state of the nation dominated Romney's summary of reasons for seeking the Presidency. He expressed concern over the widespread sense of personal futility, and added:

"We have begun to see acceptance of irresponsibility as a way of life. There is a growing aimlessness and flabbiness in our American society. The evidence is everywhere. Too frequently, family responsibilities are preempted by Government and weakened by obsolete welfare policies that cripple each generation of the poor.

"The crime rate mounts and over half the major crimes are committed by teen-agers. To avoid a society that seems to offer no cause worth serving, too many turn to drugs or alcoholism or other means of escape. Too often, young people bursting with idealism either find themselves playing a game for which they have little heart or hurling themselves into wasteful protest against the so-called Establishment."

The Michigan Governor declared that under the Johnson Administration the richest nation in the world is in a fiscal mess.

"As we have drifted away from principle at home, we have undermined the foundation of our position in the world," he said. "Once a beacon of hope for people everywhere, America is now widely regarded as belligerent and domineering.

"We are mired in an Asian land war which sacrifices our young men and drains our resources, with no end in sight. Time and again, we have been taken toward the mountaintop of hope, only to fall back into the crevices of sickening reality. False optimism and lack of candor on the part of our leaders have confused our citizens and sapped their resolve."

Governor Romney offered little in his speech or in supplemental comments in the way of a specific pattern for action to end the Vietnam war, but he declared that "a Republican President can work for a just peace in Vietnam unshackled by mistakes of the past. A Republican President can restore truth to Government and regain the confidence of the people.

"We need leadership," Romney said, "that can again elevate religion and morality to their position of paramount importance and thus eliminate growing selfishness, immorality, and materialism. We must end the spirit of 'anything goes,' and restore the importance and quality of our personal lives."

There was no doubt in George Romney's mind that he was capable of providing the needed leadership and had the broad experience required to energize the great talents of the American people.

"I have had such experience," he said with confidence. "I have worked in the fields, in construction, in independent and voluntary agencies during war and peace, in international trade and labor conferences, in two of the nation's largest corporations operating in three major industries, and in state and Federal Government.

"A new America requires leadership which by word and deed merits the confidence of the people and is worthy of God's blessing," Romney said with sincerity. Such words would have rung false in the mouths of many other national political figures, but coming from George Romney they were genuine.

The sincerity itself was a handicap for Romney in some quarters. A long-time Romney admirer declared, "George has been a great Governor, but I'm afraid he is just too damned honest to be a good President."

Although the Detroit man said he would vote for Romney, he expressed doubts about whether the Michigan Governor was "tough enough" to face Lyndon Johnson's kind of a campaign, or callous enough to initiate some of the actions a President might have to take in the international field.

While President Johnson had another kind of image problem, Romney and his aides had become aware that he was being hurt politically because he seemed too wholesome and too much the Boy Scout to deal with the evil realities presented by the Communist world.

In answering questions after announcing his candidacy, Governor Romney tried to come to grips with the problem. When his "underdog" position in the polls was noted, Romney recalled that there were widespread predictions that he would fail in American Motors because he was "not tough enough."

He declared that his detractors in the 1950's said he "didn't chew cigars" and "did not drink alcoholic beverages" and reasoned that this made him too soft to handle the problems of the business world.

It was not necessary for Romney to go into details on the real "toughness" he had exhibited in dealing with notorious financial sharks, tough and militant union leaders, and with the Big Three of the automobile industry.

Over the years, Romney has exhibited the persistent toughness of character needed by the young man who served as a missionary for an offbeat religion and took abuse and insults without faltering in his belief or changing his principles.

Gus Scholle, head of the Michigan AFL-CIO, was a tough and wily political foe by any standards, yet Romney bested him on the political platform and at the polls. The UAW-CIO political organization that Walter Reuther put together in Michigan was one of the best-financed and most competent in the country, but somehow naïve George Romney always triumphed.

President Lyndon B. Johnson, as shrewd a political wire-puller as there has been in the White House, had the one significant encounter with Romney in connection with the sending of United States troops to Detroit during the riot. The President and his top aides went through an interesting 22-hour exercise to trap Romney in a political blunder. The President even sent Cy Vance, one of his most cunning operators, to handle the dealings with Romney in Detroit. When it was over, President Johnson was exposed as a fellow who was engaged in distasteful political trickery during a serious riot, while Romney, the intended victim, emerged without injury.

When the whole pattern of George Romney's life is examined, one must conclude that while the Michigan Governor is no brilliant whiz kid, he is not a naïve idealist. He has had a wide experience in government and business, and practical experience in international financial matters.

Romney has had the inquisitiveness and the capacity to learn every job he has undertaken, and he has had the driving energy and the enthusiasm needed to imbue colleagues with a desire to overcome substantial obstacles. While some of his initial goals on each new venture have seemed a bit vague and a little too idealistic, Romney has won the admiration of colleagues and superiors for hard work, practical intelligence, and solid accomplishment.

George Romney was not the whole show at American Motors, but he was the most important figure in that great success story. He brought good men into American Motors and he relied upon them. It was Romney who did the selling job that won refinancing for American Motors at a crucial stage. It was Romney who held Louis Wolfson at arm's distance and sold that tough-minded financial raider on the theory that a Romney-directed American Motors could be a success.

Any objective analysis must conclude that it was not a Romney miracle which rescued Michigan from financial disaster. An economic boom was the major factor involved in bringing in new revenue needed to save Michigan from bankruptcy.

However, Romney must be given credit for orderly handling of the fiscal affairs of Michigan at a crucial time. He can claim credit for the constitutional reform and the tax-reform measures, and for ending union-labor domination of Michigan government. Only the most partisan Democrats would contend that Romney has not been an excellent Governor of Michigan.

Essentially all of Romney's political problems in 1967 and early 1968 can be traced to his comments on the Vietnam war. A review of the Romney statements on Vietnam certainly shows that reporters and editors were justified in concluding that the Michigan Governor vacillated on the issue. However, the Johnson Administration's position on Vietnam has certainly been an ever-changing thing, and constant complaints in Congress and the press about the Administration's misleading and inaccurate information relative to the United States' role in Vietnam and the nature of the commitment there were justified.

If George Romney felt he was brainwashed or deceived by the Johnson Administration, he was certainly not alone. The pages of the Congressional Record are filled with comments by leading doves as well as hawks who contended that the Johnson Administration had given misleading impressions on the reasons for United States involvement, the progress of the war, and the advice of the Joint Chiefs of Staff.

In the wake of editorial comment and cartoon ridicule, it must be said that the brainwashing comment was unwise and had a crushing impact on the Romney campaign in September of 1967. However, the fact that a slang word lent itself to widespread ridicule does not alone justify a broad conclusion that Romney has become unfit for the job of President of the United States. It is possible to go back to the comments of Presidents Harry S Truman, Dwight D. Eisenhower, John F. Kennedy, and Lyndon B. Johnson and find blunders on points of substance involving national security or the integrity of high government officials.

What is significant about the brainwashing incident is that Governor Romney failed to grab the initiative to explain his position, and failed to keep the attention on the credibility-gap issue that was so well documented. Governor Romney gave the credibility-gap issue a few blows and then went off to examine the conditions in the slums while his political foes in the Republican and Democratic parties tossed about dozens of political jokes all designed to destroy his image.

More than two months later, when he taped the "Face the Nation" television show for broadcast on November 19, 1967, Governor Romney had not learned how to handle the questions on Vietnam in a smooth manner. He faced an aggressive panel of reporters, all well briefed on Romney's problems with the Vietnam war, but it would have been possible for Romney to have turned nearly every question on his changing positions into a strongly documented attack on the credibility of President Johnson or Defense Secretary Robert S. McNamara. He failed to take advantage of the opportunity.

The questions aimed at Governor Romney had teeth in them, for he was fair game as an announced presidential candidate. But his answers were still vague and, though spoken with conviction, still lacked conviction. His criticism of the Johnson Administration had less of an edge of specificity than could be found in the unanimous reports of Senate and House committees and much less than could be found in criticism by leading Democrats—liberals as well as conservatives.

Some Romney advisers said the Michigan Governor was still holding back and would become a real political tiger as he moved into the first crucial primaries in New Hampshire and Wisconsin. Romney's associates declared that the New Hampshire primary was made to order for the folksy and exuberant Michigan Governor. He started his campaign in the Granite State as a two-to-one underdog to former Vice President Richard Nixon, but he had a superior organizational team and there was time for him to meet and greet nearly all the one hundred thousand voters by the March 1968 primary election date.

Victory in the primaries will not assure nomination for either Romney or Nixon any more than a series of primary victories delivered the Democratic presidential nomination to the late Senator Estes Kefauver of Tennessee. But the primaries are crucial tests for both Romney and Nixon, and consistent heavy losses will end the presidential hopes for either of the two men.

Two pesky side issues tagged Romney throughout 1967, and both are certain to be raised periodically as long as he remains in the presidential race. The first deals with Romney's birth in Mexico, and the unresolved question of whether a man born abroad of American parents is a "natural-born" citizen eligible to be elected President of the United States. It is generally accepted that his birth in Mexico will not bar Romney from the presidency, and that no court would set aside an election of a president after the voters have expressed their preference with full knowledge of the facts. However, it can be expected that there will be periodic discussions of the Romney birth stimulated by political opponents who hope to create doubts in the minds of at least a few voters.

Even more controversial is the position of the Mormon Church of excluding Negroes from the full membership symbolized by the priesthood. Political debate is certain to flare up over this discrimination. Political foes and newspaper writers will continue to press Romney to justify his membership in a church that denies the priesthood to Negroes. Governor Romney successfully avoided the issue in his Michigan campaigns by simply evading the direct question and stressing his own exemplary personal record in working for civil rights. It is doubtful if this Romney tactic could be such a total success in a bitter national political campaign. Although an opposing presidential candidate would not dare raise such a religious issue, there would be little difficulty in finding some civil-rights leaders or partisan political opportunists to ask the questions and touch off the debate.

When one views all the problems of underdog Romney, it is difficult to imagine that he could ever emerge as one of the leading candidates for the Republican presidential nomination. For a young man born in Mexico and reared in a much persecuted minority religion, Romney has gone a longer way in American politics and American business than he could have hoped in his wildest boyhood dreams in Rexburg, Idaho. Yet, whether he wins the Republican presidential nomination in 1968 or not, he may continue as a strong force in Republican politics for years.

The Michigan Governor has the vigor of a man in his forties, and he has the driving enthusiasm for work that kept his forebears active into their seventies. Win or lose, George Romney stands apart as an unorthodox political figure and as an admirable man of integrity.

It is impossible to say with any certainty that George Romney would make a great President, or even a good President. But it is possible to say that he is a man most of us would like to have as a friend or neighbor. He is a man who could be trusted with our most precious possessions. He is a man easy to follow, as his colleagues have found, and a man always willing to carry his share of the load, as his associates have found. But most important, George Romney is a man whose own life is worthy of emulation.

Bibliography

1. Fuller, Richard C., *George Romney and Michigan*. New York, Vantage Press, Inc., 1966.

2. Hess, Karl, *In a Cause That Will Triumph*. New York, Doubleday & Company, Inc., 1967.

3. Hess, Stephen, and Broder, David S., *The Republican Establishment*. New York, Harper & Row, 1967.

4. Mahoney, Tom, *The Story of George Romney*. New York, Harper & Brothers, 1960.

5. Romney, Thomas C., *Life Story of Miles P. Romney*. Independence, Missouri, Zion's Publishing Company, 1948.

6. Turner, Wallace, *The Mormon Establishment*. Boston, Houghton Mifflin Company, 1966.

7. White, F. Clifton, *Suite 3505: The Story of the Draft Goldwater Movement*. New Rochelle, New York, Arlington House, 1967.

APPENDIX A

Governor George Romney's Speech on Vietnam Delivered in Hartford, Connecticut, April 7, 1967

In the rip tide of today's heated debate on the paramount issue confronting our nation, there is one incontestable truth: It is unthinkable that the United States withdraw from Vietnam.

It is not my purpose tonight either to catalog past mistakes or to prescribe what ought to be done in the next four days, four weeks, or four months in that embattled corner of Southeast Asia that so drastically affects every American hearthstone.

Vietnam is a name that boxes the compass. It presents problems that cannot be resolved by crafty political gamesmanship that seeks to homestead the inside track on an issue that will win the American presidency.

Vietnam is not just foreign affairs, as it might have been called a generation behind us. It cuts across every vital sector of national life—urban and rural modernization, economic and social welfare, campus environments, church affairs, and the all-encompassing public morality. It affects most poignantly those American boys who are fighting and their families and loved ones at home.

Moreover, every nation around the globe judges what we are

doing in Vietnam against the way in which we comport ourselves on this issue at home.

And it is not a test of wills to see which party will be the peace party—which candidate will be the hawk or dove.

Too often the complex policies involved in South Vietnam are reduced to "Do we bomb?" "Do we withdraw?" It's not that simple.

Problem is piled on problem in a tangled heap that challenges our intelligence, our stamina, and our faith.

When people become frustrated and confusion reigns, the desire for a simple answer increases. We cannot let this desire cloud our thinking or misguide our action.

Although efforts to induce negotiations have not worked up to this point, they should be pursued vigorously. But since they haven't worked yet, demands for a sharp change of course will undoubtedly be intensified.

That change could take the direction of massive military escalation.

Many thoughtful and responsible American leaders are beginning to speak in this vein. Indeed, among the general public there appears a visible ground swell of impatience leading to a mood of "Let's get it over with; let's crush them once and for all."

This simplistic reaction is tempting but wrong.

First, by actions approaching devastation of a nonwhite Asian people, we would play into the hands of the Communists. They would use this effectively to paint us in their propaganda as ruthless oppressors and militarists—the very opposite of our true role in the world.

Second, from the point of view of stopping the expansion of communism, we must remember that a devastated Vietnam would not be a buffer. It would be a vacuum.

Third, we must never forget that substantial escalation is still possible on both sides.

Vietnam does not stand by itself in international affairs.

Others who watch the world frontiers of freedom fear a bog-down in Vietnam may make us vulnerable to Communist pressure, intrigue and subversion in Latin America, Europe, the Middle East,

Africa, and elsewhere. They wonder if America can use effectively our principles, purpose, and power for peace and progress around the world.

Before us stretch grief-laden straits that must be navigated with resolute will and genuine—and I repeat genuine—willingness to reach that solution that will lead to a just peace.

Failure to recite a catalog of past mistakes does not mean that the past cannot instruct the present and the future. It is a useful exercise to ask ourselves what are the lessons that emerge from Vietnam.

One lesson surely is that a commitment of the character and massiveness of ours in a country the size of Vietnam has the inevitable result of turning it into an American dependency.

This is as unconscionable to our tradition as it is resented by other free nations. We can hardly be happy when our every decision not merely affects but largely directs the intimate daily life of a sister nation.

We must avoid such future entrapments.

Another—and I hope well-learned—lesson is that we must avoid commitments that grow like Topsy. There has been a failure to decide what the scope and nature of our Vietnam commitments ought to be.

We now must acknowledge the wisdom of President Eisenhower's decision thirteen years ago not to deploy ground troops in Vietnam. Starting with a decision in 1954 to afford modest economic support and limited military advice, we now find ourselves totally committed—with a current force in being approaching half a million men and a direct budgetary outlay of at least $24 billion yearly, almost one fifth of our national budget.

Our interest has been defined largely by the commitment, rather than the commitment by the interest.

The final major lesson is that any Administration must be frank, open, and straightforward in counseling with the American people. Vietnam has given rise to a rupture of trust between governors and governed for which it is difficult to find a parallel in American history.

Not only has the public thus been largely excluded from its direct

sovereign role in decision-making, but Congress has been bypassed.
There is no excuse here of lack of time, or of the small nature of
the emergency. This is the fourth largest war in our history.

On this point, I am going to let Abraham Lincoln speak for all
Americans who feel that there is something terribly wrong about
this.

Lincoln, confronted with this precise issue when in Congress,
wrote to his law partner, William Herndon:

"Allow the President to invade a neighboring nation whenever he
shall deem it necessary to repel an invasion, and you allow him to
do so whenever he may choose to say he deems it necessary for
such purpose, and you allow him to make war at pleasure. Study
to see if you can fix any limit to his power in this respect, after
having given him so much as you propose. If today he should
choose to say he thinks it necessary to invade Canada to prevent
the British from invading us, how could you stop him? You may
say to him, 'I see no probability of the British invading us'; but he
will say to you, 'Be silent: I see it, if you don't.' "

Lincoln continued:

"The provision of the Constitution giving the war-making power
to Congress was dictated, as I understand it, by the following
reasons: Kings had always been involving and impoverishing their
people in wars, pretending generally, if not always, that the good
of the people was the object. This our convention understood to be
the most oppressive of all kingly oppressions, and they resolved
to so frame the Constitution that no one man should hold the power
of bringing this oppression upon us. But your view destroys the
whole matter, and places our President where kings have always
stood."

Adhering to the constitutional process could prevent similar
entrapments in the future.

But where do we stand now?

It is patently clear that the massive buildup in American and
allied might has not only made defeat unthinkable, but makes
possible the breaking of the spine of enemy-force battalions.

Our military effort must succeed. I believe that we must use military force as necessary to reduce or cut off the flow of men and supplies from North Vietnam, to knock out enemy main force units, and to provide a military shield for the South. We must give our gallant fighting men our full support.

Action in the South holds out the promise of a series of conventional military victories.

Obviously this does not mean cessation of guerrilla activity. Nor does it portend a significant breakthrough in that "other war"— the pacification program. But it does mean that, with the achievement of military dominance in the traditional sense, we will have reached a decisive moment in the course of the war.

But before that moment is reached, we must ask ourselves once again what is the shape of the peace we seek in Vietnam? What do we hope to leave behind when our task there is done?

We must recognize the danger that substantial military victories could inflate our peace aims. I find this prospect extremely disquieting.

Too often in the tides of history, men have sought to rationalize sacrifices already made by seeking wider goals. We must guard against falling into this pattern in Vietnam.

We must stand immovably against all pressures which would preclude a just peace.

Hopefully, when the time of military dominance arrives, the government of South Vietnam would be willing to negotiate a "peace with amnesty."

In a "peace with amnesty" in South Vietnam, all citizens would be allowed to participate in the political process, provided they abide by the ground rules.

Specifically, individual members of the National Liberation Front would be permitted to participate freely in the political life of South Vietnam, on condition that it abandon its use of political terrorism, its subservience to any foreign Communist organization, and then disband.

This would not mean that a coalition government involving the National Liberation Front would be forced upon the people of South Vietnam. I am opposed to any such coalition government.

It would mean that all the people of South Vietnam would be given an equal opportunity, as individuals, for peaceful participation in shaping the future of their country.

Unless we pursue this proposition or some similar solution, we will face a very lengthy and brutal struggle in winning the "other war."

It would be far wiser and more compassionate to include today's enemies in tomorrow's peace than to court the human suffering to both the South Vietnamese and our own fighting men that a drawn-out "other war" struggle would demand.

Unless "peace with amnesty" can be achieved in South Vietnam, then it would be necessary to break the spine not only of the main force battalions but of the Viet Cong guerrillas as well in order to win the "other war."

The United States is the most powerful nation the world has ever seen. But we are not omnipotent.

While there are no limits to what we can destroy, there are limits to what we can build.

The ultimate outcome of this fateful struggle depends on what the South Vietnamese do in rebuilding their own society and communities as well as on what we do in helping them.

The "other war" is primarily their war.

It combines antiguerrilla warfare, political and psychological warfare, social and economic weapons, pacification and civic action programs, and reconciliation programs to win back those Viet Cong members who are more nationalists than Communists.

The villages and hamlets, where the majority of the people live, are the very base of South Vietnamese existence, and thus the base for South Vietnam's future—either Communist or free. The Viet Cong, recognizing this, directs its primary campaign of terror and assassination against them—not against Saigon.

Our fighting men, not only in battle but in countless individual acts of consideration and concern for the suffering people of Vietnam, have proved they are truly magnificent Americans.

But it would be a tragic error to ask them to take over the "other war," as some have proposed.

Taking on the responsibility for the "other war" would tie down hundreds of thousands of American troops for many years. It would undermine the initiative and capacity of the South Vietnamese to help themselves. It would transform South Vietnam into an American military colony which America neither wants nor needs.

We have already Americanized the shooting war. We should not Americanize the "other war."

The Hanoi leaders may be holding out in the desperate hope that America will tire of the struggle, that our purpose will falter, that disillusionment and discord here at home will somehow induce us to abandon our friends and dishonor our commitments by pulling back or pulling out.

That is a false hope—and I for one will not contribute to it. I have repeatedly said that I will neither give encouragement to Hanoi's aggressive course nor undermine our President in sincere efforts to bring peace to Vietnam.

I have even heard that the leaders in Hanoi think a Republican Administration might come into power that would settle on their terms.

For what it is worth, I would like to tell them right now that here is one Republican I can speak for who will not settle on their terms under any circumstances!

Let me summarize my position on Vietnam:

1. It is unthinkable that the United States withdraw from Vietnam.

2. We must not oversimplify this conflict by talking only in terms of bombing or withdrawing.

3. The failure to induce negotiations at this time should not result in massive military escalation. We should continue to seek meaningful negotiations.

4. We must learn from the lessons of this tragic war to avoid similar involvements in the future.

5. We must give our gallant fighting men our full support. We must use military force as necessary to reduce or cut off the flow of men and supplies from North Vietnam, to knock our enemy main forces, to provide a military shield for the South, and to establish military dominance.

6. We should help South Vietnam to get an effective program

under way to help win the "other war," which because of its inherent nature is primarily their war.

7. At the point of achieving military dominance, we should encourage the government of South Vietnam to achieve "peace with amnesty" to avoid a very long and brutal "other war."

8. If "peace with amnesty" or some similar negotiated solution fails, we should continue to help the South Vietnamese win their "other war" but keep from Americanizing it as we have done the military conflict.

With our help, the South Vietnamese have made a start toward building a stable, representative, civilian government at the national level. This is encouraging.

America's major objective and contribution must be a just peace.

The political, social, and economic development of South Vietnam and of all Southeast Asia cannot really start or eventually take off without peace.

So much remains to be done—and patiently so.

Let us build stone by stone upon the dreams and concepts that have served this nation from its birth.

Let us get on with the task. Let us be ready to move our dreams and our beliefs in freedom from the drawing boards to the conference table.

Let us pursue with strength the just peace in South Vietnam that our prayers should so earnestly seek, and that may yet be within our grasp.

So doing, we can fulfill our role as "the last, best hope of earth . . . The way is plain, peaceful, generous, just."

APPENDIX B

Address on "Credibility In Government" by Governor George Romney of Michigan before the Oregon Republican House Fund-Raising Dinner, Portland, Oregon, September 7, 1967

I'm concerned about truth and credibility in government.

First, let's distinguish between them. "Truth" and "credibility" are two different things. "Truth" means sound principles—and accurate, factual statements. "Credibility" means that these principles or statements are believable and believed.

The story of the boy who cried "Wolf!" emphasizes the distinction. The first few times he shouted for help, the boy was not telling the truth, but he was believed. His cry was false but nevertheless credible, and it produced a response. The last time, when there was a wolf, he was telling the truth, but he had lost his credibility. No one believed him, and even though he told the truth, he got no response.

Two things are apparent from this simple example. First, a person can get away with untruths for a while, but he will eventually lose his credibility and with it his capacity to motivate others. Second, no matter how true something may be, if it is going to motivate people, it must be believed.

I believe we face a credibility crisis in America today. This crisis has been brought on in part by the Administration's consistent lack of candor. But even more significantly, it involves a growing disbelief in some of our nation's most basic truths.

I would like to suggest some of the challenges with which this credibility crisis confronts us as Americans, as public officials, and as Republicans.

The Administration's credibility gap has become a national embarrassment.

Its present attitude is a far cry from the day when Adlai Stevenson, accepting his first nomination, said, "Let's talk sense to the American people. Let's tell them the truth. . . ."

Today's attitude is far different. An Assistant Secretary of Defense actually told newspaper reporters in 1965, when discussing Vietnam, "If you think any American official is going to tell you the truth, then you are stupid. Did you hear that—stupid." And the Secretary of Agriculture just last year urged Democratic candidates for Congress to "slip, slide, and duck any question of higher consumer prices if you possibly can." It is ironic that the one matter about which the Administration is so candid is its own reluctance to tell the truth.

The 1966 elections showed among other things that the American people are not satisfied with the Administration's attitude toward truth in government.

And I think the 1968 elections will show that the people remember deception and are fed up with Democratic performance.

They will remember, for example, that President Johnson said during his campaign in 1964, "We don't want our American boys to do the fighting for Asian boys. We don't want to get . . . tied down in a land war in Asia." And later in the same 1964 campaign, "We are not about to send American boys nine or ten thousand miles away from home to do what Asian boys ought to be doing for themselves."

The people apparently believed this when they voted in 1964. But now we are approaching a hundred thousand American casualties in connection with the conflict in Vietnam. We have over half a million American boys tied down in a land war in Asia, with thousands more on their way to join them.

Now, it's hard for Americans to know what they can believe about our involvement in Vietnam.

I, for one, have strong reason to remember another promise President Johnson made in that same 1964 campaign, when he said, "Law must be respected and violence must be stopped," and added, "Wherever a local official seeks help or federal law is broken, I have pledged and I will use the full resources of the federal government." This pledge proved hollow for the people of Detroit and Michigan. They recently went through many anxious hours of fire, sniping, and fear while the President inexplicably delayed his response to my request and that of Mayor Cavanagh for the help of federal troops in the Detroit riot.

The reason we asked for that help, incidentally, was that we knew we had to have enough manpower so that the people of Detroit could know that they would be protected, and so that others would not be tempted to join the riot.

If law and order are to be maintained, there must be no doubt about the willingness of local, state, and federal officials to take the necessary steps to protect lives and property.

Another of Mr. Johnson's 1964 promises is important here. On September 26, 1964, President Johnson said: ". . . I have instructed the Secretary of Defense to enlarge the program of the United States Army for demonstration techniques of riot control. We will make these techniques a larger part of the training of the National Guard of the various states and we will make them available to local police forces as well."

Now, while much of the criticism of the National Guard's riot performance has been exaggerated, it is true that the Guard hasn't had as much riot training as it should. The responsibility for this failure lies squarely with the Administration, and the grim fact is that we can chalk up another Administration promise that literally went up in smoke in places like Newark and Detroit.

The credibility of the Administration's commitment to law and order has also suffered from the words of the Vice President. He seemed to actually encourage lawlessness when he said on July 18, 1966—while the fires still were burning in the Hough area of Cleveland—that if he were living in slums, ". . . I think you'd have had a little more trouble than you've had already because I've got enough spark left in me to lead a mighty good revolt under those conditions."

In light of comments like this, just which side is the Democratic leadership of this country on, anyway? The side of law and order? Or the side of the revolutionists and rabble-rousers who threaten our civil peace and our very existence?

I think the American people who are concerned about crime and law enforcement will remember the statement of the present Attorney General in May of this year when he said: "The level of crime has risen a little bit, but there is no wave of crime in the country." The FBI's Uniform Crime Reports, however, showed a 20 percent increase in seven major crimes in the first three months of 1967 over the comparable period in 1966, and a 62 percent increase in the last six years. The Attorney General may see "no wave of crime," but there is a robbery in the United States every thirty seconds, a car stolen every minute, a rape committed every three minutes, and a murder every hour. The innocent victims of these crimes may not find the Attorney General's statement very credible.

We need law-enforcement officials who can recognize a crime wave when they see it.

And I think that as the American people consider the President's request for a 10 percent federal tax increase, and look at the higher prices of everything they buy, they will remember that this is the same President who assured them time and again that we could have both "guns and butter" without serious economic dislocation.

As late as January of this year, he was predicting a federal deficit of only $8 billion; now it appears that the cost of "guns and butter," according to an August presidential message, is serious inflation and a $29 billion deficit in the current fiscal year, and the prospect of higher taxes for you and me and all taxpayers. By refusing to act on taxes when action was necessary in 1966 . . . by ignoring inflationary trends or fighting them with the popgun of credit control when the cannons of spending control or tax action on both were needed . . . by adhering to the disproved theories of continuous deficit governmental budgeting . . . the Administration has strapped us with this ugly prospect of inflation or higher taxes or both.

We need an Administration that will "talk sense to the American people" in fiscal matters—and tell them the truth even when it hurts. That's what we had to do in Michigan this year, and that's what Republicans in states all around the country have been doing.

Like the boy who cried "Wolf!" the Johnson Administration has squandered its store of credibility. Its words are now suspect. It has crippled its own capacity to motivate people, and to provide leadership.

The Administration's statements on matters of great national importance—Vietnam, fiscal policy, urban problems—have too often turned out to be unrealistic, or overly optimistic, or deceptive, or just plain false. It's no wonder that there is dissent on the Vietnam War, resistance to increased taxes, resentment of poverty programs. The people have heard "Wolf!" too often.

Government that loses the confidence and trust of the people thereby loses its ability to provide constructive leadership.

The American people are ready for new leadership. And it's up to the Republican Party, from the courthouse to the nation's Capitol, to be sure that we talk sense to the people . . . tell them the truth, and be worthy of belief.

But the failure of our national leaders to be truthful is only one aspect of the credibility crisis which confronts us. There is another and even more serious facet of the problem. For if an idea or a principle is going to move people, inspire them and give them hope, it must not only be true, it must be believed.

The hard fact is that growing numbers of people in this country no longer believe in some of the most fundamental truths of our Declaration of Independence and Constitution.

At the root of the revolt brewing in many of our cities is a conviction that the promises of equal rights and equal justice set forth in those great documents are not true. Militant demagogues like Stokely Carmichael and Rap Brown are telling Negroes that they have been tricked, and that only fools believe that the Constitution really guarantees them "equal protection of the laws."

The civil disorders which have broken out in over eighty cities this summer dramatize what can happen when large segments of our population lose faith in the truth of our basic principles.

When that happens, respect for law goes with it, and it takes armed force to maintain order.

I can tell you from painful experience what it is like to have to rely on force to maintain law and order. Violence, looting, arson, and sniping rocked Detroit for days; it took over ten thousand armed men to restore the peace. Over forty deaths occurred; hundreds were injured; over fifteen hundred fires brought millions of dollars in property loss; and over four thousand persons were arrested and jailed before an uneasy peace was restored.

No city that has been through such a holocaust wants to experience it again.

No American is justified in breaking the law. Riot and revolution cannot be tolerated. Revolution is permissible only when non-revolutionary means of righting wrongs are not possible—such as when our own nation was forged from the crucible of injustice of its day. But this is not the case today. Peaceful means *are* available to right wrongs. They take time, and are not as dramatic as revolution; but they're available and they're effective. And as long as they are, lawlessness cannot be tolerated, no matter how noble the end sought may appear.

I am absolutely committed to maintenance of law and order. In Detroit, my orders to the state police and National Guard from the beginning were to use whatever force was necessary to apprehend lawbreakers and prevent violation of law.

But no city can live as an armed camp; maintenance of law and order requires respect for law and for those who administer the law.

And this brings me back to America's credibility crisis.

Because it isn't easy to instill respect for law in people who regard the promise of the Constitution as "white man's trickery." Too many hear the noble words but just don't believe them. Their experience just has not squared with what the Constitution says.

They see building codes designed to protect tenants ignored by absentee landlords, and they get no help, or not enough help, from public officials charged with enforcing these laws.

Rightly or wrongly, many Negroes believe that the police treat them less respectfully and not as fairly as they would treat whites in the same circumstances.

They wonder why, with equal opportunity laws on the books, some jobs just don't seem to be open to qualified Negroes.

They hear about the War on Poverty, and the Great Society. They've been told that laws have been passed which will give them the good life. But with few exceptions the promises simply haven't begun to be matched by performance. So they think this is another trick.

For these people, we've got to reestablish the credibility of the Declaration of Independence and the Constitution . . . the credibility of democracy itself . . . faith in government by law . . . otherwise the very existence of our nation is at stake.

Because if our laws and principles under the Constitution are not believed, they will not be respected and honored. And if they are not respected and honored, those citizens who have lost respect for law will turn increasingly to the stimulating promise held out by violence and force, and to the irresponsible handful of demagogues who advocate them.

Credibility in democracy doesn't start with the Federal Government and trickle down. It has to be a task for every member of our society—individuals, associations, businesses, and every level of government.

Here is a great opportunity for the Republican Party. Here is a chance to apply our basic principles to one of the great challenges of our day—to demonstrate by our actions that the principles of equal opportunity, equal justice, and individual responsibility are real and true.

As some of you know, I'm going to spend the next few weeks in several of our great urban centers. I'm going to search for better ways to deal with the problems of jobs, education, housing, law enforcement, health, and human relations which must be solved if the people of our core cities are to have faith in the promise of America.

I know that much is being done about these problems. As just one example, let me tell you about a project the Republican Party has undertaken in Detroit—and which began, I might add, last April, before the summer storm.

In order to come closer to the problems of the people in the core city, we Republicans opened a Metropolitan Action Center in the core city. We invited people to come to us with their problems . . . and we are currently handling more than eighty cases a day. We have found, through the cooperation of Senator Griffin, or our Congressmen, or state offices, that we can offer meaningful help on the bulk of these problems.

Here are some of the early results.

During the riot, many agencies turned to us for emergency food and clothing rations, and within a matter of hours our volunteers were handling this necessary project for the innocent riot victims.

We have sent 171 children to camp—and followed up with them to keep them actively interested in school after camp is over.

We are engaged in price studies to determine the living costs to the poor and how to make most effective use of limited incomes.

We are studying the possibility of aiding in child-care centers, especially in the "uncovered hours" of 5 to 8 P.M., when many children are on the streets waiting for their parents to return home.

We are beginning to establish a belief that *Republicans do care,* and what's more, we do something about our concern.

Not only does this demonstrate that Republicans care, it shows what individuals, working together, can do to prove that each American does have the chance for life, liberty, and the pursuit of happiness—to provide hope for a better life.

Government has a very proper role to play. In Michigan, we've established a Human Resources Council, which is developing and encouraging voluntary programs to help solve human problems. Every community has untold resources of human energy, ability, and dedication. The role of the Human Resources Council is to bring these assets to bear on the human problems that beset so many of our citizens.

As party leaders and public officials, we must support and encourage these kinds of active concern. And in our own actions in the state houses and in city halls, we must show the same kind of concern.

Our practices must match our principles!

The Negro parent must be able to believe that his child will have as good an education as the white child.

The Negro job applicant must be able to believe that if he's turned down, it wasn't because the job was open to whites only.

The slum tenant must be able to believe that city hall will enforce building codes not just for those who live in luxury apartments, but for all citizens.

The Negro storekeeper must be able to believe that the police will give him the same protection that they give his white neighbor.

The Negro accused of crime must be able to believe that the courts will give him the same justice—no more and no less—that a white man would receive.

We know that this won't come about just by passing a federal law. It is going to take state laws, and local ordinances, and new attitudes on the part of those who administer and enforce the laws, from top to bottom.

And it is going to take a new awareness on the part of individuals and private institutions that they share the responsibility for restoring the credibility of our basic principles.

We Republicans can provide the leadership necessary to meet this credibility crisis.

It was Abraham Lincoln who said, "I have faith that when given the facts the great American people will choose the right."

There is great opportunity in America today for political leadership which will give the American people the facts on the vital issues of the day.

There is great opportunity, also, for political leadership which can breathe new life into the basic truths of the Declaration of Independence and the Constitution.

As Republicans we should seize this opportunity to restore truth and credibility to government.

If we meet this challenge, we can restore to the American people trust and confidence in their country. We can mobilize their unified support for our national purpose. And we can achieve an even more important goal.

We can restore, to those who have lost them, hope and faith in the promise of America.

APPENDIX C

Address on "Dissent"
by Governor George Romney
of Michigan at Dartmouth College,
Hanover, New Hampshire,
October 30, 1967

Tonight I want to talk with you *about dissent.*

We are exposed to dissent on all sides and on a great variety of issues. Some of this dissent is thoughtful. Some of it is cogent. Much of it is noisy. *Some of it is irrelevant.*

Dissent is a part of America's heritage. From Jefferson to Thoreau, from Oliver Wendell Holmes to Martin Luther King, Americans have contributed to the practice and to the literature of dissent.

Dissent essentially involves choice—the choice between the *status quo* and *something else, either better or worse.*

Dissent involves the choice between acceptance of what is and vision of what might be.

Dissent involves individual conscience versus collective indifference, conformity versus individualism.

The occasions for choice arise every day in our lives and each is accompanied—to one degree or another—by the opportunity for dissent. Sometimes these choices are public and dramatic, usually they are of a quieter nature. *Sometimes they are clean and clear*-cut, *more often they are subtle and complex.*

Dissent is not the sole province of the young, nor is it reserved for the oppressed, although it can be helpful to each and probably is employed more dramatically by both.

Each of us, on many occasions, must make the choice of conformity versus dissent, and we should recognize all the risks and hazards involved in both directions.

You're listening right now to a dissenter. In fact, some of the most significant turning points of my life have resulted from dissent.

When faced with a fundamental choice, I have always employed three basic tenets: search diligently, pray always, and be believing.

By "search diligently," I mean to get all the facts you can lay your hands on, pursue all the meaningful advice you can find, define the principles involved, weigh the alternatives, study the consequences, consider the risks and the likelihood of success or failure.

"Pray always" means to me that after man has done all he can to understand a problem, then is the time to seek spiritual guidance which is available to him from a power greater than himself —from God, who is omniscient and willing to respond to our prayers, if we have first searched for the answers. It is not the weak who really pray. It is those who having done all they can and are determined not to fail.

And once the decision is made, on the basis of fact and prayer, then "be believing"—proceed without faint heart and with the conviction that what you are doing *can* be done, and *should* be done.

Let me give you three instances from my own background involving the choice between conformity and dissent.

When I decided to stop working for all the car and truck companies and join one of them, I chose the predecessor of American Motors—Nash-Kelvinator. I joined them because they were developing a distinct type of car. They had decided to dissent from making cars progressively longer, wider, and bulkier. Even so, the company conformed to the basic industry practice of not commenting on the other fellow's product.

Well, when I suddenly became President of American Motors in 1954, I studied the market, the competition, and our own resources and capacities. Then we made a basic decision to dissent in selling, as well as in product. We decided to stake our whole future on a completely different design concept: the compact car. And we decided to be nonconformists in our advertising as well.

We told the people what was wrong with our competitor's cars —they were "gas-guzzling dinosaurs"—and explained why they should buy our compacts. We bucked the industry trends with enthusiasm and conviction. And our dissent had a major, constructive, continuing impact on the whole industry. All our larger competitors tried to ignore us, but within a short time, at great cost they had to pay us the high compliment of copying us.

I cite this example not only to suggest that dissent can be profitable, but also to point out that conformity can be vulnerable.

A second example from my own experience concerns public affairs. In the late 1950's, Michigan was suffering from economic and political polarization. Big Business and the Republicans were on one side and Big Unions and the Democrats were on the other. The resulting stalemate was keeping Michigan from doing many things which were badly needed. The easy course as an industrialist and a Republican would have been to conform to what most of my fellow businessmen were doing.

But I concluded that the need was for someone to speak out. The dissenting course was to organize Citizens for Michigan, which antagonized many of my colleagues in business and in the Republican Party, but which was eventually instrumental in bringing about a new constitution for the State of Michigan.

The third example is more recent, and some of you may be familiar with it. In 1964, as a relative newcomer to national Republican politics, I might have followed the political axiom that the way to get along is to go along. But I felt it was important in our 1964 platform that we speak out against extremism and that we strongly support action in the civil-rights field beyond just the federal level.

I pushed for platform amendments—one which emphasized the role of dissent in a free society but condemned extremists, and another which urged state, local, and private action on civil rights.

These were minority views in the 1964 convention, but they are supported today by virtually the entire leadership of the party. They have been adopted as official party positions.

There are certain criteria for the role of responsible dissent which come out of experiences such as these and out of the American tradition:

1. Each American has the constitutional *right* to dissent.
2. Each American has not only the right to dissent but, as Thoreau so eloquently argued, each American has the *obligation* to dissent, on principle, against injustice as he sees it.
3. Dissent must eventually involve *constructive* alternatives. Dissent must be positive and productive and not just negative. We must attack what is wrong and then we must champion what is right.
4. Dissent must be, and can be, carried out through *lawful* means. Americans have the constitutional opportunity to change laws and influence policy and should employ it accordingly. No American is justified in breaking the law to bring about change and progress.

How dissent is carried out will determine whether the end is served or defeated, whether the action is wasteful, destructive—or genuinely useful in solving the problem, responding to the need, and serving the common good in a constructive manner.

People should not be discouraged from dissenting because they don't have a solution to the problem. We have to recognize the problem and call attention to it first. Then we must produce a constructive alternative—usually provided by the leadership of a creative, innovative individual.

The means, the character of dissent, can determine whether it is constructive or destructive in its effect. Dissent for dissent's sake is no good. Passion is no substitute for reason, nor violence for discipline in dissent. Dissent should be careful not to harm the cause it is supposed to advance.

I condemn the violence brought to bear at the recent Pentagon demonstration, the wasted time, blood, and headlines, the obscenity and vilification employed. And the great irony of this event was that it undoubtedly attracted greater public support for the *policies followed by the present Administration on Vietnam.*

With the strength offered by a grand coalition such as that—any grouping of forty thousand people which includes representatives of the Episcopalian clergy, the Amalgamated Clothing Workers Local No. 1199, and the U.S. Committee to Aid the National Liberation Front is not to be sneezed at—there was pathetically little to show for it other than bad manners, viciousness, and filth.

To be effective, it is necessary to do a lot better than this demonstration did in its protest, in its dissent.

So, performance and methods count, as well as principles. High ideas don't justify their unprincipled application. In dissenting it is not just an intellectual or philosophical challenge, it's behavioral as well. It is too often sadly overlooked that our destiny will be determined not only by the strength of our conscience and the vision of our ideals but also by our method of application, by the activity with which we pursue them.

A very fundamental point about constructive dissent is that it should be carried out *within* rather than *against* the society. Positive protest should be undertaken *for* rather than *at* our community. This is an important distinction, and it involves the questions of order and stability.

If we attempt to reform by destroying our institutions and our social fabric, we will fail. The very durability of our institutions, the fidelity of our basic procedures over time should invite us to wield them as weapons of reform, not attack them as the targets of revolt.

The wisdom of our founders—guided, I believe, by what Washington called the invisible hand of Divine Guidance—wrote into our Constitution safeguards which would make unnecessary to future generations the type of illegal dissent which was forced upon our American Revolutionists.

Respect for the law is absolutely basic to our whole way of life. Injustice occurs as a result of good laws not being carried out and bad laws being enacted and enforced. The law can be changed before it is made, or after it is made through judicial and legislative processes, but laws cannot be changed by breaking them without the direst consequences.

If illegality is a permissible tool, for instance, for students protesting the governing structure of a university, it is also a permissible weapon for the so-called Minute Men or the American Nazi Party. As Montesquieu wrote: "Liberty is a right of doing whatever the laws permit, and if a citizen could do what they forbid, he would no longer be possessed of liberty because all his fellow citizens would have the same power."

The constructive dissenter and reformer recognizes that we do have a democracy and that in a democracy, freedom and order must exist in a subtle tension. His patience with the system does not preclude his indignation at its faults or his vigorous action to correct them. He attempts both to retain and to utilize the good as he roots out the bad.

He does not let his frustration with what is bad blind him from employing the very means society provides for changing and improving itself. He refuses—with undramatic prudence and common sense—to throw the baby out with the bath water.

In order to improve our society from within, we must learn in a given situation to reject the extreme alternatives opposed to one another which alienate the common humanity.

Extremism is currently stretching America apart. Extreme dissent on the left is strengthening extremist action on the right, and thus the great casualty is the potential creative progress which resides in the middle. For instance, the Stokely Carmichaels and the H. Rap Browns do not yet speak for a majority of the black community. But their hardened attitudes are mirrored in the white community. America is becoming dangerously polarized.

In an important speech on "The Politics of Stability" last month, Patrick Moynihan spoke of the need for working in unity rather than in diversity on the great problems facing America. He pointed out that liberals "must see more clearly that their essential interest is in the stability of the social order, and that given the present threats to that stability, it is necessary to seek out and make much more effective alliances with political conservatives who share that concern and who recognize that unyielding rigidity is just as much a threat to that continuity of things as is an anarchic desire for change."

American students clearly have plenty of willingness to dissent and plenty to dissent about. I am profoundly impressed by the idealism of today's students. I am deeply moved by the basic honesty and the highly developed sense of social consciousness of your generation.

I think we face some common enemies—injustice, hypocrisy, patronizing paternalism, centralized power, increasing indifference, fuzzy permissiveness, and the impersonalness of our privately and publically bureaucratized and computerized society.

I was struck recently to read in a book entitled *A Prophetic Minority* by Jack Newfield about the so-called "young radicals" at the similarity of objectives with the so-called old fogies. The New Radicalism, it is written, represents an anti-Establishment protest against the inequities of American life, a moral revulsion against the corruption in our society. Its politics are concerned with moral absolutes like love, justice, equality, and freedom, and are engaged in revolt against "remote, impersonal machines that are not responsive to human needs." The New Radicals condemn the IBM course cards of the multiuniversity, "urban renewal by technocrats," wire taps, and computer marriages. All I can say to that frame of reference is "Amen!"

I share the frustration some of you feel at the difficulty in making your own contribution to the fulfillment of principle, the obstacles faced in trying to apply the dictates of conscience to the sometimes appalling facts of your social environment, and your distress at the apparent unresponsiveness of the Establishment.

I believe that constructive, responsible, and effective dissent by the student generation of America can be of inestimable value to the improvement of the whole community. Indeed, it already exists. But, you've got to do more and do it better.

In order to tap a great potential for leadership, in order to assure greater positive results from student dissent, I think several factors should be kept in mind. I make these suggestions as a frequent dissenter, in the strong spirit of encouragement.

First, I think students should guard against self-indulgence and escapism. Selfishness isn't justified in dissent any more than anywhere else.

Second, greater emphasis should be placed on learning all the facts that can be absorbed about a problem before diving into it. Alienation is no excuse for not doing one's homework.

Third, the chosen course should be pursued in a realistic context relevant to the problem it is attempting to influence. The pursuit of an abstract "perfection" may both harm the cause and deny human nature.

We count on you for your idealistic capacity for moral feeling and your spirit of challenge—not just because it's healthy, but because it's essential and desperately needed. But, do not make the mistake of feeling that no one appreciates your mission or that no one else is trying.

I don't want to expropriate your "thing." I do want to suggest that we may be moving in the same direction.

But, you might ask, isn't the whole thing an exercise in futility? Isn't the Establishment too entrenched to beat? Doesn't the callous indifference of much of your society preempt effective channels of action?

The answers to these questions—an answer which many of you have already provided—is No. Youth must match its disenchantment and disgust with resourcefulness and imagination to find the means of constructive action. There are plenty of opportunities to take effective action—some of which you have devised.

The student generation deserves great credit for numerous dynamic undertakings which it has fostered and is now engaged in. The Student Education Corps—which has eight thousand members in Michigan alone—and the Peace Corps are the most obvious examples. VISTA, civil-rights programs, social work in slum areas, legal aid, free medical clinics are others. There are many more, and their enlargement and improvement are unlimited. This is the voluntary association of cooperating individuals, the creative force of the independent sector of society which so fascinated de Tocqueville.

The American Revolution is a continuing revolution that has barely begun, as is made clear by Father Bruckberger in his book *Image of America.*

The anvil for dynamic, creative dissent is service. The tremendous growth of service in the past several years as a basic principle and motivating purpose of the new generation is one of the most exciting developments in our modern society and one of untold value to that society.

As Richard Unsworth, formerly your own Tucker Foundation Dean, wrote while he was still at Dartmouth: "An ethic of service, which stresses sensitivity, responsibility, and usefulness, is the only thing I can see as a viable and fruitful alternative in this world of hard demands and complex choices."

And the opportunities abound: private poverty programs, youth groups, scholarship funds, conservation projects, hospitals, civic-improvement assemblies, and community organization efforts. You know them.

Private research and philanthropic foundations disperse over $750 million per year. We have 118 million church members in 320,000 churches in America. There are 33,000 Americans working in 146 countries abroad under the sponsorship of volunteer organizations.

On my recent tour of America's cities, I learned in Indianapolis of the Women's Anti-Crime Crusade, in which 50,000 women are informally organized to watch the courts, assist the police department, prevent school dropouts, and work with juveniles who might otherwise be involved in street crime.

In Illinois and Indiana, I encountered dramatic education programs developed by private groups which can give a functional illiterate the reading, spelling, and arithmetic skills of a high-school graduate in just a few short weeks.

In Harlem I saw private street academies which prepare dropouts for a college education.

In my own State of Michigan, the Republican State Central Committee decided to go where the action was—in Detroit—and launched last January a program of personal involvement with the problems of people at the neighborhood and community level. The program's first community action center was opened in April in the heart of Detroit's biggest slum area and now handles all sorts of problems brought by members of the neighborhood, from confusion on social security payments to uncertainty on how to apply for a job.

After the rioting hit Detroit on July 23, the State Committee organized a program which collected and sent to Detroit, for distribution by the Action Center, more than eighty tons of food and thousands of pieces of clothing for those left homeless, hungry, or helpless from the riots.

Here is personal involvement and individual relevance. Here are arenas of positive protest.

America's record of private effort for humanitarian causes is unmatched. Yet, we have only barely started.

Remodeling and expanding our independent, volunteer sector of society is essential in solving many urgent national problems. In this way, through the involvement of ordinary citizens, more efficient use can be made of available resources with great benefits to those giving of themselves and those securing help in helping themselves.

The potential for constructive dissent and for positive protest, as I have defined it—for the student generation as for all of us— is huge. It has not yet been effectively tapped.

The most burning area of dissent in the United States today is, of course, Vietnam. It is particularly hard to be a constructive dissenter about Vietnam, because it is such a bitterly anguishing and such an intensely complex problem. That is why the premium on constructive dissent is at its highest here.

The role of politics in foreign policy has always been a difficult one. We must realize the importance of full discussion and debate as the best way to find answers in a democracy. Yet, we also realize that internal divisiveness can contribute to miscalculations by our enemies and raise doubts among our friends as to how far they can depend on us.

I am proud of the debate on Vietnam which is presently going on within my party, and welcome it. We are not conformists, and we have real dialogue and spirited examination of United States national-security interests and policies in Vietnam.

I am a dissenter on our government's policy in Vietnam. I have said that I thought it was a tragic error to become involved in Vietnam, and to become involved in a land war in Asia. I have questioned the optimistic expectations based on our dangerous bombing policy in the North.

I have criticized the Administration for "Americanizing" both the military and the nation-building effort in South Vietnam. I have deplored the inadequate effort of the South Vietnamese. I have called for the United States to encourage Saigon to start talks with the NLF or Hanoi. I have said a solution calls for fresh leadership unshackled to the mistakes and rigidities of the past.

But, I have also stressed that we have to see the Vietnam conflict through to an honorable solution; that we must make it absolutely clear to Hanoi that no new Administration would mean the lessening of United States determination in Vietnam.

I'm not willing to throw away everything because I'm anguished or frustrated by the problem. I am looking for a real answer, not a vacuum. I'm looking for an alternative, not merely a more popular or devastating criticism of the way things are going.

Recently, on October 15, I suggested that I was exploring a plan which might bring a peaceful settlement to Vietnam—an alternative to the unacceptable outcomes I think the present policy presents us.

This plan would identify the basic components which would be involved in any settlement, whether negotiated or tacit. It would include a scenario for the various levels of negotiations and the participants.

It would provide for the support and participation of the international community—in encouraging a settlement, in helping in the process of negotiations, in setting up implementing machinery, and in guaranteeing the settlement.

Finally, this plan would make arrangements for the neutralization of the nations of the area which are directly involved in the conflict.

In my view, there will not be a solution to the Vietnam mess until we have a carefully, thoroughly developed overall plan which accommodates and coordinates the various aspects of the problem.

I don't think enough preparation has been done in setting out the basic elements which would have to be determined in any settlement, affecting such matters as: bombing, infiltration, withdrawal, repatriation, participation in the representative government of the South, elections, reunification, economic and social development, and so forth.

I don't think the international community has been sufficiently motivated before and is sufficiently encouraged now to take major responsibility in a settlement. Everyone was trying to get something different out of the Geneva Accords in 1954. The implementing machinery for that agreement was pitifully inadequate. We might make use of a number of different existing international institutions in coordinated roles, as well as perhaps develop a new, overall multilateral instrument for this purpose.

Finally, I don't think that there will be a Vietnam solution until the area is defused through neutralization, both from the cold war and as a battleground of "wars of national liberation." And I don't think that any of the participants will genuinely opt for a peaceful solution until they can see their interests served through the prospect of real economic and social development on a regional basis and free from devastation or the threat of conflict.

In this way I hope to make my Vietnam dissent constructive.

Thank you for listening to what I have said about constructive dissent, which we all participate in, but for which we place a special reliance on you. In renouncing the dropout or the flower-child route, don't on the other hand lose the zest and fervency of your convictions when you face conformity in the career you choose. If anything, that would be worse, and it is probably a greater danger.

Dissent and protest are not the exclusive property of the student, the hippie, or the picket. *Take it from a square dissenter who ought to know.*